Adolescent
Risk
Taking

Adolescent Risk Taking

edited by

Nancy J. Bell
Robert W. Bell

SAGE Publications
International Educational and Professional Publisher
Newbury Park   London   New Delhi

For information address:

SAGE Publications, Inc.
2455 Teller Road
Newbury Park, California 91320

SAGE Publications Ltd.
6 Bonhill Street
London EC2A 4PU
United Kingdom

SAGE Publications India Pvt. Ltd.
M-32 Market
Greater Kailash I
New Delhi 110 048 India

Printed in the United States of America

Library of Congress Cataloging-in-Publication Data

Bell, Nancy J.
    Adolescent risk taking / Nancy J. Bell, Robert W. Bell.
        p.   cm.
    Includes bibliographical references.
    ISBN 0-8039-5064-0.—ISBN 0-8039-5065-9 (pb)
    1. Risk-taking in adolescence. 2. Risk-taking in adolescence—
Prevention. 3. Problem youth—Behavior modification. I. Bell,
Robert Wayne. 1931- . II. Title.
RJ506.R57B45   1993
362.2′7—dc20   92-35561
                                                                    CIP

93 94 95   10 9 8 7 6 5 4 3 2 1

CONTENTS

INTRODUCTION

As we are reminded by Lola Lopes (this volume), the study of risky choice, with origins dating back to the advent of probability theory, is hardly a new endeavor. Contemporary interest in risk is ubiquitous: In one form or another it appears in the literatures of economics, management and organizational behavior, law and social policy, environmental sciences, technology, medicine, psychology, and sociology. This volume highlights contributions from the latter two disciplines, although advances in any one of the above are to some extent indebted to all of the others.

Concerted formal theory testing in risky-choice decision making by psychologists during the past two-three decades provides an important foundation for the study of adolescent risk taking (cf., Kahneman, Slovic, & Tversky, 1982; Slovic, Fischhoff, & Lichtenstein, 1977). So, too, does work in the sociology of risk, a relatively new but growing specialty area within sociology (Heimer, 1988; Short, 1984). Even more recent are the attempts to explore the value of a risk-taking perspective for an understanding of self- and socially-destructive behaviors—substance abuse, unprotected sex, crime, and the like. References to this sort of behavior as risk taking, specifically during adolescence and young adulthood, have begun to appear only in the last few years (e.g., Baumrind, 1987; Irwin & Millstein, 1986; Tonkin, 1987).

We do not imply that there has been a lack of scientific interest in the topic of youthful recklessness on the part of either psychologists or sociologists. Journals in both of these disciplines contain a wealth of information on incidence rates and correlates of adolescent and young adult "problem behaviors" as well as theoretical presentations (e.g., Jessor & Jessor, 1977). Nor has there been a void in the development of programs and policies designed to curb and reverse the trends viewed by many as alarming for society (see Dryfoos, this volume; Wilcox, this volume).

Given the plentiful amount of past research, particularly on such topics as adolescent substance abuse and delinquency, we must consider the merits of the introduction of the concept of risk taking to this literature. If the term is being used simply as a shorthand device for referring to a set of behaviors that place young people at risk, then we would expect it to have little impact upon the field. If, on the other hand, the use of the concept suggests something about a more global orientation to the study of dysfunctional, dangerous, sometimes life-threatening behaviors of youth, then its impact could be more substantial.

Contributors to this volume explore a risk-taking perspective in this second sense. By perspective, we do not refer to any particular theory or body of research; but we do mean that the theories, models, hypotheses, and research data associated with the study of risk taking are used to organize, explain, and inform the study of choices being made by adolescents and young adults. The adoption of this perspective represents a commitment to utilize the concept of risk taking in a fundamental way—to explore it as a source for new approaches to understanding these adolescent behaviors and for generating different questions than have been asked in the past.

The value of a risk-taking perspective as applied to this area of inquiry is as yet an unknown, but we speculate about the following possibilities.

1. As expressed by Irwin and Millstein (1986), "The behaviors associated with the major mortalities and morbidities of adolescents share a common theme: risk taking" (p. 82S). A risk-taking perspective discourages the examination of isolated categories of behaviors, suggesting instead that we design studies which permit tests of the "common theme" hypothesis. The interrelationships of problem behaviors and the overlap in their correlates have been documented for some time in the literature (e.g., Donovan & Jessor, 1985; Jessor, 1987; Osgood, Johnston, O'Malley, & Bachman, 1988). Thus, this admonition, while not unique to a risk-taking perspective, is consistent with conclusions of current research on adolescent problem behaviors.

2. The concept of risk taking encompasses much more than choices to engage in dysfunctional behaviors, ie., those behaviors that seem to have little long-term payoff for the individual. It also includes consideration of, for example, decisions to embark upon mountain climbing, sky diving, and race-car driving; to work in risky occupations or in jobs where high-risk decisions are made; and perhaps to be a sensation-seeker in many aspects of life (Zuckerman, 1979). The risk-taking perspective calls for comparisons between these types of risk taking behaviors; differences as well as commonalities may be informative (see Lyng, 1990; this volume).

Related to this point, normal adolescent development is characterized by increased risk taking (Baumrind, 1987). The risk-taking perspective invites, perhaps more so than some other approaches, attempts to distinguish the positive from negative aspects of risk taking as they contribute to or result from optimal cognitive, social, and emotional development during adolescence.

3. This perspective may promote commentary, ideas, and contributions from groups of scholars who would be less willing to participate in discussions of, for example, adolescent substance abuse. Some may be able to "connect" with the concept of risk taking in a way that they might not with a more narrowly-defined topic.

The contributors to this volume have diverse interests and backgrounds: adolescent medicine; social, cognitive, developmental, and health psychology; sociobiology; sociology; intervention; and public policy. Although not all contributors deal explicitly with dysfunctional risk taking during adolescence and young adulthood, all chapters contain implications for research or intervention with adolescents; in many cases, implications that would not have come from the existing adolescent literature.

The first chapter by Charles Irwin lays a foundation for subsequent chapters by summarizing past research on adolescent problem behaviors and discussing the rationale for regarding these behaviors as having a common risk-taking component. His work provides empirical support for a future emphasis on an underlying common component rather than a selective attention to particular behaviors both in research and intervention efforts.

Lola Lopes also provides a foundation for the remainder of the volume by presenting a history and critique of formal decision theories of risky choice. She gives examples from her own work to illustrate the way in which "person" variables (security- versus potential-mindedness and aspiration level) can be introduced into formal theory. This chapter contributes to the volume in two important ways. First, anyone adopting a risk-taking perspective must be informed about the extensive psychological literature in risky choice. Second, we see the glimmerings of a link between real-world decision making and formal theory in the introduction of variables suggested by the way people "think about" risky choices.

The next two chapters also discuss cognitively-based approaches to the understanding of risk taking. Many people attribute the high incidence of risky behavior during adolescence to cognitive immaturity, assuming that adolescents are less capable of understanding the consequences of their actions than are adults and suffer from exaggerated perceptions of their own invulnerability. Susan Millstein reviews perceptual, inferential, and affectively-regulated biases relevant to the above assumptions. While noting the striking absence of data pertinent to the questions raised in this chapter, she concludes that currently there is little evidence that these biases play a major role in adolescent risk taking.

If cognitive immaturity and perceptual biases are not strong contenders for explaining adolescent recklessness (recognizing that this conclusion might well change in the future), could these reckless decisions be in some sense rational? William Gardner argues that they can. He supports this argument by showing that rational choice theory, amended to take into consideration changes over the life course (increasing income and age-correlated degrees of preference for immediate versus delayed rewards) predicts heightened risk taking during youth. This chapter invites a reorientation in our thinking about adolescent competencies with implications for our research questions and our approaches to intervention.

From a different framework, that of sociobiology, Wilson and Daly make a similar point. As an explanation of gender and age differences in one type of risky behavior, homicide, they propose that risk taking has been adaptive (in the sense of increasing inclusive fitness) for males compared with females, and for younger compared with older males, in our evolutionary history. Potentially lethal confrontations with a competitor are more likely to be undertaken if the payoff is substantial, and in evolutionary terms, the payoff has been much more substantial for males, particularly young males, than for females. Wilson and Daly clearly do not propose that risk-taking behaviors adaptive in past environments are necessarily adaptive in the environments of today. Rather, contemporary risk taking is the result of psyches—emotional reactions to situations, information processing strategies, and so forth—that have been shaped by the factors contributing to inclusive fitness in evolutionary history. Once again, at least some aspects of risk taking are proposed as "rational," but in this instance from a more distal point of view.

Stephen Lyng brings a sociological perspective to these discussions of risk taking. He first poses the question of whether similarities exist between voluntary risk taking (e.g., mountain climbing) and criminal behavior. He convincingly supports the proposition that both can be characterized as "edgework," although they are distinguishable on the basis of "ecological" versus "interpersonal" edgework. Further, he proposes that edgework occurs in response to feelings of powerlessness and a loss of personal control and provides the individual with renewed feelings of control and self-actualization. The structure of modern society diminishes perceived instrumentality for many individuals and subgroups; we observe that adolescents are among those for whom edgework may be appealing.

It is inevitable in any treatment of adolescent risk taking that, lurking in the background if not in the forefront of the discussion, is the question, "What can we *do* about these things?" Joy Dryfoos gives an in-depth answer to that question. Based upon her extensive review of intervention efforts, she lists the common components of programs that have had some measure of success in reducing negative outcomes. Her proposal for the future, comprehensive community-schools, is based upon the common components and is an intriguing concept.

Public policy also is a form of intervention. Brian Wilcox's informative review covers the effects upon adolescent risk taking of legal proscription and threats, economic regulation, and information dissemination and control. In spite of the usual lack of sufficient evaluation data, he is able to draw upon his knowledge of adolescent development to comment upon the types of policies that are likely to have some impact, and those that are not. He points to the important role of research both in evaluating the effects of policies and in educating policy makers about the nature of adolescent risk taking.

The contributors to this volume were encouraged to use this outlet as an opportunity for speculation about risk taking and to include suggested priorities for research, intervention, or policy. They have more than fulfilled this request: We find these chapters to be thoughtful, scholarly, and provocative, each making a valuable contribution to the literature from a risk-taking perspective.

The volume's final chapter is intended to be an integration and extension of the ideas discussed in previous chapters. The authors discuss some major themes of these chapters, suggest additional issues for consideration, and identify what seem to be the most immediate research priorities stemming from the risk-taking perspective.

NANCY J. BELL AND ROBERT W. BELL
Texas Tech University

ACKNOWLEDGMENTS

This book is based upon a symposium held at Texas Tech University on April 5-6, 1990. Financial support for the symposium was provided by the South Plains Foundation, Lubbock, Texas; the Texas Tech University Health Sciences Center, Department of Psychiatry, Southwest Institute for Addictive Diseases; and the Texas Tech University Office of the Executive Vice President and Provost, Dean of the College of Arts and Sciences, Dean of the College of Home Economics, Dean of the Graduate School, Department of Psychology, and Department of Human Development and Family Studies.

Special thanks to Connie Rome and to the many Texas Tech University faculty and graduate students in the Department of Psychology and the Department of Human Development and Family Studies who assisted with the symposium arrangements.

REFERENCES

Baumrind, D. (1987). A developmental perspective on risk taking in contemporary America. In C. E. Irwin, Jr. (Ed.), *Adolescent social behavior and health. New directions for child development,* No. 37. San Francisco: Jossey-Bass.

Donovan, J. E., & Jessor, R. (1985). Structure of problem behavior in adolescence and young adulthood. *Journal of Counseling and Clinical Psychology, 53,* 890-904.

Heimer, C. A. (1988). Social structure, psychology, and the estimation of risk. *American Review of Sociology, 14,* 491-519.

Irwin, C. E., & Millstein, S. G. (1986). Biopsychosocial correlates of risk-taking behaviors during adolescence. *Journal of Adolescent Health Care, 7,* 82S-96S.

Jessor, R. (1987). Risky driving and adolescent problem behavior: An extension of problem-behavior theory. *Alcohol, Drugs, and Driving, 3,* 1-11.

Jessor, R., & Jessor, S. L. (1977). *Problem behavior and psychosocial development: A longitudinal study of youth.* New York: Academic Press.

Kahneman, D., Slovic, P., & Tversky, A. (Eds.). (1982). *Judgment under uncertainty: Heuristics and biases.* Cambridge, England: Cambridge University Press.

Lyng, S. (1990). Edgework: A social psychological analysis of voluntary risk taking. *American Journal of Sociology, 95,* 851-856.

Osgood, D. W., Johnston, L. D., O'Malley, P. M., & Bachman, J. G. (1988). The Generality of deviance in Late adolescence and early adulthood. *American Sociological Review, 53,* 81-93.

Short, J. (1984). The social fabric at risk: Toward the social transformation of risk analysis. *American Sociological Review, 49,* 711-725.

Slovic, P., Fischhoff, B., & Lichtenstein, S. (1977). Behavioral decision theory. *Annual Review of Psychology, 28,* 1-39.

Tonkin, R. S. (1987). Adolescent risk-taking behavior. *Journal of Adolescent Health Care, 8,* 213-220.

Zuckerman, M. (1979). *Sensation seeking: Beyond the optimal level of arousal.* Hillsdale, New Jersey: Erlbaum.

ADOLESCENCE AND RISK TAKING:
HOW ARE THEY RELATED?

CHARLES E. IRWIN, JR.

INTRODUCTION

Increasingly, the term risk taking is utilized to describe the emergence of all behaviors that are initiated during adolescence. As I have stated elsewhere, this generic terminology implies that all behaviors initiated during second decade of life are volitional and that adolescents and adults differ significantly in the behaviors they engage in (Irwin, 1990a; Irwin & Millstein, 1986; Irwin & Millstein, in press a). A brief review of the mortality and morbidity patterns of adolescents, the biopsychosocial processes occurring during adolescence and preliminary results from our cross sectional longitudinal studies will enable the reader to have a better understanding of the utility of true risk-taking behavior in the adolescent years (Irwin & Millstein, in press a).

Mortality

Age specific mortality rates for the second decade in 1987 were 26.9/100,000 for early adolescents (10–14 years old) and 84.6/100,000 for late adolescents (15–19 years old) (National Center for Health Statistics [NCHS], 1989a; NCHS, 1990). The mortality rate increases by 214% going from early to late adolescence representing the single largest percent increase in any two consecutive age cohorts. Intentional and unintentional injuries account for this major increase in mortality. Death rates from motor vehicle injuries increase by 386%, homicide and legal intervention by 525%, suicide by 587%, and other unintentional injuries increase by 75% between the early and late adolescent years. Gender and race are important factors that are associated with differences in the etiology of death. For example, blacks and other nonwhites have higher mortality rates due to unintentional injuries in the 10–14 year old age cohort. In the 15–19 year old and 20–24 year old age cohorts, whites have the highest rates of unintentional injuries with nonwhites and blacks in decreasing order. This shift in mortality patterns is due to the major increases in intentional injuries categorized as homicide and legal intervention for blacks and the increases in unintentional injuries categorized as motor vehicle accidents for whites. Male adolescents die at greater than twice the rate of females (Irwin, Brindis, Brodt, Bennett, & Rodriguez, 1991; Irwin, Cataldo, Matheny, & Peterson, 1989). The mortality rates of adults from 20 years of age to 39 years of age remain similar to adolescents. Unintentional injuries peak in the 20–24 year old cohort at 51.4/100,000 and fall to 33.3/100,000 among 35–39 year olds; suicide peaks in the 30–34 year old cohort at 15.4/100,000 and falls to 14.9/100,000 in the 35–39 year old cohort. Homicide and legal intervention peaks in the 20–24 year old cohort at 17.8/100,000 and falls to 12.0/100,000 in the 35–39 year old cohort (NCHS, 1989a, 1990). The epidemiology of mortality rates clearly indicates that the negative health outcomes beginning in early adolescence persist throughout the fourth decade of life (U.S. Preventive Services Task Force, 1989).

Morbidity

Injuries. Acute nonfatal injuries account for 15% of discharges from hospitals in the 15–44 year old category and 13.5% of discharges from hospital in the 1–15 year old age category (Graves, 1988). Injuries also contribute substantially to physician office visits in the United States: 5% of visits to pediatric practices and 8.6% of visits to internists (NCHS, 1989b&c). These data documenting physician office visits underestimate the true magnitude of the problem because they do not include visits made to emergency rooms. Studies have documented that children as early as 10 years old are being encouraged to engage in dangerous behaviors such as fights and reckless bicycle or skateboard use (Lewis & Lewis, 1984).

The 1987 National Adolescent Student Health Survey reports that 92% of students never wear a helmet when riding a bike and 50% never wear a seat belt when riding in a car (Association for Advancement of Health Education, 1989). Studies documenting specific behaviors and biopsychosocial processes associated with injuries are generally lacking. Several studies have been done documenting the basic description of epidemiologic patterns of injuries (Rivara & Wolf, 1989; Scheidt, 1988).

Sexual behavior. Sexual activity increased dramatically between 1971 and 1983 (Weddle, McKenry, & Leigh,1988). In spite of the rising concerns of sexually transmitted diseases including AIDS, rates of sexual behavior have continued to increase throughout the 1980s (Pratt, 1990). In the most recent 1988 national survey, 97%

of black males and 85% of white males had experienced coitus at least once by 19 years of age. For females, 83% of black females and 76% of white females had experienced coitus at least once by age 19 years. Differences in sexual behavior among younger adolescents of different racial groups also were noted. By age 15, 69% of black males report having had sexual intercourse while 26% of white males report having had coitus. For females, 26% of whites at age 15 years report having had sex as compared to 24% of blacks at age 15 years (Pratt, 1990). Little is known about sexual behavior other than coitus in adolescents (Brooks-Gunn and Furstenberg, 1989). The resultant negative outcomes of sexually transmitted diseases and pregnancy also have increased in the past decade. In the area of sexually transmitted diseases alone, the rates for *Neisseria gonorrhoeae* in adolescents in 1988 were 36/100,000 for early male adolescents (ages 10–14) and 96.0/100,000 for early female adolescents (ages 10–14). By late adolescence (ages 15–19), the rates are 978/100,00 for males and 1170/100,000 for females (Center for Disease Control [CDC], 1990). If sexual activity status is accounted for in the reported age-specific rates, the rates of sexually transmitted diseases in late adolescence would be the highest for any age specific cohort in the United States.

Substance use and abuse. The 1988 lifetime prevalence rates of cigarette and alcohol use remain high at 66.4% and 92% respectively. The 1988 daily use of cigarettes is reported by 18.1% of high school seniors with 10.1% reporting use of more than half a pack per day. Since 1978, females report greater daily use than males (Johnston, O'Malley, Bachman, 1989a & b). The mean age of onset is early in adolescence at 12 years old (CDC, 1989). There is increasing evidence that males may be using smokeless tobacco as a "healthy" alternative (Connolly, Winn, Hecht, Henningfield, Walker, & Hoffmann, 1986; Hunter, Croft, & Burke, 1986). Daily use of alcohol remains high at 4.2% in high school seniors in 1988 with 34.7% of this cohort reporting that they had five or more drinks at one time in the past two weeks. Initiation of alcohol also begins early in adolescence with a mean age of onset at 12.6 years. Males report greater frequency and intensity of alcohol use by a ratio of 2:1 compared to females (Johnston et al., 1989a).

The 1988 lifetime prevalence rates of marijuana and cocaine use are 47.2% and 12.1% respectively. The lifetime prevalence and daily use have decreased markedly since the peak in late 1970s for marijuana and early to mid-1980s for cocaine. The 1988 daily use of marijuana was 2.7% by high school seniors. The mean age of onset is 14.4 years old (Johnston, O'Malley, Bachman, 1987). These prevalence rates of marijuana, crack and cocaine may underestimate the true prevalence rates of these substances in the entire adolescent population because adolescents not in high school probably have much higher rates of substance use (Irwin, 1990a).

Covariation of Risk Behaviors

Certain risk behaviors (substance use, sexual activity, and recreational vehicle use) appear to be associated with each other. Investigators are now focusing on the possible mechanisms responsible for the interrelationships of the behaviors and the positive and negative health outcomes (Baumrind, 1987; Donovan & Jessor, 1985; Irwin & Millstein, 1987; Irwin & Millstein, in press a; Jessor & Jessor, 1977; Udry, 1988).

The close association between alcohol use and injuries is well established at all ages. Alcohol-related motor vehicle injuries are the leading cause of mortality in late adolescence and young adulthood (CDC, 1983; Mayhew, Donelson, Beirness, & Simpson, 1986). Alcohol is associated with a large number of other unintentional injuries resulting from water-related sports, fires, falls, bicycles, and skateboards (CDC, 1983, 1989; Friedman, 1985; Mayhew et al., 1986). Other substances have been implicated in unintentional injuries but their definitive role remains to be established.

Several studies have now documented the relationship of substance use and sexual activity. Jessor and Jessor (1977) documented the association between early sexual activity and use of marijuana, cigarettes and alcohol. With drinking status as a marker for at risk youth, Jessor and Jessor found 80% of their at risk subjects were marijuana users and better than 50% had initiated coitus. Zabin (1984) further documented the association of early sexual activity, ineffective contraceptive use, and cigarette use. Additional data from the National Survey of Youth indicate that early alcohol use in females is more predictive of early sexual activity than in males (Mott & Haurin, 1987). From longitudinal analyses of our data, we have found that the number of risk behaviors (e.g., substance use, dangerous vehicle use, etc.) reported by white females correlates positively with their intention to become sexually active (Kegeles, Millstein, Adler, Irwin, Cohn, & Dolcini, 1987). This relationship does not hold up in nonwhite females. A factor analysis of our cross sectional data on risk behaviors demonstrated the interrelationship of substance use and other physical risk behaviors in males and not in females (See Results section of paper; Adler, Millstein, Irwin, & Kegeles, 1986; Irwin & Millstein, in press a).

Beyond the association of substance use with other risk behaviors, substances are associated in predictable ways. Alcohol and/or tobacco appear to be "gateway drugs" for the use of illicit substances. Kandel and her colleagues have documented the progression in a cohort of adolescents followed through young adulthood (Yamaguchi & Kandel, 1984). The sequence of progression is as follows: Alcohol, cigarettes, and marijuana precede other illicit substances (including psychedelics, cocaine, heroin and other nonprescribed stimulants, sedatives, and tranquilizers), and the use of prescribed psychoactive drugs follows all other substances. For females, tobacco in the form of cigarettes is the drug of choice for initiation. For males, alcohol or cigarettes may precede other substance use. Newcomb and Bentler (1986) have recently documented the initiation of cocaine use and its association with other substances during a five year period in the late 1970s to early 1980s in Los Angeles County. Alcohol use preceded marijuana use by one year. Marijuana use in the preceding year was an important predictor of cocaine use in the following year.

Definition of risk taking. Behaviors associated with some of the major mortalities and morbidities of adolescents share a common theme: risk taking. Our definition of risk taking includes only volitional behaviors in which the outcomes remain uncertain with the possibility of an identifiable negative health outcome. Young people with limited or no experience engage in behaviors with anticipation of benefit and without understanding the immediate or long-term consequences of their actions (Irwin, 1990a; Irwin & Millstein, 1986). Three behaviors fit our definition: 1) sexual behaviors; 2) substance use; and 3) motor recreational vehicle use. We deliberately exclude behaviors that are inherently pathogenic (e.g., suicide, eating disorders) or result from the overwhelming forces of the environment, e.g., homicide (Irwin, 1990a).

These behaviors are initiated during early adolescence with a marked increase in frequency from early to late adolescence, are prevalent in all socioeconomic and racial/ethnic groups, differ by gender and racial/ethnic groups, and account for the majority of morbidity during adolescence (Blum, 1987; Irwin & Millstein, 1986; Irwin & Vaughan, 1987, 1988). Mortality patterns and hospital discharge rates also indicate that traumatic injuries and substance use account for the two largest discharge categories when one excludes pregnancy (Irwin, 1986). The prevalence of these three risk behaviors has remained high over the past decade. Many clinicians consider these risk behaviors to be normative in spite of the well-recognized short- and long-term health problems (Irwin, 1987). Increasingly, there is a recognition of the covariation of these three behaviors, with some investigators postulating a developmental trajectory of behaviors (Irwin, 1987; Irwin, Millstein, Adler, & Turner, 1988).

Adolescence and Risk Taking

Adolescence is a critical developmental period in the life cycle (Lerner, 1987; Petersen, 1987, 1988). With major changes occurring in biological, cognitive, psychological, social and environmental processes, exploratory behavior and experimentation with a wide range of behaviors is essential for normal adolescent development (Irwin, 1987; Irwin & Vaughan, 1988). Learning how to take the initiative is one of the critical tasks of development (Baumrind, 1987). With the onset of these maturational changes, risk-taking behavior emerges as a component of normal adolescent development. The major problem for investigators and clinicians is to distinguish between normal transitional risk-taking behaviors that are developmentally enhancing and those same behaviors that, by their frequency or intensity, are pathological expressions for which there is little evidence of secondary gain for the teenager (Baumrind, 1987; Irwin, 1987; Irwin & Ryan, 1989).

Biopsychosocial Models of Risk Behaviors

Several models have been proposed that integrate adolescent developmental principles with risk factors for the emergence of risk-taking behaviors (Irwin and Millstein, 1986; Jessor and Jessor, 1977; Udry, 1988). Jessor and Jessor have proposed a problem behavior framework that includes an interaction of factors that arise within and between each of three systems: the personality system, the perceived environment and the behavior system (Jessor, 1984; Jessor & Jessor, 1977). There is increasing evidence that sex hormones, especially testosterone and androgenic steroids, have a major independent and interdependent role in the onset of sexual behavior in males and females and other risk behavior in males (Udry, 1985, 1988; Udry and Billy, 1987). More recently, Udry has proposed a model for males that includes the effects of sex hormones. Serum levels of free testosterone added significant variance to a social model when using a factor of five behaviors

(Udry, 1988). Other psychosocial variables added little variance to the model. In girls, there were no specific biological effects. Other models draw heavily from the concept of sensation seeking as a personality trait that correlates with risk behaviors (Daitzman & Zuckerman, 1980; Zuckerman, 1987) and the risk perception constructs (Slovic, 1987). Our model (as depicted in figure 1) draws from the Jessor and Jessor constructs, the biological effects demonstrated by Udry, and integrates the knowledge we have gained from the literature on the psychosocial effects of timing of pubertal maturation. To understand our model, a brief review of the literature on effects of pubertal timing on psychosocial functioning is essential (for an extensive review of the model and the variables in the model, see Irwin & Millstein, 1986 and Irwin & Ryan, 1989). The effects of timing of puberty have their greatest effects in the areas of self-perceptions (body image and self-esteem), developmental needs (family independence, heterosocial relationships, peer affiliation); school performance (academic performance and problem behaviors associated with school functioning); and environmental responses (family, peer, and teacher expectations). These psychosocial effects are related to gender, the relationships of the adolescent's pubertal status to that of his or her peers, timing of pubertal maturation and psychosocial constructs definitions utilized, and the risk behavior under investigation (for extensive review and discussion see Brooks-Gunn, 1989; Brooks-Gunn, Petersen, & Eichorn, 1985; Eichorn, Clausen, Haan, Honzik, & Mussen, 1981; Irwin & Millstein, 1986; Steinberg, 1987). The most negative effects have been reported for early maturing females (Brooks-Gunn, 1989). Recent work has shown that the effects of early maturation may be detrimental for both genders, with early maturation in males being associated with the early initiation of sexual activity (Irwin, Millstein, & Turner, 1989; Westney, Jenkins, Butts, & Williams, 1984).

According to our model, the timing of biological maturation affects cognitive scope, self-perceptions, perceptions of the social environment, and personal values. These four variables are hypothesized to predict adolescent risk-taking behavior through the mediating effects of risk perception and peer-group characteristics. In a series of studies now being conducted in our division, we are analyzing the strength of the various components of the model in a heterogeneous urban sample of adolescents (Irwin et al., 1988, 1989; Irwin & Millstein, 1987, in press a).

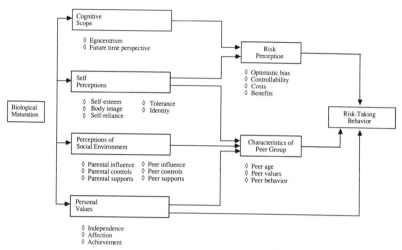

FIG. 1.   Causal model of adolescent risk-taking behavior. Modified and adapted
from: Irwin and Millstein (1986).

My colleagues and I are particularly interested in the interrelationships among behaviors and the mechanisms that influence
their onset, progression and cessation. Our research has focused
on the relationships among these behavior, changes in frequency
and intensity over time, and the adolescents' perceptions and expectations of specific behaviors. Beyond the quantitative issues of
the risk behaviors and pubertal measures, of critical importance to
us was the meaning ascribed to pubertal change and the specific
behaviors.

CURRENT RESEARCH PROGRAM

Basic to all of our data collection is a general philosophy driving
our research program: Adolescents are actively involved in our research process and they have the opportunity to learn more about
their development and risk behaviors through the process of participating in our research. Therefore, all of our research has a
feedback component for the teenagers.

Our subjects come from two Bay Area high schools, one middle
school, a longitudinal sample at the middle school and a small
cohort of the original middle and senior high school sample that
we have brought into the Medical Center for more in depth interviews and physical assessments. The Bay Area high school and middle school data are collected using a modified version of the
Centers for Disease Control Teen Health Risk Appraisal Form, a
self staging pubertal assessment form, and a supplemental form

which gathers information regarding sexual behaviors and intentions to engage in behaviors during the next year. The Teen Age Health Risk Appraisal forms have the added benefit of providing adolescents with an individualized computerized feedback form which gives them a lifestyle score based upon the number of health damaging and health promoting behaviors in which they have engaged. During the feedback session with the class our staff provides information to the young people regarding where to seek help for a variety of health related problems. The Health Risk Appraisal feedback form has been modified to eliminate the life style score. The current form provides information regarding health promoting and damaging behaviors and mechanisms by which the adolescents may change their health damaging behavior.[1] This feedback form encourages accurate reporting due to the feedback sheet: Students were informed that the only way to obtain useful feedback was to provide correct information about their behaviors.

The pubertal self assessment form also was developed to provide computerized feedback information to young persons regarding their current sexual maturation stage (Tanner staging), anticipated changes in overall biological development over the next two years, and a projected growth curve giving them their anticipated height at 19 years of age. The supplemental teen health risk form includes questions regarding sexual behaviors and intentions to engage in 18 risk behaviors over the next year.

All instruments are administered in required classrooms of the middle and high schools by an Adolescent Medicine fellow or faculty physician and a graduate student in health psychology or a health psychologist. The program was presented to the young people as one that was trying to understand more about the health and development of young people. Informed consent was obtained through parental notification with letters sent by the principals of the schools and the principal investigators. Parents, teachers and students understand that all data collected are confidential and no information will be shared with parents and teachers without permission from the students.

The university data are collected in two initial sessions of five hours duration and one follow up session eighteen months later. The initial data at the Medical School includes a session focusing on qualitative issues regarding risk and pubertal changes and a physical examination. The second session includes quantitative measures of psychosocial functioning. The final data session (18 months later) focuses on quantitative data regarding intensity and frequency of risk behaviors and qualitative data regarding risk behaviors and major demographic changes. There are five data points as listed below.

Data Point	Year	Middle School	High School
		(N)	(N)
T1	1985	124	100
T2	1986	813	600
T3	1987	332	
T4	1987–88	100	100
T5	1989–90	100	200

Findings

Our preliminary findings are presented in four areas: frequency of initial behaviors (T2), assessments of behavioral risk (T1); interrelationships of behaviors (T2); and anticipatory assessment of consequences.

Frequencies of specific behaviors. The frequencies of 13 health risk behaviors are listed in table 1. The data are provided by school type: middle or high school. Four behaviors (drinking alcohol, taking chances on a bike or skateboard, not using a seat belt in a car, and driving/riding in a car over the speed limit) are reported by over 50% of the sample in middle school. Greater than 20% of the middle school sample report using marijuana, having sexual intercourse, and driving with an impaired driver. The only behaviors that are not engaged in by approximately 20% of the high school sample are driving a car or motorcycle under the influence. Even though the data are cross sectional, there are major differences between middle and high school indicating the importance of the transition time between middle and senior high school.

Interrelationships of behaviors. The 18 behaviors on the CDC Teen Health Risk form were subjected to factor analysis with varimax rotation (Adler et al., 1986; Irwin & Millstein, in press a). The 18 behaviors include: smoking cigarettes, drinking beer, drinking wine, drinking mixed drinks, using controlled substances (e.g., marijuana, cocaine, LSD, etc.), motorcycle driving or riding, using seatbelts, taking physical risks, having broken bones, being knocked unconscious, engaging in dangerous behaviors (e.g., carry a knife, argue with strangers, seek entertainment in high crime area), eating high sugar foods, eating cholesterol/high fat foods,

TABLE 1.—*Percentage of middle and high school aged adolescents engaging in risk behaviors.*

Health Risk Behavior	Middle School(a)	High School(b)	Total(c)
Alcohol (ever used)	71.8%	84.4%	78.4%
Alcohol (≥ 1×month)	13.8%	42.8%	28.7%
Marijuana (ever used)	31.9%	61.4%	47.1%
Marijuana (≥ 1×month)	9.4%	33.0%	21.6%
Sexual intercourse	21.4%	43.9%	33.3%
Casual sex	8.0%	19.7%	14.4%
Unprotected Sex	11.0%	32.6%	22.8%
Take chances on bike/skateboard	68.0%	59.5%	63.3%
Use bike/skateboard under influence	7.7%	19.5%	14.0%
Not use seat belt in car	56.9%	71.9%	64.0%
Drive/ride car over speed limit	63.8%	73.4%	70.7%
Passenger in car with impaired driver	36.9%	58.3%	48.3%
Drive car/motorcycle under influence	3.9%	9.4%	6.8%

(a) n = 640; ages 11-14
(b) n = 680; ages 14-18
(c) n = 1,320

going for dental check-ups, sleeping eight hours per night, exercising, getting into a fight.

Five factors emerged which accounted for 53% of the variance for the males and 49% of the variance for the females. Each behavior had to have a factor loading of .30 or above to be considered a separate factor (Adler et al., 1986; Irwin & Millstein, in press a). The factors for males and females are not identical since different items failed to meet this criterion for any one factor for each sex. For males three of the five factors related to injuries and preventive behavior. The first male factor to emerge consists of three items relating to alcohol use (frequency of use of mixed drinks, wine, and beer) and the item regarding substance use. The second male factor includes beer, substance use, cigarette use, hours riding a motorcycle, and frequency of being knocked unconscious. The third male factor consists of fat servings and sugar servings per day. The fourth male factor includes seat belt use, servings of high fiber foods, and frequency of dental check-ups suggesting that diverse preventive behavior may be linked. Finally, the fifth male factor reflects potential for interpersonal violence, including fights and a number of dangerous behaviors in which the respondent usually engages.

For females a slightly different structure emerged. Two of the five factors relate to alcohol and substance use and two factors relate to injury and prevention. Alcohol use is more differentiated for females than for males. For females beer ingestion is associated with cigarette and controlled substance use. Wine and mixed drinks and cigarette use fall on a separate factor. The third female factor is the same junk food factor seen with males linking fat and sugar servings. The final female factor is a health prevention factor which includes two of the three items in the comparable factor for males. For females it includes seat belt use, exercise, and dental check-ups. The differences in the male and female factor structure suggest a broader range of behaviors (including physically dangerous behaviors as well as substance abuse and sexual behavior) in males as compared with females in which the behaviors are primarily substance abuse behaviors.

Sexual behavior was not included on the CDC Teen Health Risk Behavior form, but was included in our supplemental risk behavior form. In some preliminary analyses of the relationship of sexual activity to other risk behaviors, we used the six risk behaviors with the highest frequency in the sample (i.e., having driven a car fast, using marijuana, having drunk alcohol, having ridden in a car when the driver had used alcohol or drugs, having done fancy tricks on a skateboard or bicycle, and having taken dares (Kegeles et al., 1987).

Among our sample, 29% were sexually active, 18% were not sexually active but intended to become sexually active in one year, and 53% were not sexually active and intended to remain inactive in one year. Significantly more black males and females were sexually active than their white counterparts. Sexually active youths of both races engaged in significantly more other risk behaviors than did adolescents who were not sexually active. Among both blacks and whites, sexually active adolescents and those who intended to initiate sexual activity engaged in the same number of risky behaviors. Among white adolescents, those who anticipated initiating sexual activity in the next year engaged in more risk behaviors than did sexually inactive youths. This difference was not found among the black youths. Risk behaviors were important predictors of intention to initiate coitus in white adolescents, but were not predictors in black adolescents. Among black adolescent

females, age was a better predictor than risk behaviors for intention to initiate coitus (Kegeles et al., 1987).

Assessment of behavioral risk. Invulnerability and adolescence
often have been closely linked, and our own definition of risk
taking has the basic assumption that adolescents do not have the
basic knowledge about health, illness, and risk. In our early investigation we attempted to understand whether adolescents were
able to make differential judgments about risk behaviors and the
way in which age, gender and sexual maturation status affects the
adolescents' assessments of the severity of risk behaviors. Also, we
were interested in how these perceptions change over time.

The results relating to health and illness behaviors are reported
extensively elsewhere (See Millstein & Irwin, 1988). Subjects were
224 middle and high school students ranging in age from 11 to 19
years (mean = 14.2 years, SD = 1.8). The interview included quantitative and qualitative measures of health, illness, and risk, as well
as a self-assessment of sexual maturation status (Tanner staging)
and of their age as perceived by adults. Subjects were asked to
quantify 11 risk behaviors on a six point scale from not at all risky to
extremely risky. The 11 behaviors included drinking beer/wine,
drinking hard liquor, smoking cigarettes, using drugs, being a passenger in a car whose driver has had a few drinks, being a passenger
in a car whose driver is driving too fast, riding a bike or skateboard
recklessly, having sexual intercourse, not seeing a physician in the
presence of a health problem, eating poorly, and not exercising.
For each of the behaviors, subjects also were asked to rate whether
the degree of risk would be less, the same, or more as they got older.
Drug use was perceived as being the most risky, and not exercising
being the least risky (however still ranking a 3.4 on a six-point
scale). All behaviors except exercising ranked better than 4.2 on
the six-point scale. Overall, females perceived significantly greater
risk than did males. Older adolescents and more physiologically
mature adolescents perceived significantly less risk across the 11
behaviors than did younger adolescents. Specific behaviors for
which older adolescents perceived less risk were: engaging in sex;
smoking cigarettes; drinking beer/wine; drinking hard liquor; and
using drugs.

The more physiologically mature adolescents (as defined by
sexual maturation status), when compared with less mature adolescents perceived less risk for the following specific behaviors: driving and drinking; engaging in sex; smoking cigarettes; drinking
beer and wine or hard liquor; and using drugs.

In order to begin to understand how risk perception changes with age, adolescents were asked to anticipate how the risk of certain behaviors would change with advancing chronologic age. Having sexual intercourse and smoking cigarettes were viewed as becoming less risky with age by greater than 50% of the sample. Not seeing a physician when you had a health problem and not exercising were seen as becoming more risky with advancing age by 50% of the sample. Four behaviors (drive and drink, drive fast, reckless vehicle use, drug use) were reported as remaining the same risk by greater than 50% of the sample (Irwin & Millstein, 1987, in press a; Millstein & Irwin, 1985).

Adolescents have been characterized as risk takers without an understanding of how adolescents themselves perceive risk. These results suggest that gender, chronologic age and physiologic age need to be considered for a further understanding of the meaning of risk. Older adolescents in this study perceived less risk than younger adolescents for behaviors representing many of the major morbidities/mortalities of youth including substance use and sexual activity.

Older adolescents' perceptions of diminished risk may reflect actual differences in the prevalence of these behaviors as a function of age. Studies of risk perception in adults have shown that individuals who engage in risk behavior perceive less risk associated with those behaviors than do individuals who do not engage in risk behavior (Weinstein, 1984). Alternatively, the perception of less risk by older adolescents may reflect expectations formed at an earlier age. More than half of this sample perceived the risk of cigarette smoking and sexual intercourse as becoming less risky with a advancing age. This anticipatory risk assessment could account for some of the variance in actual risk assessments. Although these data cannot provide information about developmental changes in risk perception, the risk perceptions associated with different age groups do correspond to some of these anticipatory perceptions (Irwin & Millstein, 1987, in press a; Millstein & Irwin, 1985).

Other correlates of risk taking. The national morbidity and mortality patterns point out that males are at greater risk. In our data sets, males engage in more risks and at a greater intensity (Adler et al., 1986; Irwin & Millstein, 1987; Irwin & Millstein, in press a; Millstein & Irwin, 1988).

Preliminary analyses of our data also has demonstrated the importance of timing of biological maturation and expectations of outcome of risk behavior. Early maturing males and females engage in a greater number of risk behaviors (Irwin, Millstein, & Turner, 1989). Positive and less negative expectations of outcomes of risk behaviors have differential effects on the onset of certain risk behaviors. Positive expectations appear to be associated with physical risk behaviors (Irwin et al., 1988).

SUMMARY

Adolescents are engaging in behaviors with a high probability of negative outcomes in early adolescence. Behaviors cluster together in specific patterns for females and males. Early in adolescence, teenagers make differential assessments of risk behaviors. There appears to be a tendency to reduce the estimate of risk associated with the behavior as the adolescent gets older. This may be associated with experience and a better understanding of risk. The adult literature tells us that adults who participate in risky behaviors tend to underestimate the risks associated with these behaviors (Weinstein, 1984). Perhaps the same phenomenon operates in adolescents. It is unclear from our data, what is responsible for the anticipation of diminished risk associated with certain behaviors. It may be that they have already anticipated diminished risk prior to engaging in the behavior. Recently, Johnston and his colleagues have followed the changes in marijuana use over the past decade and its correlation with increased perception of risk of danger associated with marijuana (Johnston et al., 1989a). This is the only clear data that points out cross sectional changes in risk behavior associated with increased risk perceptions. It is important to recognize that Johnston and his colleague's data come from high school seniors.

INTERVENTION MODEL

Figure 2 integrates our model with results from a number of studies focusing on environmental factors contributing to risk behaviors. This model is presented as a useful tool for those who want to consider risk behaviors in a unified manner. The model highlights the importance of biopsychosocial factors which are primarily endogenous and environmental factors that are primarily exogenous. The model further delineates the importance of predisposing factors that increase the vulnerability of the adolescent and, finally, precipitating factors that are more immediate and may be the final pathway causing the adolescent to initiate the behavior.

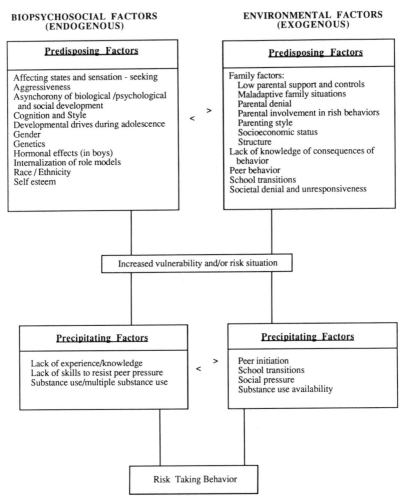

FIG. 2.   Principal factors in risk-taking behaviors. Modified and adapted from: Irwin and Millstein (1986) and Irwin and Ryan (1989).

Biopsychosocial Factors

Biopsychosocial factors include gender, attitudes and beliefs about consequences, role modeling, affective states including sensation seeking, aggressiveness, self-esteem, and developmental drives during adolescence. Attitudes, perceptions, motivations, and intentions all predict the onset of behaviors. Personality factors include high values on independence, decreased expectation for academic performance, and less involvement in conventional activities such as religiosity. Generally decreased cognitive competence has been associated with the onset of risk behaviors; however, Baumrind has demonstrated the association of increased competence and initiation of risk behaviors (Baumrind, 1987). Participating factors in the biopsychosocial area include substance use, lack of experience and knowledge associated with lack of skills to resist peer pressure.

Environmental Factors

The role of the social environment remains an important predictor in the onset of risk behavior including the school and its structure (Simmons & Blythe, 1987). The protective role of supportive environments must be acknowledged during adolescence (Irwin, 1987; Irwin & Vaughan, 1988). Family and peer factors remain crucial with parental behavior and style being important correlates of onset (Baumrind, 1987; Irwin, 1987). Precipitating factors include substance use availability, peer onset and multiple social transitions including school.

CONCLUSION

The mechanisms for onset of risky behaviors is complex. A better understanding of the differences in the mechanisms presents the challenge for investigators in attempting to understand risk behaviors in adolescence and developing effective intervention and prevention strategies for separate risk behaviors as well as groups of behaviors (Irwin, 1990a & b).

During the past several years, there has been considerable movement away from studying single behaviors to studying groups of behaviors. In addition, interventions have begun to focus on multiple behaviors. Little attention has been directed toward understanding the mechanisms responsible for the initiation, meaning, and natural history of specific behaviors. The literature and conventional wisdom speak about the functional role risk taking serves, yet there is little or no work done trying to understand the functional nature that risk behaviors may serve in the developmental process of adolescence (Baumrind, 1987; Irwin & Millstein, 1986, in press a; Millstein, 1989). The risk behaviors initiated during adolescence persist throughout the fourth decade of life as the causes of mortality and morbidity (Irwin, 1990b; U.S. Preventive Services Task Force, 1989). A better understanding of injuries, sexual behavior and substance use warrants our attention if we are to make a difference in the health of adolescents and adults.

ACKNOWLEDGMENTS

The author would like to thank Dulce Padilla for her numerous hours of work with the manuscript, Susan Millstein who has worked with me for over ten years in conceptualizing many of the ideas presented in this paper, Rebecca Turner for a number of the analyses presented here, and the large number of psychology graduate students and Adolescent Medicine fellows who have been involved in our research program.

Portions of this paper were presented at a conference on Risk taking on April 27, 1990 at Texas Tech University, Lubbock, Texas. The results presented in this paper and some of the conceptual ideas are to appear in a chapter entitled Correlates and Predictors of Risk Taking Behavior During Adolescence by Charles E. Irwin, Jr. and Susan G. Millstein in L. P. Lipsitt and L. L. Mitnick (Eds.) Self Regulatory Behavior and Risk Taking Causes and Consequences, Norwood, New Jersey: Ablex Inc.

The author was supported in part by grants from the William T. Grant Foundation and the Bureau of Maternal and Child Health (MCJ000978 and MCJ060564).

NOTE

[1]All questionnaires are available from the author.

REFERENCES

Adler, N. E., Millstein, S. G., Irwin C. E., Jr., & Kegeles, S. M. (1986). *Risk factors and health behaviors in adolescents.* Paper presented at annual meeting of the Society for Behavioral Medicine, San Francisco.

Association for Advancement of Health Education (1989). *National Adolescent Student Health Survey: A Report of the Health of America's Youth.* Oakland, CA: Third Party Publishing Co.

Baumrind, D. (1987). A developmental perspective on risk taking in contemporary America. In C. E. Irwin, Jr. (Ed.), *Adolescent social behavior and health. New directions for child development,* No. 37. San Francisco: Jossey Bass.

Blum, R. (1987). Contemporary threats to adolescent health in the United States. *Journal of the American Medical Association, 257,* 3390-94.

Brooks-Gunn, J. (1989). Pubertal processes and the early adolescent transition. In W. Damon (Ed.), *Child development today and tomorrow.* San Francisco: Jossey-Bass, 155-176.

Brooks-Gunn, J., & Furstenberg, F. F., Jr. (1989). Adolescent sexual behavior. *American Psychologist, 44,* 249-257.

Brooks-Gunn, J., Petersen, A. C., & Eichorn, D. (1985). The timing of maturation and psychosocial functioning in adolescence. *Journal of Youth and Adolescence, 14,* 3-4.

Centers for Disease Control (1983). Alcohol as a risk factor for injuries United States. *Morbidity & Mortality Weekly Report, 32,* 61-65.

Centers for Disease Control (1989). Psychosocial predictors of smoking among adolescents. *Morbidity & Mortality Weekly Report, 45,* 1S-45S.

Centers for Disease Control (1990). *Sexually transmitted diseases,* unpublished data.

Connolly, G. N., Winn, D. M., Hect, S. S., Henningfield, J. E., Walker, B., & Hoffmann, D. (1986). The reemergence of smokeless tobacco, *New England Journal of Medicine, 314,* 1020-1024.

Daitzman, R., & Zuckerman, M. (1980). Disinhibitory sensation seeking, personality and gonadal hormones, *Personality and Individual Differences, 1,* 103-112.

Donovan, J. E., & Jessor, R., (1985). The structure of problem behavior in adolescence and young adulthood, *Journal of Consulting and Clinical Psychology, 53,* 890-906.

Eichorn, D. H., Clausen, J. A., Haan, N., Honzik, M. P., & Mussen, P. H. (Eds.) (1981). *Present and past in middle life.* New York: Academic Press.

Friedman, I. M. (1985). Alochol and unnatural deaths in San Francisco youths. *Journal of Pediatrics, 76,* 191-193.

Graves, E. J. (1988). *Summary: National Hospital Discharge Survey. Advance data from vital and health statistics,* No. 185. Hyattsville, Maryland. National Center for Health Statistics 1990, Department of Health of Human Services Publication No. (PHS) 90-1250.

Hunter, S. M., Croft, J. B., & Burke, G. L. (1986). Longitudinal patterns of cigarette smoking and smokeless tobacco use in youth: The Bogalusa heart study. *American Journal of Public Health, 76,* 193-195.

Irwin, C. E., Jr. (1986). Why adolescent medicine? *Journal of Adolescent Health Care, 7(Suppl),* 1S-12S.

Irwin, C. E., Jr. (1987). *Adolescent social behavior and health. New directions for child development,* no. 37. San Francisco: Jossey-Bass.

Irwin, C. E., Jr. (1990a). Risk taking during adolescence. In M. Green & R. J. Haggerty (Eds.). *Ambulatory pediatrics III.* Philadelphia: W. B. Saunders, 24-26.

Irwin, C. E., Jr. (1990b). The theoretical concept of at-risk adolescents. *Adolescent Medicine: State of the Art Reviews, 1,* 1-14.

Irwin, C. E., Jr., Brindis, C., Brodt, S., Bennett, T., & Rodriguez R. (1991). *The health of America's youth: A prelude to action. Bureau of Maternal & Child Health.*

Irwin, C. E., Jr., Cataldo, M. F., Matheny, A. P., & Peterson, L. (1989). *Health consequences of behavior: Injury prevention model, 'Consensus' Paper from conference on research in behavioral pediatrics: Current approaches and future directions,* National Institute of Child Health & Development Bureau of Maternal & Child Health, Columbia, Maryland. Paper currently under review.

Irwin, C. E., Jr., & Millstein, S. G. (1986). Biopsychosocial correlates of risk-taking behaviors during adolescence: Can the physician intervene? *Journal of Adolescent Health Care, 7(Suppl),* 82S-96S.

Irwin, C. E., Jr., & Millstein, S. G. (1987). The meaning of alcohol use in early adolescents. *Pediatric Research, 21,* 175A.

Irwin, C. E., Jr., & Millstein, S. G. (in press a). Correlates and predictors of risk-taking behaviors during adolescence. In L. P. Lipsitt & L. L. Mitnick (Eds.), *Self regulating and risk taking behavior: Causes and consequences.* Norwood, New Jersey: Ables Inc.

Irwin, C. E., Jr., & Millstein, S. G. (in press b). Risk taking behaviors during adolescence. In R. Lerner, A. Petersen, & J. Brooks-Gunn (Eds.): *Encyclopedia of adolescence.* New York: Garland Publishing.

Irwin, C. E., Jr., Millstein S. G., Adler, N. E., & Turner, R. (1988). Predictors of risk taking behaviors in early adolescents. *Pediatric Research, 23,* 201A.

Irwin, C. E., Jr., Millstein, S. G., & Turner, R. (1989). Pubertal timing and adolescent risk taking: Are they correlated? *Pediatric Research, 25,* 8A.

Irwin, C. E., Jr., & Ryan, S. A. (1989). Problem behaviors of adolescence. *Pediatrics in Review, 10,* 235-246.

Irwin, C. E., Jr., & Vaughan, E. (August 1987). *Emerging national issues and trends in adolescent health.* Plenary session, regional institute on high priority issues in maternal and child health, Region IX: Department of Health and Human Services.

Irwin, C. E., Jr., & Vaughan, E. (1988). Psychosocial context of adolescent development: Study group report. *Journal of Adolescent Health Care, 9(Suppl),* 11-20.

Jessor, R. (1984). Adolescent development and behavioral health. In J. D. Matarazzo, S. M. Weiaa, I. A. Herd, N. E. Miller, & S. M. Weiss (Eds.), *Behavioral health: A handbook of health enhancement and disease prevention.* New York: John Wiley, 69-90.

Jessor, R., & Jessor, S. L. (1977). *Problem behavior and psychosocial development: A longitudinal study of youth.* New York: Academic Press.

Johnston, L. D., O'Malley, P. M., & Bachman, J. (1987). *National trends in drug use and related factors among american high school students and young adults: 1975-86.* National Institute on Drug Abuse, Department of Health and Human Services Publication No. (ASM) 87-15350. Government Printing Office, Washington, D.C.

Johnston, L. D., O'Malley, P. M., & Bachman, J. G. (1989a). *Drug use, drinking and smoking: National survey results from high school, college and young adult populations.* Department of Health and Human, Services Publication No. (ADM) 89-1638, Washington, D. C.: U.S. Government Printing Office.

Johnston, L. D., O'Malley, P. M., & Bachman, J. G. (1989b). *Illicit drug use, smoking, and drinking by America's high school students, college students and young adults.* Department of Health and Human Services Publication No. (ADM) 89-1602, Washington, D.C.: U.S. Government Printing Office.

Kegeles, S. M., Millstein, S. G., Adler, N. E., Irwin, C. E., Jr., Cohn, L., & Dolcini, P. (1987). The transition to sexual activity and its relationship to other risk behaviors. *Journal of Adolescent Health Care, 8,* 303.

Lerner, R. (1987). A life-span perspective for early adolescence. In R. Lerner & T. Foch (Eds.), *Biological-psychological interactions in early adolescence.* Hillsdale, New Jersey: L. Erlbaum Associates, 9-34.

Lewis, C. L., & Lewis, M. A. (1984). Peer pressure and risk-taking behaviors in children. *American Journal of Public Health, 74,* 580-584.

Mayhew, D. R., Donelson, A. C., Beirness, D. J., & Simpson, H. M. (1986). Youth, alcohol and relative risk of crash involvement. *Accident Analysis & Prevention, 18,* 273-287.

Millstein, S. G., & Irwin, C. E., Jr. (1985). Adolescent's assessments of behavioral risk: Sex differences and maturation effects. *Pediatric Research, 19,* 112A.

Millstein, S. G., & Irwin, C. E., Jr. (1988). Accident-related behavior in adolescents: A biopsychosocial view. *Alcohol, Drugs and Driving, 4,* 21-30.

Mott, F. L., & Haurin, R. J. (1987). The inter-relatedness of age at first intercourse, early pregnancy and drug use among American adolescents: Preliminary results from the national longitudinal survey of youth labor market experience. Paper presented at Population Association of America, Chicago, Illinois.

National Center for Health Services Research (1988). *Health United States.* Department of Health and Human Services Publication No. (DHS) 89-1232 (1989). Washington, D.C.: U.S. Government Printing Office.

National Center for Health Statistics (1989a). Vital Statistics of the U.S., 1987, *Volume II, Mortality, Part B.* Department of Health & Human Services Publication No. (PHS) 891102, Public Health Service, Washington, D.C.: Government Printing Office.

National Center for Health Statistics (1989b). Advance data from Vital and Health Statistics, U.S. Dept. HEW, Ambulatory Medical Care Rendered in Pediatrician's Offices during 1975, *National Center for Health Statistics Vital Health Statistics, 16(13),* 1-7.

National Center for Health Statistics (1989c). Advance data from Vital and Health Statistics, U.S. Dept. HEW, Ambulatory Medical Care Rendered in Pediatrician's Offices during 1975, *National Center for Health Statistics Vital Health Statistics, 16(12),* 1-11.

National Center for Health Statistics (1990). Vital Statistics of the U.S., 1987. *Volume II, Mortality, Part A.* Department of Health & Human Services Publication No. (PHS) 90-1101, Public Health Service, Washington, D.C.: Government Printing Office.

Newcomb, M. D., & Bentler, P. M. (1986). Cocaine use among adolescents: Longitudinal associates with social context, psychopathology and use of other substances. *Addictive Behaviors, 11,* 263.

Petersen, A. C. (1987). The nature of biologicalpsychological interactions: The sample case of early adolescence. In R. Lerner & T. Foch (Eds.), *Biological-psychological interactions in early adolescence.* Hillsdale, New Jersey: L. Erlbaum Associates, 35-57.

Petersen, A. C. (1988). Adolescent development. In M. R. Fosenzweig & L. W. Portere (Eds.), *Annual Review of Psychology, 39,* 583-607.

Pratt, W. (1990). National survey of family growth, cycle IV for 1988, Unpublished tabulations, Ohio State University, Columbus Ohio.

Rivara, F. P., & Wolf, M. E. (1989). Injury research: Where should we go from here? *Journal of Pediatrics, 84,* 180-181.

Scheidt, P. C. (1988). Behavioral research toward prevention of childhood injury. *American Journal Disabled Children, 142,* 612-617.

Simmons, R. G., & Blyth, D. A. (1987). *Moving into adolescence: The impact of pubertal change and school context.* New York: Aldive Press.

Slovic, P. (1987). Perceptions of risk. *Science,* 236, 280.

Steinberg, L. D. (1987). The impact of puberty on family relations: Effects of pubertal status and pubertal timing. *Developmental Psychology, 23,* 451-460.

Udry, J. R. (1985). Androgenic hormones motivate serum sexual behavior in boys. *Fertility and Sterility, 43,* 90-94.

Udry, J. R. (1988). Biologic predispositions and social control in adolescent sexual behavior. *American Sociological Review, 53,* 709-722.

Udry, J. R., & Billy, J. O. G. (1987). Initiation of coitus in early adolescence, *American Sociological Review, 52,* 841-855.

U.S. Preventive Services Task Force (1989). Guide to clinical preventive services: An assessment of the effectiveness of 169 interventions. *Report of the U. S. Preventive Services Task Force,* Baltimore, MD: Williams and Wilkins.

Weddle, K. D., McKenry, P. C., & Leigh, G. K. (1988). Adolescent sexual behavior: Trends and issues in research. *Journal of Adolescent Research, 3,* 245-257.

Weinstein, N. D. (1984). Why it won't happen to me: Perceptions of risk factors and susceptibility. *Health Psychology, 3,* 431-457.

Westney, Q. E., Jenkins, R. R., Butts, J. D., & Williams, I. (1984). Sexual development and behavior in black adolescents. *Adolescence, 19,* 558-570.

Yamaguchi, K., & Kandel, D. B. (1984). Patterns of drug use from adolescence to young adulthood: III. Predictors of progression. *American Journal of Public Health, 74,* 673-681.

Zabin, L. S. (1984). The association between smoking and sexual behavior among teens in U. S. contraceptive clinics. *American Journal of Public Health, 74,* 261-263.

Zuckerman, M. Sensation seeking and the endogenous deficit theory of drug abuse (1987). In S. I. Szara (Ed.): *Neurobiology of behavioral control in drug abuse.* National Institute on Drug Abuse Research Monograph 74. Department of Health and Human Services Publication No. (ADM) 86-1506, Washington, D.C.: U.S. Government Printing Office.

REASONS AND RESOURCES:
THE HUMAN SIDE OF RISK TAKING

LOLA L. LOPES

Of all the subfields of psychology, the study of risky choice is at
once the newest and the oldest. If one inspects modern sources
such as *Psychological Abstracts,* advertising brochures for scholarly
publishers, and tables of contents of introductory psychology
textbooks, it would appear that the area first began to emerge
sometime in the early 1950s and only became prominent in the
1970s and 1980s. On the other hand, if one studies the content
and structure of the most popular theories of risky choice, it is apparent that there are unbroken links going back to the last half of
the 17th century when probability theory first emerged as an intel-
lectual discipline.

There is a further paradox in this juxtaposition of old and new in
that psychology itself emerged as a separate discipline only sometime in the second half of the 19th century. Thus, the theoretical
ideas that form the basis for most present-day research on risky
choice originated outside psychology and, arguably, have not even
yet been tellingly influenced by psychological data. Although
there is ample evidence that modern-day versions of these early
theories do not adequately describe human behavior under risk,
modifications to the theory have been generally timid and insuffi-
cient, changing superficial features of the theory without ever
questioning its fundamental form.

The research summarized here sprang from the conviction that
adequate psychological theory must begin with description not
only of behavior (that is, of final choices among risks) but also of
the process of choosing and the reasons that people have for their
choices. Although my narrow research goal has been to provide a
formal or mathematical account of risky choice, and thus, is clearly
in keeping with the goals of earlier researchers, I have looked for
formal structures that describe the process of choosing as well as
the outcome of choice.

At one time, I believed that my work would lead me to formal
structures that were unrelated to anything that had gone before.
More recently, I have come to see that there are similarities as well

as differences between my work and that of my predecessors. In this chapter, I will describe my own theory of risky choice, SP/A theory, against the backdrop of competing theoretical ideas that originated in the 17th, 18th, mid-20th and late 20th centuries.

FOUR FUNDAMENTAL IDEAS ABOUT RISKY CHOICE

Principle of weighted averaging. The earliest model for risky choice was the expected value model which proposes that people choose so as to maximize expected value. This model originated as early as the idea of expected value itself, being commonly assumed by early probabilists in the 17th century.

The expected value model embodies what I shall call the principle of weighted averaging which is the idea that the composite value of a risky option corresponds mathematically to an average in which the various possible outcomes are each weighted by their probabilities of occurrence. This idea can be illustrated by considering the set of six experimental lotteries presented in figure 1. Each lottery consists of a set of five possible outcomes, as listed at

$200 IIII		$200 IIIIIIIIIIIIIIIIIIII	
$165 IIIIIIIIII		$150 IIIIIIIIIIIIIIIIIIII	
$130 IIIIIIIIIIIIIIII		$100 IIIIIIIIIIIIIIIIIIII	
$95 IIIIIIIIIIIIIIIIIIIIIIII		$50 IIIIIIIIIIIIIIIIIIII	
$60 IIIIIIIIIIIIIIIIIIIIIIIIIIIIIII		$0 IIIIIIIIIIIIIIIIIIII	
RISKLESS		**RECTANGULAR**	

$200 IIII		$200 IIIIIIIIIIIIIIIIIIIIIIIIIIIII	
$150 IIIIIIIIIIIIIIIIII		$150 IIIIIIIIIIIIII	
$100 IIIIIIIIIIIIIIIIIIIIIIIIIIIIIIIIIIIIIIIIIIIIIIII		$100 IIII	
$50 IIIIIIIIIIIIIIIIII		$50 IIIIIIIIIIIIII	
$0 IIII		$0 IIIIIIIIIIIIIIIIIIIIIIIIIIIII	
PEAKED		**BIMODAL**	

$140 IIIIIIIIIIIIIIIIIIIIIIIIIIIIIIII		$348 IIII	
$105 IIIIIIIIIIIIIIIIIIIIIIII		$261 IIIIIIIIII	
$70 IIIIIIIIIIIIIIII		$174 IIIIIIIIIIIIIIII	
$35 IIIIIIIII		$87 IIIIIIIIIIIIIIIIIIIIIII	
$0 IIII		$0 IIIIIIIIIIIIIIIIIIIIIIIIIIIIIIIII	
SHORT SHOT		**LONG SHOT**	

FIG. 1. Set of six experimental lotteries. Each has 100 lottery tickets (tally marks) and each has a $100 expected value.

the left, and a set of 100 lottery tickets, here represented by tally marks arranged in rows to the right of the outcomes. The tickets represent the probabilities that each of the various outcomes will be won. For example, the lottery at the top, labeled "riskless," has 38 tickets that win $60, 28 tickets that win $95, 19 tickets that win $130, 11 tickets that win $165, and 4 tickets that win $200. If we multiply the various outcome values by their probabilities, we find that the expected value of the riskless lottery is $100. The same is true for each of the lotteries in the set: although the shapes of the various lotteries differ radically from one another, each has a $100 expected value.

From the beginning, it was understood that the expected value of a gamble or lottery represents the average amount that would be won per trial if the lottery were to be played many, many times. It is, in other words, a long run average and thus is a good measure of a gamble's worth in long run situations. However, the earliest probabilists also supposed that the expected value of a gamble measures the value of a single play and were surprised that their own intuitions or gut reactions to gambles did not agree, and neither did the reactions of most people. For example, the six lotteries in figure 1 all have the same expected value and thus should be equally valued, but most people have clear preferences among them, tending to prefer them in roughly the order riskless > peaked > short shot > rectangular > bimodal > long shot. This tendency has been called "risk aversion," and its explanation is the focus of the second historically significant idea in risky choice theory and the first that can be said to be fundamentally psychological.

Principle of diminishing marginal utility. In the expected value rule, outcomes are valued according to their absolute magnitudes. Thus, the receipt of $200 is assumed to be twice as positive as the receipt of $100. This is equivalent to the hypothesis that the subjective value of money is proportional to its objective magnitude or, putting it another way, that the receipt of $100 has the same impact for a rich person (who may already have many hundreds of thousands of dollars) as for a poor person (who may have nothing).

It was Daniel Bernoulli (1738/1967) who questioned this assumption about the subjective value of money. He proposed that the value of additional constant absolute increments of money provide diminishing increases in subjective value or utility. Thus, if a poor person is given $1,000, that will undoubtedly provide some increase in the person's utility. If a second $1,000 is given, that should also increase the person's utility, but to a somewhat smaller

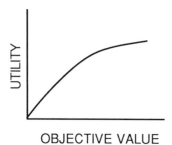

OBJECTIVE VALUE

FIG. 2. Bernoullian utility scale. The negative acceleration signals the diminishing marginal utility of money.

degree than the first $1,000. Likewise, a third increment of $1,000 provides a still smaller increment in utility, and so forth up the utility scale. Bernoulli's notion of diminishing marginal utility can be graphed as shown in figure 2. Absolute dollar amounts are shown along the abscissa and subjective values (utilities) are shown on the ordinate. The critical theoretical feature is that the curve is negatively accelerated: constant increments along the abscissa define diminishing increments on the ordinate.

Bernoulli's proposal is a sensible one that almost certainly must be true over large money ranges. Thus, for most people, winning $20 million would be little different from winning $19 million even though there is a large difference between $1 million and nothing. However, the theoretical principle is mathematically operative over all money ranges, including the $100 ranges involved in the lotteries of figure 1. As is easy to verify, if one replaces the dollar values in the lotteries of figure 1 by values generated according to a negatively accelerated utility function (such as the log or the square root of the dollar values) and then computes expected utility by multiplying utility values by probabilities, it follows immediately that the lotteries are not equivalent to one another in expected utility and do, indeed, tend to decrease in expected utility from the riskless to the long shot.

The idea of diminishing marginal utility was invented in order to account for people's risk averse preferences, and it does this effectively, if not necessarily correctly. This effectiveness is, however, also the idea's greatest pitfall since people are not uniformly risk averse. Sometimes they prefer risky options as in the case of recreational gambling and when facing certain kinds of potential losses. These kinds of preferences cannot be accounted for by Bernoulli's kind of function, which brings us to the third historically important idea.

Principle of inflected utility. If risk aversion can be accounted for by diminishing marginal utility, then risk seeking (as the preference for riskier options is generally called) can be accounted for by regions in the utility function that are marginally increasing, that is, regions in which constant increments in absolute value produce

FIG. 3.   Two examples of inflected utility functions. The left function was proposed by Friedman and Savage (1948) and the right function by Kahneman and Tversky (1979).

increasing increments in subjective value. What needs to be specified, however, is where such regions lie on the value/utility dimension.

Figure 3 shows two proposals for placement of the inflection point. The graph on the left was proposed by Friedman and Savage (1948). It was the first example of a utility function in which both risk aversion and risk seeking could be explained. This particular function was designed to explain why people both buy insurance (i.e., are risk averse) and buy lottery tickets (i.e., are risk seeking). The basic trick is to see that people who have assets that place them at position X on the figure will avoid risks that might lower their standard of living considerably but will be willing to take very small risks (a few dollars) for options that might move them across the convex region of the utility curve to a very high asset level.

The function on the right was proposed by Kahneman and Tversky (1979) to account for what has been called "risk seeking for losses." This refers generally to the fact that people will often prefer riskier to safer options when outcomes are negative. For example, in figure 1, if people are given a choice between versions of the "short shot" lottery and the "long shot" lottery in which the outcomes are all losses, many of them will prefer the riskier long shot.

Kahneman and Tversky's function differs from those of Bernoulli and Friedman and Savage in that it is centered on the status quo. The curve is negatively accelerated above this point which predicts that people will be risk averse for options involving gains. Below the status quo, however, the curve is positively accelerated which predicts that people will be risk seeking for options involving losses. Thus, opposite patterns of preferences are predicted for gains and for losses, what Kahneman and Tversky have termed "reflection in preferences."

Although an S-shaped utility function can account for reflection when it occurs (which is not by any means universally, see e.g., Hershey & Schoemaker, 1980; Schneider & Lopes, 1986), wiggily utility functions in general cannot account for all human preferences since there are some common patterns of human preference that are disallowed by any form of expected utility model no matter what shape the utility function is given. These preferences imply that the weights assigned to outcomes in the weighted averaging process are not simple probabilities but are instead nonlinear functions of probabilities. This leads us to the fourth and final important idea in risky choice theory.

Principle of probability weighting. In the 200 years after Daniel Bernoulli invented expected utility theory, the principle of diminishing marginal utility came to be accepted almost universally by scholars who thought about human preferences under risk (most of whom were economists and philosophers rather than psychologists). But the full model of expected utility maximization fell into some disfavor due to the difficulty of measuring utility on more than ordinal scales. Since there were alternative theories available that did not require such measurement, the expected utility model could be and largely was forgotten until the 1940s.

In 1944, however, John von Neumann (a mathematician) and Oskar Morgenstern (an economist) developed an axiomatic theory of expected utility that solved the measurement problem in a way that mathematically sophisticated scholars (now including some psychologists) found extremely satisfying and elegant (von Neumann & Morgenstein, 1947). Thus was born the interest of psychologists in testing mathematical theories of decision making drawn from economics and (eventually) from other normatively oriented fields such as statistics and logic.

The mathematical crux of saying that someone maximizes expected utility is that their preferences will be linear in probability. Thus, changes in the probabilities of outcomes that are linear transformations of the original probabilities should not change the order of preferences among gambles. This point was seen most clearly by Maurice Allais in 1952 (1952/1979). Allais believed that this assumption was wrong and that people's preferences would not be invariant over linear transformations of probabilities.

To illustrate his beliefs, Allais invented two kinds of problems, now called the Allais paradoxes, that focus on transformation of probabilities. For purposes of this chapter, I will concentrate on only one of these problems which has come to be called the constant ratio paradox.

Consider two gambles: Gamble A gives you $6,000 with probability .45 and zero otherwise; Gamble B gives you $3,000 with probability .90 and zero otherwise. Which gamble do you prefer? According to Kahneman and Tversky's (1979) data, 86% of people prefer Gamble B. Now consider two new gambles: Gamble A' offers $6,000 with probability .001 and zero otherwise, while Gamble B' offers $3,000 with probability .002 and zero otherwise. Which gamble do you prefer? According to Kahneman and Tversky (1979), 73% of people now prefer Gamble A'. But Gambles A' and B' are identical to Gambles A and B (respectively) except that the probabilities of winning have been divided by 450 in the former case. Since division by a constant is a linear transformation, people who prefer B to A should also prefer B' to A' if they are maximizing expected utility.

Allais had intended through his paradoxical problems to falsify expected utility theory but he was unsuccessful in this quest because economists, even while acknowledging that expected utility theory was wrong descriptively, believed that it was right normatively. In other words, it was a theory of what people ought to do and should, therefore, be the theory that economists focused on in their work.

Psychologists, on the other hand, considered the descriptive problem to be more interesting and thought about what modifications would have to be made on expected utility theory in order to make it correct descriptively. As early as 1962, Ward Edwards proposed that the weights of probabilities in the expected utility equation would have to be different from the probabilities themselves and would, in fact, have to be a quite particular function of probability magnitudes (Edwards, 1962).

Edwards' ideas were not, however, worked out in detail or made accessible to the general psychological public. That was done in 1979 by Kahneman and Tversky who incorporated a probability weighting function into their modification of expected utility theory, which they called prospect theory.

The prospect theory weighting function is shown in figure 4. Objective probability is on the abscissa and the decision weight of probability is on the ordinate. The function is convex upward with discontinuities at both ends. (These are exaggerated in the figure but in general represent probabilities near enough to to one so

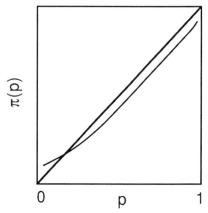

FIG. 4. Probability weighting function proposed by Kahneman and Tversky (1979).

that they are treated as certain and near enough to zero so that they are treated as impossible.)

For values greater than about .12, the decision weight of a probability is less than the probability itself. Put another way, large probabilities are underweighted. Below .12, there is overweighting, with decision weights being greater than their associated probabilities. There is also a tendency for the function to flatten out as it goes from larger probabilities to smaller probabilities. Most important for present purposes, it is this flattening that is used to explain the constant ratio paradox since the ratio of π (.002) to π (.001) is nearer to unity than the ratio of π (.90) to π (.45) despite the fact that the objective ratios are 2:1 in both cases.

Prospect theory's probability weighting function was designed to account for the Allais paradoxes. Taken in conjunction with the S-shaped utility function which accounts for both risk aversion and risk seeking, it can be claimed (and has been) that prospect theory provides a reasonable first approximation to a descriptive theory of risky choice. There are costs, however, to prospect theory's strategies for accounting for risky choice, one of which is extreme complexity and theoretical inelegance. Readers who are interested in such matters may wish to look at Lopes (1990) for a critique focusing on elegance and explanatory power.

The present chapter focuses on a more crucial critique, that being the basic correctness of the account. In the next section, three recent experiments will be described that cast doubt on three of the central ideas just presented, all of which are used in prospect theory. These are specifically the notions of probability weighting, inflected utility, and diminishing marginal utility.

HOW THREE OF THE FUNDAMENTAL IDEAS FAIL

Testing the decision weight function. Prospect theory's decision weight function was designed with one goal in mind, predicting the patterns of known responses to the Allais paradoxes. However, the function predicts other preference patterns that have yet to be

				FIG. 5. Two lotteries to test
−$200	‖	−$200	‖‖‖	the principle of probability
−$100	‖‖‖	−$100	‖‖‖	weighting. The test involves
$0	‖‖‖‖‖‖‖‖	$0	‖	changing a $200 loss ticket to a
$100	‖‖‖	$100	‖‖‖	$200 gain ticket. Which change
$200	‖	$200	‖‖‖	produces the greater improve-
				ment?

tested. One such testable implication concerns the flattening out of the decision weight function.

Consider the two lotteries in figure 5. Each has 20 tickets and each has an expected value of zero. You must draw a ticket from one of these lotteries, but before you do you will be allowed to change one of the $200 loss tickets to a $200 gain ticket. The question is this: in which lottery would the change of this one ticket produce the largest improvement, the "peaked" gamble on the left or the "bimodal" gamble on the right?

According to expected value theory and expected utility theory, there is no difference between the moves, but there is a difference according to prospect theory. The difference between the two gambles in terms of the prospect theory equation involves whether the weight of the worst outcome drops from π (.10) to π (.05) [and the weight of the best outcome goes from π (.10) to π (.15)] or the weight of the worst outcome drops from π (.25) to π (.20) [and the weight of the best outcome goes from π (.25) to π (.30)]. If the probability weight function really does flatten out, then the improvement will be greater in the bimodal gamble.

When this question was asked of subjects, their responses did not confirm the prospect theory predictions[1]. Of a group of 56 subjects who were asked to make this choice, 84% said the improvement would be greatest in the peaked lottery. Moreover, the same general pattern was observed in a second experiment in which people were asked to rate the amount of improvement in the two cases. The explanation offered by subjects for their responses reflected the fact that moving one ticket in the peaked lottery makes the probability of the worst outcome almost zero (i.e., 5%) whereas the same movement in the bimodal lottery still leaves a very high probability of the worst event (20%). This reasoning is consistent with the psychophysics of magnitude but not with prospect theory's decision weight function.

Testing for inflected utility. Prospect theory's S-shaped utility function was designed to account for risk seeking for losses, most of the evidence for which comes from carefully chosen instances in which risk seeking choices are made[2]. As it happens, the idea of S-shaped utility can also be tested by considering a task in which subjects are asked about their preferences for moving tickets in lotteries from bad outcomes to good outcomes.

Consider the lottery in figure 6. It is rectangular with 21 tickets in all and ranges from -$300 to $300 with an expected value of zero. You must draw a ticket from the lottery but before you do so you will be allowed to move a single ticket up one category. For ex-

−$300 III ample, you might move a -$300 ticket to the

−$200 III -$200 category, or a -$100 ticket to the zero category or a $200 ticket to the $300 category.

−$100 III The question of interest is, in which order do subjects prefer to move the tickets?

$0 III According to expected value theory, there is no difference. According to Bernoullian

$100 III utility theory, on the other hand, the -$300

$200 III ticket should be most preferred, followed (in order) by the -$200, -$100, 0, $100, and $200

$300 III tickets. The S-shaped utility function of

FIG. 6. A lottery testing the principle of inflected utility. One ticket will be moved up one category. Which ticket would you choose to move?

prospect theory makes still different predictions. Although it is not possible to say exactly how tickets from the two sides of the gambles (gains and losses) will be related, on the loss side the preference order should be -$100, -$200, and -$300 and on the gain side the preference order should be 0, $100, and $200.

The data do not confirm the prospect theory predictions[1]. Of 42 subjects tested on this lottery, only nine preferred the prospect theory order for losses, and their order for gains was essentially flat or suggestive of a U-pattern. Ten more subjects had a scalloped pattern (with the -$300, -$100, and $200 moves being most preferred) and 23 were essentially Bernoullian in their preferences except that the $200 ticket move was quite well preferred. (Essentially the same results were obtained in a second experiment using different subjects and a slightly different form of the lottery).

Testing for diminishing marginal utility. Although it is virtually certain that there is diminishing marginal utility over very large outcome ranges, it is not clear that the risk aversion observed in small outcome ranges is produced by diminishing marginal utility. In fact, when one examines the issue directly, it appears strange that the theory that is used to explain risky choice has no way to define the notion of risk itself (since diminishing marginal utility is merely concerned with the psychophysics of magnitude and not with the effects of outcome uncertainty).

Deidre Huckbody and I (Lopes & Huckbody, 1988) wanted to test the idea of diminishing marginal utility directly by seeing what would happen to people's preferences if we shifted lotteries by adding constants to all their outcomes. Our standard lotteries were the lotteries in figure 1 and our shifted lotteries were the same except that $50 was added to each outcome.

According to the idea of diminishing marginal utility, a shift of this sort should not affect people's preferences over the various gambles since the utility function is convex everywhere and thus produces uniform risk aversion. However, data from a group of 80 subjects disconfirms this prediction. As shown in figure 7, preferences for the shifted gambles are tilted toward risk seeking, a phenomenon that subjects explain in terms of being willing to take more risks when there is the assured safety of winning at least $50[3].

Rethinking and Enriching the Idea of Weighted Averaging

The experiments just described cast serious doubt on all of the major theoretical moves that have been taken in explaining risky choice since Bernoulli. The particular decision weight function needed to handle the constant ratio paradox has been shown to be wrong. The S-shaped utility function used to explain risk seeking for losses has also been directly disconfirmed. Even the basic Bernoullian explanation of risk aversion has been shown not to pass the test of the $50 shift.

What about the idea of weighted averaging itself? In the remaining pages of this chapter, I will present a theory that rethinks and reclaims the notion that one's evaluation of a gamble reflects a probability weighted average of its outcomes. However, as will also be shown, this notion by itself is not sufficient to account for all of risky choice, and it must be supplemented by a completely different principle based on the idea of maximizing one's likelihood of achieving an aspiration level. Working together, these two ideas provide a simple and powerful account of risky choice which has the added benefit of being compatible with the reported experiences of people actually making risky choices. (For more extensive discussion of the experiential aspects of the theory, see Lopes 1987.)

Data from protocols. In my experiments on risky choice, I have sometimes asked subjects to explain their choices in writing. The

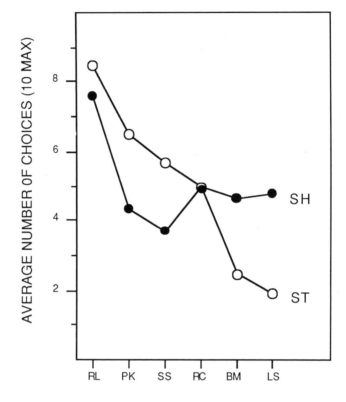

FIG. 7. A comparison of preferences for standard lotteries (ST) versus lotteries that have been shifted (SH) by having $50 added to each outcome. The shift in preference toward riskier lotteries cannot be accounted for by diminishing marginal utility. (RL = riskless, PK = peaked, SS = short shot, RC = rectangular, BM = bimodal, LS = long shot)

reasons they have provided have been illuminating of several theoretical points. Two of the most crucial to the development of my own theory have been the related observations that first, subjects tend to talk about gambles or lotteries in cumulative form, and second, that risk averse and risk seeking subjects tend to differ primarily in whether they focus on the worst outcomes in gambles or the best outcomes.

Figure 8 gives examples of written protocols provided by typical risk averse and risk seeking subjects choosing between a short shot and a long shot lottery. In the first protocol, the subject groups the lower outcomes in the short shot ("a little something") and com-

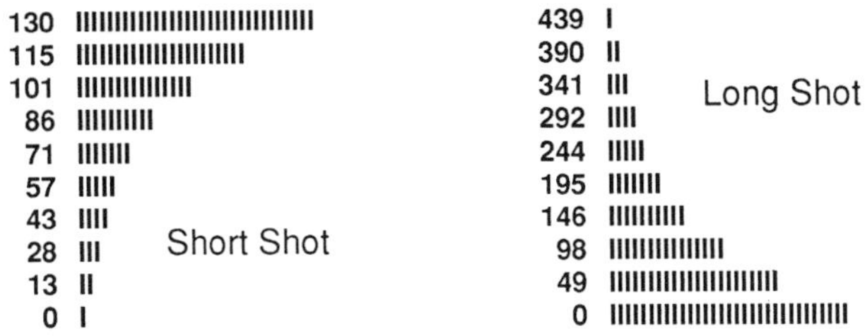

```
130  IIIIIIIIIIIIIIIIIIIIIIIIIIII          439  I
115  IIIIIIIIIIIIIIIIIIIII             390  II
101  IIIIIIIIIIIIIII                   341  III     Long Shot
 86  IIIIIIIIII                        292  IIII
 71  IIIIIII                           244  IIIII
 57  IIIII                             195  IIIIIII
 43  IIII                              146  IIIIIIIII
 28  III       Short Shot              98   IIIIIIIIIIIIII
 13  II                                49   IIIIIIIIIIIIIIIIII
  0  I                                  0   IIIIIIIIIIIIIIIIIIIIIIIIIIIIIII
```

RISK AVERSE SUBJECTS: TAKE SHORT SHOT

I'd rather have greater chances of winning a little something than greater chances for nothing. The triple jackpot [in the long shot] doesn't make me want to go for it cuz the odds are too great.

I choose the [short shot] because there is only one chance of me losing and the best odds indicate a good chance of winning $71 or more. The [long shot] has too many opportunities to lose – it is too risky.

In the [long shot], 32% do better than the best in the [short shot], but 31% get nothing at all. The [short shot] is the better risk.

RISK SEEKING SUBJECTS: TAKE LONG SHOT

The chance of winning nothing is small with the [short shot] but since the dollar amount in the [long shot] is attractive, I run the risk of losing and go for the [long shot].

The top prize money of the [long shot] is better. You still have a good chance of winning some money in the [long shot] as well as having a shot at the top prize money. The in-between prize money in the [long shot] is not all that bad, and is greater than the top prize money of the [short shot].

I'll take the added risks of losing it all or getting a lower number for the chance of the higher prizes.

FIG. 8.   Protocols illustrating reasons for risk-averse and risk-seeking choices.

pares them to the large zero category of the long shot. Although she realizes that the top prize in the long shot ("the triple jack pot") is much larger than the top prize in the short shot, its probability is too small to tempt her.

The second subject explicitly considers the cumulative probability of winning $71 or more in the short shot as well as that lottery's very small chance of winning nothing. The long shot is rejected because it has too many zero tickets.

The third subject compares the cumulative probability of exceeding $130 in the long shot ("32% do better than the best") against the simple probability of getting nothing. She concludes that the bad aspects of the long shot outweigh its good aspects.

The risk seeking subjects make similar comparisons but their values focus on achieving the high outcomes offered by the long shot. For example, the first risk seeking subject notes that the short shot has a small chance of winning nothing but then chooses to go for the high prizes in the long shot. The third risk seeker makes a similar decision.

The second risk seeker is more analytical. He compares the long shot to the short shot on three separate features: the chance of winning at all, the chance of winning top prizes, and the size of the intermediate prizes. The long shot is chosen because it is at least acceptable on all three.

Moving from protocols to formal models. Protocols such as these may seem at first glance to contain little in the way of mathematical structure. If one examines them, however, with an eye to mapping verbal features onto mathematical features of explicit models such as the expected utility model, there are interesting points to be noted.

The first line of figure 9 shows the expected value model in symbolic form with a simple three-outcome example just below. Symbolically, the expected value of a gamble is equal to the sum of the i outcome values each multiplied by its own probability of occurrence. For the example given, this equals 15.

Note that in the example, each term consists of a value times a probability. Although the various terms are listed here smallest to largest, the final result in no way depends on the order in which terms are computed and summed. If subjects were using reasoning that was structurally related to the first equation, we should expect to find verbal evidence of the weighting of individual outcome levels by their own probabilities of occurrence.

This is not what the protocols reveal. With the exception of references to zero outcomes and sometimes to top outcomes, most subjects group outcomes into categories that usually have reference to either the top or the bottom of the outcome range. Vague phrases such as "winning some money" and "getting a lower number"

$$EV = \sum_i p_i v_i$$

$$.25(9) + .60(15) + .15(25) = 15$$

$$EV = v_1 + \sum_{i=2}^{n} (\sum_{j \geq i} p_j)(v_i - v_{i-1})$$

$$9 + .75(6) + .15(10) = 15$$

$$EU = u(v_1) + \sum_{i=2}^{n} (\sum_{j \geq i} p_j)(u(v_i) - u(v_{i-1}))$$

$$RDV = v_1 + \sum_{i=2}^{n} h(\sum_{j \geq i} p_j)(v_i - v_{i-1})$$

FIG. 9. Two ways of writing the expected value and expected utility models.

tend to refer to cutoff points or regions in the outcome space while probability values are frequently processed in terms of the relative magnitudes of cumulative values (e.g., "greater chances of winning a little something," "good chance of winning $71 or more," "32% do better than the best").

As it happens, it is possible to rewrite the equation for expected value in a cumulative form that maps much more easily onto human protocols. The alternative equation is shown in the third line of figure 9.

It is easiest to understand this equation by reference to the sample computation on the next line which uses the same problem as we used above. We begin with the observation that no matter what happens, the worst outcome, v_1, or $9, will be received for sure. There is, however, a .75 probability (.60 + .15) that one will receive at least an additional $6 ($15 - $9). Moreover, there is a .15 probability that one will receive still an additional $10 ($25 - $15). Putting these terms together yields, as we expect, $15 overall just as we found with the standard formula. Once written in the new form, we are in a position to reexamine and rethink the notion that risk attitude (i.e., risk aversion and risk seeking) is a byproduct of the shape of the function that maps objective values or dollars onto subjective value or utility. The fifth line of figure 9 shows how the expected utility model can be written in cumulative form. It differs from the cumulative form of the expected value model only in that objective value, v, has been replaced in every case by utility, u(v).

In the new form, however, it is apparent that there is an alternative transformation that might be done on the equation. Instead of replacing objective value by utility, one might replace objective cumulative probability by some subjective analog, in this case represented by the function h. The interpretation of such a transformation would involve differential attention paid to outcomes at various regions in the outcome space[4].

For example, consider someone who pays the most attention to the worst possible outcome in gambles, with decreasing attention paid to better and better outcomes. Such a person would have an h function that (relatively) overweights large cumulative probabilities (which are attached to the lower outcomes) and underweights small cumulative probabilities (which are attached to large outcomes). Such a person would have preferences very much like those of a Bernoullian risk averter, but these preferences would arise from a quite different mechanism.

In the same way, another person might have an h function that (relatively) overweights small cumulative probabilities and underweights large cumulative probabilities. Someone like this would appear to be a risk seeker but they would not need to have a positively accelerated utility function.

Finally, it is possible to imagine people having hybrid h functions that overweight both extremely large and extremely small cumulative probabilities. Such people would appear to pay greater attention to extreme outcomes than to intermediate outcomes.

SP/A THEORY: A DESCRIPTIVE THEORY OF RISKY CHOICE

Security vs. potential. The h-weighted cumulative equation is a starting point for a mathematical theory of risky choice. Figure 10 illustrates this notion in a more intuitive way. The figure shows a hypothesized dimension of personality that I call security-versus-potential. This is a bipolar dispositional factor that is related to whether a person tends to be motivated to avoid bad outcomes (which we can think of as a kind of risk aversion) or to achieve good outcomes (which we can think of as a kind of risk seeking). I will speak of the former kind of person as security-minded and the latter as potential-minded.

Three characters are arrayed on the dimension. At the far left stands a "little old lady from Pasadena" (LOLFP). She represents the extreme of security-mindedness and would always choose whichever option of an available option set provided the best worst outcome. In other words, she would rank distributions lexi-

LOLFP   JOHN DOE   NICK THE GREEK

SECURITY   POTENTIAL

FACTOR 1: SECURITY vs. POTENTIAL

A bipolar dispositional factor related to whether a person tends to be
motivated to avoid bad outcomes (risk aversion) or to achieve good
outcomes (risk seeking).

FIG. 10.   The security-versus-potential dimension of SP/A theory. The "little
old lady from Pasadena" (left) represents pure security-mindedness. "Nick the
Greek" represents pure potential-mindedness. "John Doe" is the typical case being
mostly security-minded but willing to take a chance when security differences are
small.

cographically according to a maximin rule, choosing always on the
basis of a bottom-up process.

For example, in the lotteries of figure 1, she would most prefer
the riskless lottery since it has a minimum outcome of $60, which is
more than any other minimum outcome. The remaining lotteries
all have zero as their minimum outcome, but they can still be distinguished by considering probability. The peaked and the short shot
each have four zero tickets, and thus are tied. But if we move up
one ticket, we find that it is worth $50 in the peaked lottery and
only $35 in the short shot. Thus, our little old lady would prefer the
peaked lottery. The rectangular, bimodal, and long shot lotteries
come next. The rectangular is most preferred since it has the
fewest zero tickets, and the long shot is least preferred since it has
the most zero tickets.

The character on the far right is "Nick the Greek," representing
the maximum of potential-mindedness. Nick always chooses on
the basis of the best possible outcome. In other words, he is a maxi-
maxer. He would prefer the long shot above all others due to its
high maximum outcome. The bimodal, rectangular, riskless, and
peaked lotteries would be next in preference in that order. Each

has a maximum of $200 with the bimodal being most likely to yield it. The tie between the riskless and the peaked would be broken by considering the second highest outcome, with the preference going to the riskless since it pays $165. The short shot would be least preferred due to its small maximum outcome.

The third character, whom I have called "John Doe," stands to the left of center, but not so far left as the little old lady. He represents a typical subject, being mostly security-minded when there are moderate to large differences in security between lotteries, but being willing to take some risks in the pursuit of potential when security differences are small. For example, John Doe might easily prefer the long shot to the bimodal because there are almost the same number of zero tickets in the two lotteries, but the long shot has clearly better outcomes on its nonzero tickets.

The security-potential dimension relates directly to the kinds of reasons that subjects give when asked to explain their choices among lotteries (Lopes, 1987) and it easily can explain both risk aversion and the purchase of lottery tickets. It also forms the basis for a theory of risk perception in which the riskiness of a lottery is seen to be the complement of its security level (Lopes, 1984). However, security-potential by itself would not be able to explain the instances in which people prefer riskier lotteries for losses than for gains. For example, when the lotteries of figure 1 are defined as involving losses, they are preferred in the order long shot > bimodal > rectangular > short shot > peaked > riskless (Lopes & Huckbody, 1988). This is just opposite to the preference order observed for gains and would be an instance of what Kahneman and Tversky call reflection.

Aspiration level. In prospect theory, reflection occurs due to an S-shaped utility function. But as we have seen previously, that idea fails under explicit testing. The alternative hypothesis that I wish to advance is that reflection, when it occurs, reflects the influence of a second major factor in risky choice, that being the operation of an aspiration level mechanism.

Figure 11 illustrates the fact that aspiration level is assumed to be a situationally influenced factor that represents the demands and opportunities of the current situation. The assumption is made that people will, in general, be motivated to choose so as to satisfy their immediate needs and goals. In the case portrayed, the woman needs $120. Although she might ordinarily prefer the lotteries in figure 1 in the order given, if she is motivated to maximize the chances of paying her past due bill, she would prefer them in

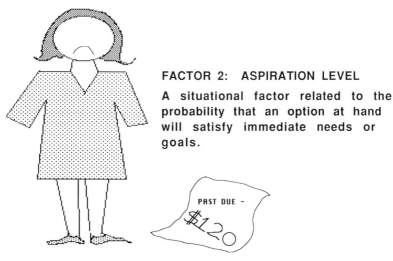

FACTOR 2:   ASPIRATION LEVEL

A situational factor related to the probability that an option at hand will satisfy immediate needs or goals.

PAST DUE -
$120

FIG. 11.   The aspiration level dimension of SP/A theory. This represents people's desire to fill immediate needs and goals.

the order bimodal > rectangular > short shot > riskless > long shot > peaked.

Aspirations often arise from externally driven necessity, as in the case of our unhappy character. However, aspirations may also be generated during the choice process as subjects assess what is available to them. For example, when the riskless lottery of figure 1 is compared to other lotteries, its minimum $60 outcome often provides a target against which the subject compares other lotteries, as though the value has become an aspiration level because it is available with certainty.

In other cases, the aspiration level is less conscious, being simply the desire to win "a little something" or to avoid "getting nothing at all." In these situations, the influence of the aspiration level may be difficult to distinguish from security-mindedness.

How SP and A fit together. Although the two factors of SP/A theory individually predict simple patterns of preference, they jointly produce quite complex patterns of behavior. Figure 12 illustrates how the factors fit together for John Doe, the typical subject.

In terms of the security-potential dimension, John Doe assesses both security and potential, but clearly prefers security (note the larger arrow) when there are large security differences between options. John Doe also evaluates the likelihood of achieving his aspiration level and integrates this into the final lottery evaluation.

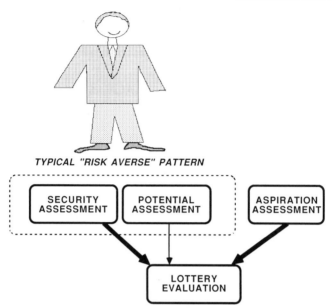

FIG. 12.   The relative influence of security, potential, and aspiration for John Doe, the typical subject. Security and aspiration (heavy arrows) receive higher weight than potential (light arrows).

The possible complexity of the process can be illustrated by considering the two lotteries in figure 13. Let us suppose that for gain lotteries like these, John Doe has a modest goal of winning "at least $25." In terms of security, he would prefer the short shot (top) since it has fewer zero tickets. In terms of aspiration level, he would also prefer the short shot since it has a larger probability of achieving $25. Thus, security and aspiration level work together. This would produce an easy and confident choice for John Doe.

For losses, however, the situation is complicated. The security choice is still the same: the short shot has a worst outcome of -$130 which is clearly more secure than the -$439 worst outcome of the long shot. But if we suppose that John Doe aspires to lose no more than, say, $25 (which is not an atypical aspiration level for real subjects), he would be better off to choose the long shot since it has the highest probability of a loss less than $25. Thus, for loss gambles, in most cases there should be conflict between the security-potential and aspiration level factors and the resulting choice should reflect this conflict.

Two types of evidence tend to confirm the existence of conflict concerning losses. For the particular lotteries shown in figure 13, most subjects pre-selected for strong risk aversion preferred the

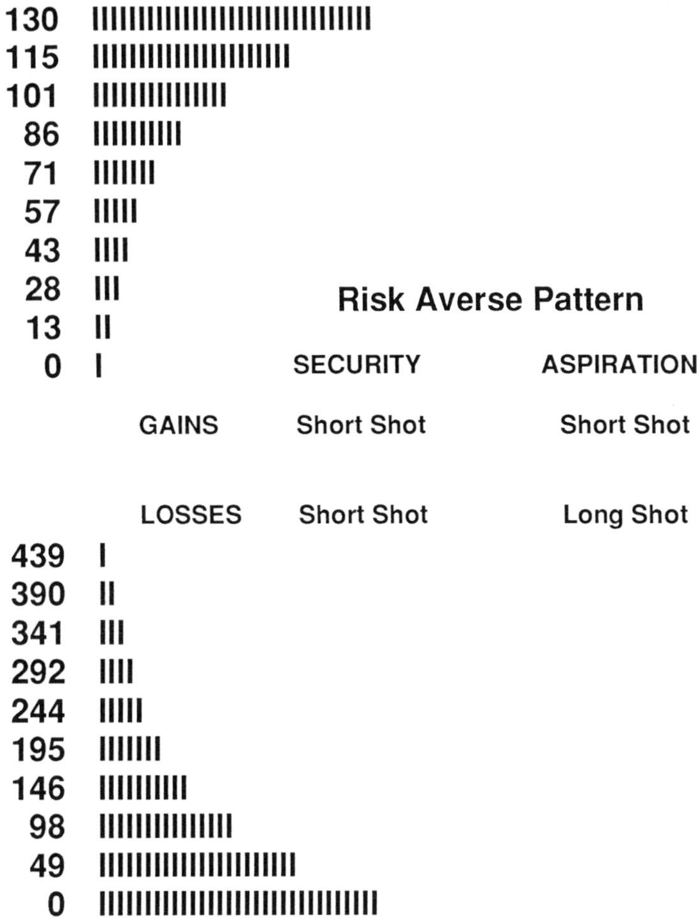

		Risk Averse Pattern	
		SECURITY	ASPIRATION
GAINS		Short Shot	Short Shot
LOSSES		Short Shot	Long Shot

```
130  IIIIIIIIIIIIIIIIIIIIIIIIIIIIII
115  IIIIIIIIIIIIIIIIIIIIII
101  IIIIIIIIIIIIIIII
 86  IIIIIIIIIII
 71  IIIIIII
 57  IIIII
 43  IIII
 28  III
 13  II
  0  I
```

```
439  I
390  II
341  III
292  IIII
244  IIIII
195  IIIIIII
146  IIIIIIIII
 98  IIIIIIIIIIIIII
 49  IIIIIIIIIIIIIIIIIIII
  0  IIIIIIIIIIIIIIIIIIIIIIIIIIIIII
```

FIG. 13. Two lotteries illustrating the joint influence of security and aspiration in choice.

short shot over the long shot for gains. When the same lotteries were defined as loss lotteries, however, almost 40% switched their preference to the loss lottery (Schneider & Lopes, 1986).

A similar result obtained for the lotteries in figure 1. When these were presented as gain lotteries to unselected subjects, the group preference function was quite steep, as shown in figure 7. When they were presented as loss lotteries, however, the preference function reversed slope (as would be predicted by an S-shaped utility function) but also flattened out, consistent with disagreement among subjects about lottery attractiveness. Such breakdowns of homogeneity of preference between subjects is suggestive, at least, of the predicted pattern of conflict within subjects. The role of conflict in producing this flattening of the preference function can also be confirmed by looking at the effect of a negative shift, i.e., subtracting $50 from every outcome. Although an S-shape utility function would continue to predict risk seeking, this is not what occurs. For negatively shifted lotteries, subjects preferences shift toward security (i.e., risk aversion). This is consistent with the idea that the reflection that occurs for the standard (unshifted) lotteries is due to subjects' attempts to achieve zero losses.

More direct evidence of conflict within subjects has been obtained from analysis of written protocol data. In protocols, subjects sometimes express unsolicited comments concerning the ease or difficulty with which they have made a particular choice. Figure 14 illustrates two such protocols from risk averse subjects choosing between the loss lotteries shown. The first subject chooses the short shot, but is uncertain about the choice. The second subject chooses the rectangular lottery, but complains of the difficulty of the choice. In the study from which these protocols were taken[5], spontaneous self-assessments were found in 58 protocols. Of

-200	IIIII	-130	IIIIIIIIIIIIIIIIIIIIIIIIIIIIII
-189	IIIII	-115	IIIIIIIIIIIIIIIIIIII
-178	IIIII	-101	IIIIIIIIIIIIIII
-168	IIIII	-86	IIIIIIIIII
-158	IIIII	-71	IIIIIII
-147	IIIII	-57	IIIII
-136	IIIII	-43	IIII
-126	IIIII	-28	III
-116	IIIII	-13	II
-105	IIIII	0	I
-94	IIIII		
-84	IIIII		
-74	IIIII		
-63	IIIII		
-52	IIIII		
-42	IIIII		
-32	IIIII		
-21	IIIII		
-10	IIIII		
0	IIIII		

Chances of losing ≤ $100 are about same for both, but [rectangular] has higher possible loss, so I picked [short shot]. I realize [short shot] gives less chance of a very low loss, which reduces my certainty about choice.

Another difficult one. I chose the [rectangular] lottery because the odds are equal on each dollar amount, whereas the [short shot] shows the odds in favor of a loss of $70 or more, and very good odds of losing $130. The [rectangular] seems to be a safer risk despite the potential for a higher loss, i.e., $200 max.

Fig. 14. Protocols illustrating conflict in choices among losses.

these, almost half (48%) were complaints about the difficulty of choosing between loss lotteries.

FINAL REMARKS AND CONCLUSIONS

The formal study of risky choice has, for the most part, concentrated on monetary outcomes presented to subjects in the form of gambles or lotteries. This is a narrow stimulus domain and we might fairly ask whether theories derived on this base can hope to shed serious light on the many important risky choices that people must make in situations where they have little previous personal experience.

I think the answer is yes and no. On the no side, I would cite situations in which the probabilities and/or outcomes are not well understood. Many applied researchers have focused in recent years on how people decide about risks when probabilities are very, very small as they are in many natural and technological hazard situations. The thrust of much of this work has been to point out that people surely cannot appreciate the relative differences among such small magnitudes and hence must have their unaided judgment supplemented or even replaced by the judgments of experts.

I have no complaint about the speculation that people cannot easily understand differences among small quantities, but I am less convinced that the judgments people make in such cases need to be educated by the experts. Often it seems, as in the case of the much touted disagreement between the public and the experts on the desirability of nuclear energy, the differences boil down to politics and not to probabilities.

Another aspect of probability that has received some attention from researchers is the issue of how people process vague probabilities (Lopes, 1983). What generally has been shown is that people (including both naive subjects and insurance actuaries) become more cautious when probabilities are vague. This seems eminently sensible to me and is, in fact, a predictable consequence of processing risky options in terms of their cumulative probabilities (i.e., in terms of a security weighting mechanism).

Even more interesting is the case where outcomes are not well understood by choosers. This case has been virtually unexplored by psychologists, but there is a very interesting research study in progress at Dartmouth Medical School headed by Jack Wennberg and his colleagues. The Wennberg team is producing an interactive video that helps men facing possible prostate surgery understand the various risks and benefits of the procedure. Although much of the interactive portion of the video concerns the presentation of probabilities that are conditionalized on factors such as the individual patient's age and symptoms, the most dramatic portion of the video is a series of open-ended interviews with various men who have either chosen the surgery or chosen to avoid surgery. Hearing their spontaneous description of the outcomes of their choices, both good and bad, immediately sharpens one's own value scheme and makes salient the subjectiveness of experience and the resources that people have for coping with less-than-perfect outcomes.

Another risky choice situation where personally relevant knowledge of outcomes is essentially absent concerns the consequences of unprotected intercourse among teenagers. Both the short term and the long term consequences of pregnancy for young women are largely unimaginable, as has been so clearly illustrated by the experience of teens who have worn "pregnancy simulators" for any length of time.

As Lita Furby and Ruth Beyth-Marom (in press) have pointed out in a recent excellent review of the literature on adolescent risk taking, adults and adolescents may differ profoundly in their identification of the possible consequences of actions. In the case of pregnancy, adults may focus on reduced opportunities for college and careers, social stigma, and financial difficulty. Teens may focus on the interpersonal and symbolic aspects of intercourse and parenthood. Educational programs that focus on parents' fears may be far less effective in preventing teenage pregnancy than the first hand discovery (by means of the simulator) that pregnancy is uncomfortable and, at least temporarily, ruins one's figure.

Furby and Beyth-Marom (in press) also point out that most studies of adolescent risk taking focus on the consequences of engaging in risky behavior (often since adults wish to prevent the behavior) but rarely consider the consequences to the teenager of not engaging in the behavior. In areas as diverse as intercourse, drug and alcohol use, and criminal activity, they suggest that adolescents may focus more on the opportunity for gain (potential) and less on the opportunity for loss (security). Although they acknowledge that these particular activities may have quite bad consequences for teens, they point out that this generalized tendency to focus on potential may be quite appropriate during this period when teens must define their own future identities.

It should be evident from the description of my own work that I do not think that there is a necessary conflict between seeking a reasonably formal theory of risky choice, on the one hand, and doing justice to the complexity and richness of the human experience of risk, on the other. But I do think that much of the formal work in the area of risky choice has been misguided in both its sources and its ends.

Formal theory always abstracts reality. That is a given. But abstraction does not require trivialization or distortion of reality. On the contrary: abstraction should sharpen and highlight fundamental aspects of reality. For this to happen, however, theory must rest on a firm descriptive base, one that is rich in detail and respectful of the object of study, which is in this case the behavior of human beings under risk.

Most formal theory in the area of risky choice has arisen out of regard for mathematical ideas that have been proven again and again to be incapable of describing human choice processes. Even the most psychological of such theories focus insistently on how and why people's preferences fail to conform to the expected utility model. We get a picture of the ground but not of the figure. In the long run, such theoretical programs are doomed to extinction, and I say, the sooner the better.

NOTES

[1] Data are from a recent unpublished experiment.

[2] In fact, several parametric studies (Hershey & Schoemaker, 1980; Schneider & Lopes, 1986) have cast strong doubt on the ubiquity of reflection over all ranges of stimuli (though these results seem not to have dampened the enthusiasm with which some researchers assert that people are known to be risk seeking for losses.)

[3] Note that control stimuli run in this experiment but not reported here can rule out explanations based on inflected utility or nonlinear decision weights.

[4] It is critical to note that this transformation is not related to the probability transformation used in prospect theory. In prospect theory, first order probabilities are replaced by decision weights. Thus, the weight of a .05 probability is always the same wherever it appears in a gamble. In this transformation, a .05 probability can have a very heavy weight if it is attached to one of the worst outcomes in a gamble or a much smaller weight if it is attached to one of the better outcomes.

[5] Illustrative protocols from this study have appeared in Lopes, 1987, and Lopes, 1990, but the detailed analysis of the protocols is as yet unpublished.

REFERENCES

Allais, M. (1952/1979). The foundations of a positive theory of choice involving risk and a criticism of the postulates of the American School. In M. Allais & O. Hagen (Eds.), *Expected utility hypotheses and the Allais paradox*. Dordrecht, Holland: Reidel.

Bernoulli, D. (1738/1967). *Exposition of a new theory on the measurement of risk.* Farnsborough Hants, England: Gregg Press.

Edwards, W. (1962). Subjective probabilities inferred from decisions. *Psychological Review, 69,* 109-135.

Friedman, M., & Savage, L. J. (1948). The utility analysis of choices involving risk. *Journal of Political Economy, 56,* 279-304.

Furby, L. & Beyth-Marom, R. (in press). Risk taking in adolescence: A decision-making perspective. *Developmental Review.*

Hershey, J. C., & Schoemaker, P. J. H. (1980). Prospect theory's reflection hypothesis: A critical examination. *Organizational Behavior and Human Performance, 25,* 395-418.

Kahneman, D., & Tversky, A. (1979). Prospect theory: An analysis of decision under risk. *Econometrica, 47,* 263-291.

Lopes, L. L. (1983). Some thoughts on the psychological concept of risk. *Journal of Experimental Psychology: Human Perception and Performance, 9,* 137-144.

Lopes, L. L. (1984). Risk and distributional inequality. *Journal of Experimental Psychology: Human Perception and Performance, 10,* 465-485.

Lopes, L. L. (1987). Between hope and fear: The psychology of risk. *Advances in Experimental Social Psychology, 20,* 255-295.

Lopes, L. L. (1990). Re-modeling risk aversion: A comparison of Bernoullian and rank dependent value approaches. In G. M. von Furstenberg (Ed.), *Acting Under Uncertainty: Multidisciplinary Conceptions.* Boston: Kluwer.

Lopes, L. L., & Huckbody, D. L. (1988, November). *The role of security motivation in risk preference.* Meeting of the Psychonomic Society. Chicago, Illinois.

Schneider, S. L., & Lopes, L. L. (1986). Reflection in preferences under risk: Who and when may suggest why. *Journal of Experimental Psychology: Human Perception and Performance, 12,* 535-548.

von Neumann, J., & Morgenstern, O. (1947). *Theory of games and economic behavior.* (2nd ed.). Princeton: Princeton University.

PERCEPTUAL, ATTRIBUTIONAL, AND AFFECTIVE PROCESSES IN PERCEPTIONS OF VULNERABILITY THROUGH THE LIFE SPAN

Susan G. Millstein

During adolescence, young people are given increasing responsibility for making decisions. Some of these decisions involve minimal risk and help foster adolescents' developmental needs for independence and limit-testing (Baumrind, 1987). However, other decisions can have serious and irrevocable consequences. These include decisions to engage in unprotected sexual behavior, the use of dangerous substances, and reckless driving—behaviors that are associated with much of the morbidity and mortality in this age group (Blum, 1987; Millstein & Litt, 1990).

While the negative outcomes associated with these behaviors are well documented, effective strategies for intervention are less clear. Pertinent to this issue is the degree to which adolescents recognize the risk inherent in certain behaviors and the degree to which they perceive themselves to be personally vulnerable to negative outcomes. Most descriptions of adolescent cognition make reference to adolescents' beliefs in their own invulnerability to harm, viewing adolescents as unable to perceive risk accurately. According to Elkind (1967, 1978), adolescents, particularly younger adolescents, are egocentric in how they view themselves vis a vis others. Adolescent egocentrism is responsible for a "personal fable"—the belief that one is special and in some way immune to the natural laws that pertain to others. The belief in this personal fable is thought to result in adolescents' tendencies to view themselves as invulnerable to harm, this tendency becoming less evident as the adolescent matures cognitively.

The concept of adolescent "invulnerability" is often used as an explanation of adolescents' decisions to engage in potentially harmful behavior. Unfortunately, there is little or no empirical support for the notion (Melton, 1988). The question of whether adolescents perceive themselves as vulnerable has implications for theory as well as for application. On a practical level, it has implications for a wide range of decision-making tasks that adults allow and expect adolescents to make. If adolescents are unable to view themselves realistically in terms of potential outcomes, should they be allowed to make potentially hazardous decisions? If adolescents are unable to see themselves as vulnerable, they are almost certain not to fulfill the legal criteria for informed consent. This could have a significant impact on treatment services for adolescents as well as on their ability to consent for participation in research.

Perceived vulnerability also has theoretical relevance to risk-taking behavior. Perceived vulnerability is viewed as a crucial element affecting health behavior in numerous theoretical models (Cummings, Becker, & Maile, 1980; Kirscht, 1983; Wallston & Wallston, 1984) including the Health Belief Model (Becker, 1974; Janz & Becker, 1984) and the Theory of Reasoned Action (Fishbein & Ajzen, 1975). In empirical tests of these theories, evidence has accumulated showing that perceptions of vulnerability are associated with a variety of health-promoting behaviors such as utilization of health services, appointment keeping, treatment compliance, and engaging in preventive activities, as well as with a variety of health-compromising behaviors such as cigarette smoking and substance abuse (Becker, 1974; Janz & Becker, 1984; Wallston & Wallston, 1984).

The degree to which individuals perceive themselves as vulnerable or at-risk is not always rationally-based. Risk assessment is inherently subjective and is known to be subject to significant bias. Even experts demonstrate biases under certain conditions. The biases that have been identified appear to be pervasive in adults and to follow fairly predictable rules (Fischhoff, 1988; Slovic, Fischhoff, & Lichtenstein, 1980).

PERCEPTUAL BIASES

Kahneman and Tversky (Kahneman & Tversky, 1972; Tversky & Kahneman, 1973, 1974) have shown that individuals use specific heuristics or rules in how they think about risk, and that these rules are associated with bias in risk perception. Two of the more important heuristics are those of availability (Tversky & Kahneman, 1973) and representativeness (Kahneman & Tversky, 1972).

Availability bias. The availability heuristic refers to the tendency to estimate the frequency of an event by how easily it is brought to mind (Tversky & Kahneman, 1973). Factors that influence how easily a specific event is brought to mind include the actual frequency of the event, personal experience with the event, the memorability of the event and the vividness of the event. All other things being equal, events and occurrences that are common are more easily brought to mind, and thus tend to be overestimated in terms of their actual frequency of occurrence. However, the perception that an event is common can be altered in a variety of ways, such as through media coverage of specific events. As media coverage increases, the salience of specific outcomes, and thus their availability, is increased. This partially explains why individuals rate the risk of death from tornadoes as being greater than the risk of deaths from asthma, despite the fact that asthma causes approximately 20 times as many deaths as tornadoes. Tornadoes, like other spectacular natural disasters, generate a great deal of media coverage, thus increasing the availability of these events. Media coverage also serves to increase the vividness of events. Outcomes that are particularly vivid and easy to imagine are viewed as being more common than those which are difficult to conjure up. Public service announcements about substance use or AIDS do more than inform the public about preventive measures or sources of further information; they also serve to increase the availability of these problems. Similarly, intervention programs that bring people with AIDS into school classrooms are attempting to increase the availability of AIDS. The availability bias also highlights the role that experience plays in risk assessment. Personal experience with a particular event undoubtedly increases the salience and availability of the event and makes it easier to imagine it occurring again. One might speculate that individual differences in the ability to visualize easily might also be associated with differences in general risk perception.

Representativeness. The representativeness heuristic describes the tendency of individuals to ignore information on base rates when they have information about correlates of events (Kahneman & Tversky, 1972). For example, when asked to judge the cause of death in a 60 year old man as being a heart attack or AIDS, one would normally consider the much higher base rates for coronary heart disease and use this in one's forecast. If, however, the man who dies is identified as being homosexual, AIDS is more likely to be considered the cause of death, even though it may still be a lower probability event for a 60 year old man. In this case, an attribute (homosexuality) that is perceived as being highly correlated with a particular outcome (AIDS) serves to bias the assessment of risk because of a failure to take into account the critical information about base rates. We are so powerfully affected by the correct belief that most AIDS cases are homosexual that we fail to take into account the fact that AIDS is still a rarer cause of death in 60 year old men than are heart attacks.

Heimer (1988), and others (Taylor, 1982) have suggested that events that are subject to stereotypic thinking may be more likely to generate bias. Stereotypic thinking is, after all, a reflection of people's perceptions of correlations that exist in the world. To the degree that these correlations overshadow our ability to consider other relevant information such as base rates, one would expect increased bias. Specifically, stereotypic sets that describe negative attributes would be expected to generate greater perception of "invulnerability" than would descriptive sets that are positive in tone. The limited research in this area supports the notion that events which generate stereotypic thinking in adults compared to those that do not are subject to greater bias (Taylor, 1982; Weinstein, 1980), but a small pilot study conducted with adolescents failed to show such a relationship (Millstein, 1989).

INFERENTIAL BIASES

In addition to bias in judging the prevalence of events, people also demonstrate clear biases in their perceptions of the likelihood that they will personally experience a negative outcome. A fundamental bias that pervades the way people think about risk is the tendency of individuals to overestimate the probability that good things will happen to them and underestimate their own vulnerability to negative events. In comparative risk assessment as well, individuals show a persistent bias in viewing their own risk status as more favorable than the risk status of others. People view themselves as better than average drivers, more likely to live past 80 years of age than others, less likely to die as a result of various factors and less likely to be harmed by the products they use (Slovic et al., 1980). They typically underestimate their own risk of disease, and perceive themselves as being at less risk than their peers. In a series of studies on this "optimistic bias," Weinstein (1980, 1983, 1984) has demonstrated that people make comparative risk assessments in an egocentric manner, paying little attention to the risk status of others when asked to determine their relative risk standing.

In fact, some evidence suggests that in order to maintain a position of low risk on the comparative scale, individuals change the reference group to whom they are comparing themselves. In a study of women with breast cancer, Taylor, Lichtman, and Wood (1984) noted that the reference group for comparison underwent change whenever the risk status of the patient deteriorated. Women with breast cancer viewed themselves as better off than other women with breast cancer. When the cancer reappeared, these same women viewed themselves as better off than other women with reappearing cancer. Similar results have been reported in adolescents with hemophilia (Kamler, Irwin, Stone, & Millstein, 1987). Although these youth are relatively realistic when they are asked about disease-relevant risks for themselves compared with other adolescents, they demonstrate a clear optimistic bias when asked to compare themselves with other hemophiliacs, or when asked about the probability of non-disease relevant risks.

ATTRIBUTIONAL BIASES

Individual's perceptions about the causes of certain outcomes, and the degree to which these causes are perceived as controllable, are also important determinants of risk perceptions. Based on studies of attributional sets (Weiner, 1979), perceptions of controllability have been identified as critical elements of the self-serving bias, affecting how individuals think about risk, how they view the risk status of others, and how they behave (King, 1982; Lau & Hartman, 1983).

Research on attributions of success and failure have shown that individuals attribute their personal failures to external, non-controllable factors, while attributing their successes to internal factors. In contrast, failures of other people are viewed as being due to personal inadequacies, while the successes of others are perceived as being caused by external events. Similar results have been demonstrated in studies of vulnerability. Optimistic bias in both absolute and relative risk assessment is particularly likely to emerge when the risk factors in question are viewed as being controllable, such as via personal and psychological attributes (Weinstein, 1980, 1984). People underestimate their susceptibility to negative outcomes when the cause of the outcome is perceived as being under their own control. For example, individuals view themselves as less likely to die in an auto accident than their peers. Accidents are viewed as being controllable, presumably through their driving skill. Given that they also believe that they are better drivers than others, it is easy to see why they fail to acknowledge their vulnerability.

In addition to underestimating the effects of personal behavior in increasing risk, people also demonstrate a self-serving bias in how they view the personal actions they take to avoid risk. Most people view the "preventive" behaviors they engage in as being far more risk-diminishing than they actually are (Weinstein, 1984). Similarly, individuals give themselves credit for positive outcomes when they see those positive events as controllable.

Two additional models propose affective rather than perceptual explanations for optimistic bias. The first holds that the mechanism underlying optimistic bias is a form of defensive denial (Kirscht, Haefner, Kegeles, & Rosenstock, 1966). In order to avoid anxiety about negative outcomes, individuals simply fail to acknowledge that the outcome could happen to them. If this were the case, one would expect outcomes with a high "dread" factor to be more subject to bias than those without the attendant emotional response, which is supported by some research (Slovic et al., 1980). Studies attempting to show the anxiety-bias link more directly have been unsuccessful (Weinstein, 1984), which is unsurprising if the mechanism is true defensive denial.

A second affect-regulation hypothesis holds that people show optimistic bias in order to enhance or maintain self-esteem (Weinstein, 1984). By making downward comparisons between themselves and others, via optimistic bias, people feel better about themselves.

ADOLESCENT RISK PERCEPTION

In exploring the issue of adolescent risk perceptions it is useful to examine the theoretical models that have been used for viewing adults' perceptions and to speculate about the predictions these theories would make for adolescents.

The primary cognitive-perceptual biases that have been utilized to explain bias in risk perception are the availability and representativeness heuristics. The mechanism by which the availability bias operates is to increase people's perceptions of vulnerability by increasing their ability to recall and/or image negative outcomes via personal experience or the vividness of the event. Personal experience with a particular event undoubtedly increases the salience and availability of the event and makes it easier to imagine it occurring again. For this reason, adolescents, who have had less experience than adults with observing certain types of negative outcomes, may be unable to imagine them occurring and subsequently judge them as unlikely. Repeated episodes that disconfirm the linkage between risk behaviors and outcomes (for example, episodes of drinking while intoxicated and *not* having an accident) serve to strengthen the bias.

The representativeness bias operates primarily through stereotypic thinking and its effects on how we consider base rates. It may also have an affective component in that highly stereotypic phenomena may be emotionally charged for people. To the degree that these emotionally charged stereotypes are negative, one would expect people to reject the idea that they are part of the stereotypic class. Thus, if strong negative stereotypes exist about "the kind of people who get AIDS," we would expect to see increased bias. It is not clear, however, that adolescents are any more likely to engage in stereotypic thinking than are adults. In fact, given the lower rates of exposure to "life correlates" among adolescents, one might hypothesize lower rates of stereotypic thinking in this age group.

Research on inferential and attributional biases indicates that people underestimate their own vulnerability to negative events. They also tend to underestimate their vulnerability when the cause of the outcome is perceived as being under their own control rather than being due to external factors beyond their control. However, currently there is no evidence that adolescents are more prone to these biases than are adults.

The affect regulation model suggesting defensive denial as a basis for optimistic bias does not suggest that adolescents are more likely than other groups to be optimistically biased, since there is no evidence that adolescents have heightened levels of defensive denial (Fiske & Taylor, 1984). An exception might be early adolescents in cases where they have heightened emotional responses to certain issues.

Nor does the self-esteem explanation offer clear implications for heightened optimistic bias during adolescence. Early adolescents do experience a drop in global self-esteem around age 12 (Simmons, Rosenberg, & Rosenberg, 1973), but whether actual self-esteem levels predict bias is not known. According to the self-esteem enhancement hypothesis, a negative outcome would be a greater threat to self-esteem if it is regarded as controllable via personal actions. Self-esteem is likely to be diminished, for example, in smokers who continue to smoke despite the recognition that smoking (a controllable behavior) increases ones risk for cancer. To avoid this dilemma one needs only to consider oneself at less risk than others.

Although these theories provide a context in which to view optimistic bias, they do not specifically entertain the issue of *adolescent* invulnerability and why it might or might not differ along the life span. Only the cognitive-developmental perspective, which holds that concepts of vulnerability vary as a function of age, offers a position on this question (Elkind, 1978). The theory is a compelling one, and many papers on adolescent risk taking accept as fact the notion that adolescents, by nature of their developmental status, perceive themselves as being invulnerable to harm.

Although there has not been strong research support for these predictions from cognitive developmental theory (Melton, 1988), some research on adolescent decision making has indicated that very young adolescents (i.e., under age 14) do differ from adults in their ability to imagine risks and future consequences of hypothetical treatments (Lewis, 1981), and in their ability to consider multiple factors simultaneously (Weithorn & Campbell, 1982). It is possible that the ability to imagine risks and consider multiple factors would translate into more realistic risk assessments. But this is clearly not automatically so. After all, bias in adults exists despite their increased ability to imagine consequences (Lewis, 1981). Having reviewed the research on adults bias, one might want to question whether adults should be held up as the gold standard against which one would want to compare adolescents.

Current research does not allow us to answer the question of whether adolescents are more likely to perceive themselves as invulnerable than are adults, since comparative studies specifically exploring bias in perceptions of vulnerability have not been done.

Some studies have included comparable ratings of individuals' perceptions of their own likelihood of experiencing negative outcomes relative to others of the same age and gender. Data from four different samples are presented in table 1. On the two questions (regarding drug and alcohol problems) that have been asked of younger adolescents (ages 12 to 18), college students, and adults (ages 18 to 65), an informal comparison of means indicates less optimistic bias among the young adolescents than among the college student and adult groups. That is, younger adolescents rate themselves as slightly more likely than do college students and adults to experience drug and alcohol problems, relative to others of their age and gender. Consequently, there is no evidence from this data of exaggerated optimistic bias during adolescence.

CONCLUSIONS AND FUTURE RESEARCH NEEDS

Some theories relevant to risk perception suggest that adolescents might perceive risk differently than do adults. The developmental perspective argues for increased perceptions of

TABLE 1.—*Comparison of studies examining optimistic bias in adolescent and adult populations.*

Type of Outline[1]	Type of Sample[2]			
	Adolescents		College Students	Adults
	(a)	(b)	(c)	(d)
Likelihood of				
Getting a sexually transmitted disease	-1.37	-1.54		
Having drug problems	-1.94		-2.13	-2.17
Having alcohol problems	1.42		-1.45	-2.02

[1]Likelihood estimates for measuring optimistic bias were obtained by asking subjects "Compared to others of your age and sex, how likely are you to experience this during the next year?" Responses were scored on a +3 (much more likely) to –3 (much less likely) scale in all samples. The midpoint value of 0 = same risk as others of my age and sex.

[2](a) Unpublished data available from author. School-based sample of 140 adolescents, ages 12 to 18 years old.

  (b) From Moscicki et al. (1988). Clinic-based sample of 746 sexually active adolescents, ages 13 to 19 years, primarily female.

  (c) From Weinstein (1982). Sample of 100 college students.

  (d) From Weinstein (1987). Sample of 296 New Jersey adults, ages 18 to 65 years.

invulnerability during adolescence compared with adulthood based upon the concept of adolescent egocentrism. Among perceptually-based theories, the availability bias provides an explanation for heightened adolescent perceptions of invulnerability resulting from adolescents' inexperience, relative to adults, in observing negative outcomes. However, there are no clear implications for age differences in perceptions of invulnerability from the literature on other types of perceptual and inferential biases discussed in this review, nor from the affect regulation models. Further, preliminary data, taken from several sources, does not show more optimistic bias among adolescent compared with adult samples.

One hesitates to dismiss lightly the widely-held assumption that adolescents perceive risk differently than do adults. Research on adolescents' concepts of vulnerability has been almost non-existent. No studies have compared directly the perceptions of vulnerability in adolescents and adults or have attempted to delineate heuristic rules that might apply in the adolescent population. It is possible, for example, that there are age differences in the way in which probabilities are calibrated, "small chance" having one meaning for adults and another for adolescents.

Whatever the explanatory approach, it is clear that we will be limited in our ability to further understand adolescent risk perception until empirical studies are conducted. These future studies are likely to have important implications for our views of adolescent risk taking, adolescents' decision-making capabilities, and for intervention with this age group.

REFERENCES

Baumrind, D. (1987). A developmental perspective on risk taking in contemporary America. In C. E. Irwin, Jr., (Ed.), *Adolescent social behavior and health. New directions for child development,* No. 37. San Francisco: Jossey-Bass.

Becker, M. H. (Ed.) (1974). The health belief model and personal health behavior. *Health Education Monograph, 2,* 324-508.

Blum, R. (1987). Contemporary threats to adolescent health in the United States. *Journal of the American Medical Association, 257,* 3390.

Cummings, K. M., Becker, M. H., & Maile, M. C. (1980). Bringing the models together: An empirical approach to combining variables used to explain health actions. *Journal of Behavioral Medicine, 3,* 123-145.

Elkind, D. (1967). Egocentrism in adolescence. *Child Development, 38,* 1025-1034.

Elkind, D. (1978). Understanding the young adolescent. *Adolescence, 13,* 127-134.

Fischhoff, B. (1988). Judgment and decision making. In R. J. Steinberg & E. E. Smith (Eds.), *The psychology of human thought.* New York: Cambridge.

Fishbein, M., & Ajzen, I. (1975). *Beliefs, attitudes, intention, and behavior: An introduction to theory and research.* Reading, MA: Addison-Wesley.

Fiske, S. T., & Taylor, S. E. (1984). *Social cognition.* Reading, MA: Addison-Wesley.

Heimer, C. A. (1988). Social structure, psychology, and the estimation of risk. *Annual Review of Sociology, 14,* 491-519.

Janz, N. K., & Becker, M. H. (1984). The health belief model: A decade later. *Health Education Quarterly, 11(1),* 1-47.

Kahneman, D., & Tversky, A. (1972). Subjective probability: A judgment of representativeness. *Cognitive Psychology, 3,* 430-454.

Kamler, J., Irwin, C. E., Stone, G. C., & Millstein, S. G. (1987). *Optimistic bias in adolescent hemophiliacs.* Anaheim, CA: Society for Pediatric Research.

King, J. B. (1982). The impact of patients' perceptions of high blood pressure on attendance at screening. *Social Science and Medicine, 16,* 1079-1091.

Kirscht, J. P. (1983). Preventive health behavior: A review of research and issues. *Health Psychology, 2(3),* 277-301.

Kirscht, J. P., Haefner, D. P., Kegeles, S. S., & Rosenstock, I. M. (1966). A rational study of health beliefs. *Journal of Health and Human Behavior, 7,* 248-254.

Lau, R. R., & Hartman, K. A. (1983). Common sense representations of common illnesses. *Health Psychology, 2,* 167-185.

Lewis, C. C. (1981). How adolescents approach decisions: Changes over grades seven to twelve and policy implications. *Child Development, 52*, 538-544.

Melton, G. B. (1988). Adolescents and prevention of AIDS. *American Psychologist, 19(3)*, 403-408.

Millstein, S. G. (1989). *Perceived vulnerability to sexually- transmitted disease: The role of stereotypic thinking.* American Psychological Association, New Orleans, LA.

Millstein, S. G., & Litt, I. (1990). Adolescent health and health behaviors. In S. S. Feldman and G. Elliott (Eds.), *At the threshold: The developing adolescent.* Harvard University Press.

Moscicki, B., Millstein, S. G., Broering, J., & Irwin, C. E. (1988). *Adolescent beliefs and behaviors concerning sexually transmitted disease (STD) and acquired immunodeficiency syndrome (AIDS).* Society for Adolescent Medicine, New York, NY.

Simmons, R. G., Rosenberg, M., & Rosenberg, F. (1973). Disturbance in the self-image at adolescence. *American Sociological Review, 39(5)*, 553-568.

Slovic, P., Fischhoff, B., & Lichtenstein, S. (1980). Facts versus fears: Understanding perceived risk. In R. Schwing & W. A. Albers (Eds.), *Societal risk assessment: How safe is safe enough?* New York: Plenum Press.

Taylor, S. E. (1982). The availability bias in social perception and interaction. In D. Kahneman, P. Slovic, & A. Tversky (Eds.) *Judgement under uncertainty: Hueristics and biases.* New York: Cambridge University Press.

Taylor, S. E., Lichtman, R. R., & Wood, J. V. (1984). Attributions, beliefs about control, and adjustment to breast cancer. *Journal of Personality and Social Psychology, 46*, 489-502.

Tversky, A., & Kahneman, D. (1973). Availability: A heuristic for judging frequency and probability. *Cognitive Psychology, 5*, 207-232.

Tversky, A., & Kahneman, D. (1974). Judgment under uncertainty: Heuristics and biases. *Science, 185*, 1124-1131.

Wallston, B. S., & Wallston, K. A. (1984). Social psychological models of health behavior: An examination and integration. In A. Baum, S. E. Taylor, & J. E. Singer (Eds.), *Handbook of psychology and health.* Vol 4: *Social psychological aspects of health.* Hillsdale, NJ: Lawrence Erlbaum Associates.

Weiner, B. (1979). A theory of motivation for some classroom experiences. *Journal of Educational Psychology, 71(3)*.

Weinstein, N. D. (1980). Unrealistic optimism about future life events. *Journal of Personality and Social Psychology, 93*, 806-820.

Weinstein, N. D. (1982). Unrealistic optimism about susceptibility to health problems. *Journal of Behavioral Medicine, 5(4)*, 441- 460.

Weinstein, N. D. (1983). Reducing unrealistic optimism about illness susceptibility. *Health Psychology, 2*, 11-20.

Weinstein, N. D. (1984). Why it won't happen to me: Perceptions of risk factors and susceptibility. *Health Psychology, 3(5)*, 431-458.

Weinstein, N. D. (1987). Unrealistic optimism about susceptibility to health problems: Conclusions from a community-wide sample. *Journal of Behavioral Medicine, 10(5)*, 481-500.

Weithorn, L. A., & Campbell, S. B. (1982). The competency of children and adolescents to make informed treatment decisions. *Child Development, 53*, 1589-1598.

A LIFE-SPAN RATIONAL-CHOICE THEORY
OF RISK TAKING

WILLIAM GARDNER

The belief in the recklessness of youth is more than folk wisdom: It is a foundation of our social institutions. Every nation exploits the recklessness of the young by placing them in the front ranks of its military. And not every youth who has gone to war was coerced or fooled: lacking the opportunity for warfare, some will find other ways to place their lives at risk. Consider the exceptional group, primarily but not exclusively male, who practice extreme forms of mountaineering. The military historian Keegan observes that "of the first 70 climbers who attempted the *Eigerwand* between 1935 and 1938, 17 were killed on it . . . Two of these, Hinterstoisser, after whom one of the most difficult traverses on the face is called, and Kurz, whose heroism in death has become one of the legends of Alpine climbing, were . . . both taking leave from the German army to tackle the climb. Their regiment . . . was that subsequently chosen, during the airborne invasion of Crete in May 1941, to crashland on to the runway at Maleme airport under the guns of the defending New Zealanders, perhaps the single most reckless operation of the war . . . and in doing so suffered . . . an 18% [casualty] ratio, contrasted with 24% for the first 13 Eiger attempts. Thus an operation of war of the most 'extreme' kind was actually proved slightly less dangerous to the unit involved than the chosen diversion of its bravest spirits." (1976, pp. 301-302; for the similar history of climbing on K2 see Curran, 1987). As the example suggests, the extreme risk taking of certain youths requires neither coercion nor ignorance of the likely consequences.

Adolescents and young adults suffer substantial morbidity and mortality as a result of voluntary risk-taking behaviors, but there is no compelling account of why this should occur. Both experts and laypersons view young people as risk takers, more willing than adults to accept catastrophic gambles, like reckless driving, and insensitive to the long term health consequences of deleterious habits, like smoking. In *Parham v. J.R.* (1979), Chief Justice Burger wrote that "Most children, even in adolescence, simply are not able to make sound judgments concerning many decisions, including their need for medical care or treatment" (p. 603; see Gardner, Scherer, & Tester, 1989; Melton, 1984). On the contrary, a central developmental change from youth to full adulthood is thought to be the acquisition of a responsible concern for one's health.

This chapter presents a theoretical explanation for life-span changes in risk taking with respect to one's health, specifically contrasting the young with the adult. I will take "youth" to refer to a broad age range, perhaps 15-25, including but not confined to the period of late adolescence. To explain why young people take health-related risks, I present a model for decision making about health-compromising behaviors based on a rational choice theory of behavior (see Gardner & Herman, 1991, for a discussion of how the theory applies to sexual risk taking and AIDS risks).

I begin with a summary of the data supporting the view that young people are risk takers. A description of rational choice theories of decision making follows. I then offer a theory that explains why different attitudes toward health risks are rational choices at different points in the life-span in the sense of maximizing lifetime expected utility. Oddly, ordinary economic models for life-span health-related decision making actually predict *less* risk taking in youth than adulthood. These theories fail because they do not include *developmental change* in the decision maker or the *ecological context* of health related choices. I present a model of a decision maker who, although rational, makes decisions in a life-span context that provides limited but developmentally changing information about the self and the consequences of choices. Risk taking is optimal for the young because they make decisions in light of judgments about their futures which are discounted in light of uncertainty.

RISK-TAKING BEHAVIOR AMONG THE YOUNG

Data on age differences in risk taking. There is abundant evidence that adolescents and young adults take serious risks with their health as compared with both older adults and younger children. In 1985, the primary causes of mortality among 15- to 24-year olds were accidents (53.5%), suicides (13.5%), and homicides (10.7%), events which either result from or are closely related to behavioral choices (Blum, 1987; Halperin, Bass, Mehta, & Betts, 1983; Irwin & Millstein, in press; Millstein, 1989, 1991). Deleterious patterns of behavior including the abuse of drugs, alcohol, and tobacco frequently have their onset during youth (Kandel & Logan, 1984). Millstein (1991) reviews data on the sexual behavior of adolescents and the mor-

TABLE 1.—*Homicide death rates by age groups, race, and sex: United States, 1986*

Race	Sex	10-14	15-19	20-24	25-29	30-34	35-39	40-44	60-64
White	Male	1.2	8.6	16.0	15.2	14.1	11.7	11.4	4.8
	Female	1.1	3.3	5.1	4.9	3.8	3.5	3.5	2.1
Black	Male	4.6	51.5	107.7	114.0	101.2	88.6	66.5	30.4
	Female	2.0	12.1	20.1	24.1	19.4	15.9	13.2	6.7
Other	Male	3.8	44.2	91.0	93.6	81.1	70.8	52.5	25.9
	Female	1.7	10.8	18.0	20.6	16.5	13.4	11.3	5.9

Note: Rates per 100,000 population in specified group. Homicides include deaths by legal intervention, meaning, presumably, people shot by police. Data are from U.S. Department of Health and Human Services (1988).

bidity they experience due to sexually transmitted diseases (see also Bell & Hein, 1984), events which either result from or are closely related to behavioral choices. Adolescents and young adults also are more likely to participate in and be the victims of violent crimes (U.S. Department of Health & Human Services, 1988; U.S. Department of Justice, 1988). Although the level of crime varies as a function of gender, historical period, ethnic group, and culture (Land, McCall, & Cohen, 1990), the overrepresentation of adolescents and young adults is a remarkable constant (Hirschi & Gottfredson, 1983; Shavit & Rattner, 1988). Table 1 shows that deaths due to homicide are highest in the 20s and 30s and are dramatically higher for males and non-Whites (see also Wilson and Daly, this volume). Finally, the typical adolescent will score higher than an adult on personality measures associated with risk taking such as the psychopathic deviance score of the Minnesota Multiphasic Personality Inventory (Archer, 1987) and on measures of sensation seeking (Zuckerman, 1979).

The data on motor vehicle accidents are particularly interesting because they can be linked clearly to specific risk-taking behaviors. Young people experience more accidents of all kinds than adults (U.S. Department of Health and Human Services, 1988). The leading cause of accidental death is motor vehicle accidents, although drownings, poisonings, and firearm accidents are also important. When corrected for number of miles driven, the relative risk of a casualty accident decreases monotonically with age, differences that persist when experience is controlled, and is higher for males (Jonah, 1986). There is evidence from both surveys (Jonah & Dawson, 1987) and observational studies showing that young drivers are more likely to perform risky maneuvers such as tailgating (Evans & Wasielewski, 1983) or pulling out into intersections (Jonah, 1986). Similarly, they neglect precautions such as wearing seatbelts (Centers for Disease Control, 1986). The young drive faster in hazardous conditions on driving simulators, in roadside observation studies, and they receive more speeding tickets per mile driven (Jonah, 1986). It thus seems that young people behave more recklessly in automobiles than adults and that these behaviors help explain their high rate of casualty accidents.

Risk-taking behavior and theoretical explanation. The data reviewed above are consistent with the view that many young people are disposed to take risks with their health. These behavioral differences often are explained by attributing different psychologies to the young and the adult. For example, the conventional lay explanation for adolescent risk taking is that "they think they are immortal" or, more plausibly, that adolescents perceive less personal risk in dangerous behaviors than do adults. There are some data that support this view. Finn and Bragg (1986) found that 18-24 year old male drivers rated videotaped driving situations as less dangerous than did adults. Both Finn and Bragg (1986) and Matthews and Moran (1986) found that young male drivers were more likely than adult males to be optimistically biased regarding their accident risks and driving ability, that is, to rate themselves as being more skillful and less likely to have an accident than same age peers. The causal significance of these findings is difficult to determine. Young males could take motor vehicle risks because they fail to perceive the relevant risks (but see Millstein, this volume). It is equally plausible, however, that perceptions of risk are affected by a disposition to behavioral risk taking. It may be that (as the theory developed here predicts) young people are disposed to more impulsive decision making than adults, and that reports of less personal risk simply rationalize reckless choices.

The decision-making competence of adolescents is a matter of significant legal controversy (Gardner, Scherer, & Tester, 1989), so it is important to note that there is no definitive psychological research about age differences in decision making processes. Although there are studies that suggest there are *differences* between the decision making processes of young people and adults (see also Tester, Gardner, & Wilfong, 1987), there is no evidence of a fundamental *deficit* in the abilities of young people that would render them incompetent to make decisions in their own best interest (Furby & Beyth-Maron, in press).

For the sake of argument, however, let us accept that adolescents have a psychology which makes them prone to accept choices which are more dangerous than adults. This would not be a sufficient explanation of age differences in risk taking because we also need an ecological explanation that would make this life-span pattern adaptive. Suppose it were confirmed that young people simply perceive less risk, in the sense that a color blind person receives different information than a person who perceives the normal chromatic range. Because it would appear that a person who was either intrinsically cautious or responsive to tuition about risk would be at an advantage compared to a "risk blind" youth, we would look for some reason why this costly perceptual anomaly was not selected out. Or, suppose that the young were shown to be intrinsically impulsive. Similar arguments would suggest that competitors who could either better regulate their behavior or remove themselves from situations of temptation would have obvious advantages. The point is not that the psychological differences are epiphenomenal, but that a complete explanation requires *both psychological mechanisms and an account of how they function in an ecological context.*

A RATIONAL CHOICE THEORY OF LIFE-SPAN CHANGE IN RISK TAKING

Goals of the rational choice theory. To place people in an ecological context we need a theory about choice, or what Coleman (1986) calls a voluntaristic theory of action (see also Becker, 1976, Cohen & Machalek, 1988; Elster, 1986; and Tooby & Cosmides, 1989, for alternative statements that, although diverging on many points and discussing diverse topics, share a common insistence on the primacy of action). This theory assumes that individuals are purposeful and goal-directed, attempting to satisfy their interests subject to constraints imposed by biological, economic, social, and—in this case—demographic, epidemiological, and informational ecologies. The theory describes patterns of choices that would consistently fulfill these goals so far as is possible given the environmental constraints. In many cases, people have several incompatible goals that must be traded off. Unfortunately, many of the necessities and pleasures of life entail risk. Although we can improve our chances for a long life by reducing our exposure to risk, it usually requires sacrificing other things.

Expected utility. The tradeoff between health and other goals can be formalized using expected utility theory, a mathematical model that describes how a consistent decision maker with stable goals will act under constraints on possible actions. If human behavior were sufficiently consistent, then one could find a set of numbers that described how people value future time in terms that would be comparable to the values they assign to other things. The choices of a consistent decision maker are characterized by the following properties (Luce & Raiffa, 1957). First, he or she can order every alternative. That is, the person knows that either $A \geq B$ or $B \geq A$, where A and B are outcomes of choices and $\geq$ is the relation "likes at least as much." Second, these preferences are transitive; if $A \geq B$ and $B \geq C$, then $A \geq C$. Third, preferences are continuous. This means that if $A \geq B \geq C$ and A and C are divisible, there is some mixture of A and C, say $uA + (1-u) C$, where u is a value between 0 and 1, that has equivalent value to B. Fourth, when confronted with a choice between two alternatives, each consisting of several components, any component that is common to both alternatives will be irrelevant to the choice. Fifth, compound probabilities describing the chance of a random outcome are reducible to simple probabilities (a coin flip to win a chance at a coin flip to win a dollar is the same as a 25% chance to win a dollar). Sixth, when comparing two gambles differing only in the probability of winning, the higher probability gamble is chosen. If decision making is consistent in this sense, then utilities can be assigned to the outcomes of choices and a person's choices can be modeled as an attempt to maximize expected utility.

The rational choice theory is not concerned with how people process information, and no one claims that people make everyday choices by assigning numbers to outcomes and calculating utilities. The claim is that an outsider observing a sufficiently consistent pattern of choices could find numbers describing the person's values that would rationalize the choices. It is *as if* the person used a utility scale to rate the value of moments of future time, then calculated the amounts of utility they expected to accumulate in each of the alternative future lives consequent to the present decision, and then made the choice that returned the maximum expected lifetime utility.

Objections to rational choice theory. Systematic violations of the consistency discipline underlying expected utility have been reported by many observers (Kahneman & Tversky, 1984; Schoemaker, 1982). For example, preferences among risky surgical operations are affected by framing choices as chances of survival or death (McNeill, Pauker, Sox, & Tversky, 1982). We do not know, however, whether risk-taking behavior is affected by these inconsistencies. Moreover, there are empirical studies showing that expected utility theory can provide useful insights into risk-taking behavior. Miyamoto and Eraker (1985, 1988; see also McNeill, Weichselbaum, & Parker, 1981) found that the preferences of inpatients among future lives of varying lengths and qualities could be explained by multiplying the scaled utility of health quality by the risky duration of life. (Some patients were unwilling to trade off reduced duration of life for superior health when the expected duration of life was short.) Moreover, expected utility models can provide useful insights into real world health risk taking behavior. For example, Brookshire and his colleagues (Brookshire, Thayer, Tschirhart, & Schulze, 1985) studied the effect of earthquake risks on the Los Angeles housing market and found a price gradient favoring less risky areas that was consistent with an expected utility model (see Thaler & Rosen, 1975, for a discussion of the tradeoff between wages and job safety).

A more compelling objection is that viewing health risk taking as a rational action seems contrary to common sense. Rational choice theory assumes a well organized individual, but this seems to be exactly what one should not assume. It is common sense that many risky acts are performed thoughtlessly, in states of distraction or passion, without calculation or even deliberation. What becomes apparent from descriptions of crime (Gottfredson & Hirschi, 1990; Reuter, 1983; Wilson & Daly, 1985) is that contrary to its glamorous televised image, the typical criminal act is not just uncalculated, but also disorganized, incompetent, and frequently *stupid*. This objection, however, mistakes the purpose of rational choice theory. The claim is not that people's choices are reasoned, because the theory is not concerned with the quality of mental processes (but see Elster, 1979, for another view). Rationality is a quality of choices: that they are instrumental means to a person's goals in a given context.

An expected utility model of a risky choice. Imagine a society where the passage from youth to adulthood was marked by a dangerous but voluntary ordeal. Some of those who choose to undergo the ordeal will perish, but those who participate and survive will obtain a reward unavailable to nonparticipants. Those who forego the ordeal miss the reward, but they are spared the risk of dying in the ordeal.

Health-risk choices are often like this: you have alternatives where one choice leads to an immediately available good at the price of a small death risk and the other avoids the risk at the cost of foregoing the reward. Narcotics, high exposure rock climbing, and armed robbery provide immediate rewards paired with small but non-negligible death risks. But more prosaic choices embody the same tradeoffs. A person who drives faster to arrive promptly at an appointment is accepting a small increase in risk of death on the road in order to protect whatever interest would be damaged by arriving late.

How would a rational decision maker approach our hypothetical ordeal? It seems clear that the choice of whether to participate in the ordeal will depend on both its danger and on how much you value your lot if you forego the risk relative to what you obtain if you participate and survive. If the ordeal is almost certainly fatal, you would not participate but would rest content with the risk-free outcome. Conversely, there is almost certainly some risk of dying that is small enough that you would participate. So if you are consistent and can discriminate fine degrees of risk, there will be some probability of dying that would leave you indifferent whether you participate. This point can be used to develop a numerical scaling of your evaluation of the three outcomes of the choice. The numbers representing the values assigned to choices will be arbitrary to the degree that any positive linear rescaling would lead to the same choices. The worst outcome is to choose the ordeal and die, so I (arbitrarily) assign this outcome the value 0. The best outcome is to choose the ordeal, survive, and receive the reward; I assign this the value 1. Intermediate between these is the outcome of foregoing the ordeal and enjoying a diminished but risk-free outcome, s, the value of life without the reward. Defining p as the probability of surviving the ordeal, you will participate in the ordeal if $p < s$, that is, if survival probability is greater than your valuation of life without the reward.

The point is that under favorable terms of exchange a rational decision maker will exchange exposure to death risks for the satisfaction of other goals. People sometimes say that a human life is priceless, but they regularly contradict the assertion by exposing themselves to deadly risks for the sake of other goals. Their behavior suggests that their future lifetimes have finite values, in that they are willing to accept threats to those futures in exchange for other things (Fuchs, 1986; Grossman, 1972; Thaler & Rosen, 1975).

LIFE-SPAN RISK TAKING

The next task is to extend this model for a risky choice to describe how the optimal health-related decisions of a rational decision maker would change across the life span. The question is: Does the decision maker's best choice change depending on where the person is in the life span? The answer depends on the assumption one makes about how the decision making context changes across the life span. The model is developed in two stages. The first step involves a decision maker whose life contains a series of risky choices that are identical. By identical, I mean that at time 1 (t_1) and time 2 (t_2) the (real or perceived) hazards of the dangerous choice, the rewards of taking the dangerous choice and surviving, and the outcomes of foregoing the dangerous choice are the same. The only thing that changes from choice to choice is that the amount of life span remaining for the person declines as they age. Under these circumstances, risk taking becomes increasingly attractive as the person ages, a problematic conclusion to say the least. In the second step, I will assume that the decision maker's income and knowledge about self and environment increase with age. Under these more realistic assumptions, a pattern of youthful risk taking followed by adult prudence becomes rational.

Risk-taking in an unchanging life-span ecology. Now imagine a society where the life-span is divided into youth, adulthood, and old age, with voluntary ordeals at both the transition from youth to adulthood (time t_1) and the transition from adulthood to old age (t_2). It is now harder to determine what the optimal choice at t_1 is, because it is dependent on what the person will choose to do at t_2. The optimal sequence of decisions is found using the logic of dynamic programming (Clark, in press). The idea is to work backwards through the life span, beginning by determining the choice you will make at t_2 if you are still alive then. Given pre-commitment to a plan of action at t_2, we can then determine the best choice at t_1.

For the moment, suppose that the ordeal is identical at both times. That is, if you do not participate in the t_1 ordeal you receive a outcome valued $s < 1$ during adulthood (the period when $t_1 < t \le t_2$). If you do participate, you survive with probability p, and this outcome has a value 1. Similarly, if you do not participate in the t_2 ordeal you receive outcomes valued s during old age ($t_2 < t$), and so on. We examine the case where the payoff at t_2 favors participation in that ordeal and where it does not.

Suppose that $p > s$ so that you will choose the ordeal if alive at t_2. Then you should choose the ordeal at t_1 only if the expected value of participation at t_1 is greater than if you forgo participating at t_1 (supposing in both cases that it will pay to participate at t_2). This occurs if $s + p > p(1 + p)$ or $p^2 > s$. So a rational youth might not participate at t_1 even when the odds and outcomes favor participating at t_2 (if $p^2 < s$), but if it paid to participate at t_1 (that is, $p^2 > s$) it must also pay at t_2 ($p > s$).

Conversely, suppose that the ordeal does not pay at t_2, that is, $p < s$. Then you would never participate at t_1 because the expected value of participating at t_1, given that you will not participate if alive at t_2 is $p(1 + s)$, which must be less than the expected value of not participating at t_1, which is $2s$. So only the following life-span patterns of risk taking are rational: participate in both ordeals if $s < p^2$, participate at t_2 but not t_1 if $p^2 < s < p$, and never participate if $p < s$.

In summary, under the assumption that the ordeals are identical at both times, the pattern of taking the risk in youth but not adulthood is never rational. The criterion for participating is more stringent at t_1 because the young have more to lose: at t_1 they risk both your adulthood and old age and at t_2 only your old age is at stake. Ippolito (1981) derived the same result, but failed to notice that it diverges from the data on youthful risk taking. Peltzman (1975) noted that expected utility considerations seemed to imply that the young should be the safest drivers, as they had the highest ratio of future to present incomes. He noted the paradox and attributed it to an unexplained desire for risky driving among the young. Clearly the premises of this model are wrong, specifically, that the decision maker and the decision making context are identical at t_1 and t_2.

A model with increasing income and positive time preferences. Now consider a model which incorporates a more realistic view of both the changing life-span context of decision making and of the decision maker. First, we let income increase across the life span. Specifically, suppose that the t_2 non-participant's outcome is still s, but the outcome at t_1 is cs, with $c < 1$.

Second, the value of the t_2 outcomes should be partially discounted, when evaluated at t_1, relative to their value at t_2, because delays in the receipt of a good diminishes its perceived benefit, a phenomenon known as positive time preferences. A preference for immediate as opposed to delayed rewards is ubiquitous in studies of both animal and human behavior (Ainslie, 1975). Strotz (1956) viewed positive time preferences as deriving from a perceptual error: people view the future myopically, as if looking down the wrong end of a telescope so that distant objects are even smaller than they should be. Many authors have viewed strong preferences for immediate rewards as reflecting impulsivity or other defects of character (Maital & Maital, 1977). Irving Fisher (1930), for example, argued that positive interest rates and credit purchases are explained primarily by the impatience of consumers because positive time preferences imply that you are willing to trade a large future consumption for a smaller present consumption. Fisher attributed poverty to the inability of the poor to delay gratification (see J. Wilson & Herrnstein, 1985, and Gottfredson & Hirshi, 1990, for related arguments about the causes of crime). To implement positive preferences in this model, suppose that t_2 outcomes evaluated at t_1 are multiplied by a factor $d < 1$.

Time preferences and increasing income will affect the choice to participate in the t_1 ordeal when $p < s$, that is, an ordeal that does not pay at t_2. The value of participating at t_1 but not t_2 is now $p(cs + 1 - s + ds)$, while the value of forgoing both ordeals is $cs + ds$. The first pattern is preferable to the second when

$$\frac{p}{1-p} > (c+d)\frac{s}{1-s}.$$

This means that you could rationally accept a health risk during youth and prudently forgo it during adulthood if $c + d$ is sufficiently less than 1. It follows that when people have positive time preferences and income increases with age, a life-span pattern of youthful risk taking followed by adult prudence may be a rational choice.

It is important to see that both positive time preferences and an increase in income with age are essential to this explanation. If you have positive time preferences but a constant future income flow, the perceived value of the future life placed at risk in the ordeal still declines with age as your life expectancy shrinks. Thus impulsivity *per se* is not a sufficient explanation for the risk taking of the young. If you have income increasing with age but no preference for immediate rewards, you increase the incentives to be prudent in youth so as to protect your future cornucopia. Thus, the deprivation of youth alone is also not a sufficient explanation for youthful risk taking.

To summarize, with positive time preferences and increasing future incomes, there are incentives to take risks as a youth that would not pay later in life. When young, the outcomes for non-risk-takers are unimpressive and the better times to come are obscured by the discounting of delayed income. Risk taking declines with passage through the life span because of the rise in value of outcomes that are not contingent on risk taking (for example, income) and, as will be argued in the next section, because attitudes toward the future change to reduce the preference for immediate outcomes.

Life-span change in impulsivity. The model in which decision makers have positive time preferences and increasing incomes across the life span assumed that time preferences are the same at all ages, that is, that adults are just as impulsive as the young. It is also possible, however, that the young are more impulsive. If positive time preferences are stronger among youths than adults, the value of one's future life and with it the implicit costs of risk taking will increase with age. Decreasing impulsivity would account for much of the observed pattern of risk taking in youth followed by prudence in adulthood.

But why should the young be more impulsive than adults? In a nutshell, because a focus on the immediate rather than the long-term consequences of a decision is a rational response to uncertainty about the future. Suppose that, as a youth, you do not fully know what your future will be like. Specifically, suppose that s depends on some qualities of yourself and your future situation summarized by a, according to some function $s = f(a)$. I will call a "ability", but it could just as well include luck. At t_1, your luck, your ability, and so on will be partially unknown to you. Although you do not know what your abilities are, you may have some ability to predict them, perhaps based on the distribution of a you observe among adults in your community. I formalize this by assuming that you know the mean (say, α) and variance (σ^2) of the probability distribution of your future abilities, with larger σ^2 indicating less certainty about your future self.

To my knowledge, age differences in the ability to predict one's future circumstances never have been studied, but it is hard to doubt that they would show that the young are far less certain of their futures than adults because their lives are, in fact, much less certain. Duncan (1984) shows that spells of unemployment are more common in youth than adulthood. Evidence summarized by Sørensen (1975, 1977) shows that income changes most rapidly among the young and, for most jobs, begins to asymptote in middle age. A young person leaving the family has little information about the income that his or her skills will command in the marketplace, or what social network he or she will inhabit. As young people pass through the transition from youth to adulthood, they are likely to obtain information that will allow at least an intuitive estimate of their future income trajectories, estimates that will improve as aging slows the youth's intra-generational social mobility.

The relation f between s and ability is also important. I suppose that $f'(a) > 0$, meaning that having more a will allow you to satisfy more of your goals. Also, $f''(a) < 0$, meaning that there are diminishing increments of s returned with each additional increment of a. The force of this assumption might be clearer if it were restated in terms of increasing losses of s with incremental loss of a. Under this assumption, for example, events which are merely dysphoric for the rich can be catastrophic for the poor.

Returning to the youth choosing whether to participate in the t_1 ordeal, this uncertainty about the future will affect his or her valuation of the future available to non-participants (s). Instead of knowing s, the youth must use the estimate $E[s] = E[f(a)]$. By Taylor's theorem, the unknown value of $f(a)$ will be related to the known $f(\alpha)$ as follows:

$$f(a) \approx f(\alpha) + f'(\alpha)(a - \alpha) + \frac{f''(\alpha)}{2}(a - \alpha)^2.$$

Hence when considering what value of s you expect in adulthood, the youth's best guess is

$$E[s] \approx E[f(\alpha) + f'(\alpha)(a - \alpha) + \frac{f''(\alpha)}{2}(a - \alpha)^2]$$

$$= f(\alpha) - \left| \frac{f''(\alpha)}{2} \right| \sigma^2.$$

Uncertainty is painful because a negative fluctuation in a is more deleterious than a positive fluctuation is beneficial. So if things get bad fast as a gets small (that is, $f''(a)$ is sharply negative), then the greater the uncertainty about your future (σ^2) the more you should reduce your valuation of the outcomes for non-participants, even if the average value of a remains constant (for related arguments in ecology see Caraco, 1980; Real, 1980; Rubenstein, 1982). This discounting of the future in the face of uncertainty should leave you disposed to accept health risks in exchange for the satisfaction of other goals.[1]

DISCUSSION

Discounting the value of the future when young may be neither a perceptual error nor a defect of character, but simply a rational response to uncertainty about the future. In a sense, having positive time preferences as a youth is not profligacy but rather an interesting sort of prudence motivated, paradoxically, by risk aversion (Arrow, 1984; Pratt, 1964). Foregoing the consumption of a dangerous good is, from the expected utility perspective, an investment. You are buying increased life expectancy—the benefits of which are, by definition, received in the future—and paying for it with present consumption. Uncertainty about the future makes this investment risky and therefore decreases its value as compared to present consumption. It is aversion to *this* risk which motivates discounting and, therefore, the decision to engage in dangerous present consumption. This argument shows that in situations where a decision maker's knowledge about and ability to predict the future increases with age, aging should bring decreasing positive time preferences. Thus a greater degree of risk taking during youth is an optimal life-span pattern for a rational decision maker who must gain knowledge of self and environment through experience.

I believe that the theory offered here is a sufficient explanation for youthful risk taking, but I do not think that it is the complete explanation. It is also very plausible that the young are more impulsive than adults because self-control is a costly activity (Thaler & Shefrin, 1981) and effective methods of self-control are skills that must be learned (Bandura, 1977; Mischel & Mischel, 1976). From this perspective, it follows that one could reduce risk taking among the young through interventions designed to increase their self-control, either by teaching self-control skills or affecting some other variable such as self-esteem. This may be correct and it is certainly worth the effort to try. But it is possible that a predisposition to risk taking may be intrinsic to youth and will, in some measure, escape every effort to reform it.

ACKNOWLEDGMENTS

Research related to this article was supported by contract #P88-12149 from the National Institute of Child Health and Human Development and a FIRST award from the National Institute of Mental Health (R29 MH42807). Special thanks to Joe Allen for several discussions of these issues; thanks also to Roger Bakeman, Susan Brodt, Bill Johnson, Jon Jonides, Michael Lamb, Michael Kubovy, Bob Ketterlinus, Marion Meyer, John Mullahy, Deborah Phillips, Emily Rissman, Steve Stern, Bill Thompson, and Tim Wilson. Correspondence about this article should be sent to William Gardner, Department of Psychiatry, School of Medicine, University of Pittsburgh, Pittsburgh, PA, 15213; electronic mail to wpg 1@ pitt. edu.

NOTE

[1]Notice that there is nothing in this argument that would limit its application to either modern times or our species, which suggests that it could be applied to understanding the natural selection of behavioral life histories (Stearns, 1977). Because the reproductive success of males has much greater variance than females the theory predicts that there would be natural selection for male recklessness. Male recklessness is easily the most important pattern in the data on health risk-taking (see also Wilson & Daly, 1985).

REFERENCES

Ainslie, G. (1975). Specious reward: A behavioral theory of impulse control. *Psychological Bulletin, 82,* 463-496.

Archer, P. (1987). *Using the MMPI with adolescents.* Hillsdale, NJ: Erlbaum.

Arrow, K. (1984). The theory of risk aversion. In K. Arrow, *Collected papers of Kenneth J. Arrow. Volume 3: Individual choice under certainty and uncertainty.* Cambridge, MA: Harvard University Press. (pp. 147-171). (Originally published in 1965).

Bandura, A. (1977). Self-efficacy: Toward a unifying theory of behavioral change. *Psychological Review, 84,* 191-125.

Becker, G. (1976). *The economic approach to human behavior.* Chicago: University of Chicago Press.

Bell, T., & Hein, K. (1984). Adolescents and sexually transmitted diseases. In K. Holmes, P. Mardh, P. Sparling, & J. Wiesner, (Eds.), *Sexually transmitted diseases.* New York: McGraw-Hill.

Blum, R. (1987). Contemporary threats to adolescent health in the United States. *Journal of the American Medical Association, 257,* 3390-3395.

Brookshire, D., Thayer, M., Tschirhart, J., & Schulze, W. (1985). A test of the expected utility model: Evidence from earthquake risks. *Journal of Political Economy, 93,* 369-389.

Caraco, T. (1980). On foraging time allocation in a stochastic environment. *Ecology, 61,* 119-128.

Centers for Disease Control (1986). Seat belt use—United States. *Injury Epidemiology and Control Reprints.* Atlanta, GA: Centers for Disease Control.

Clark, C. (in press). Modeling behavioral adaptations. *The Behavioral and Brain Sciences.*

Cohen, L., & Machalek, R. (1988). A general theory of expropriative crime: An evolutionary ecological approach. *American Journal of Sociology, 94,* 465-501.

Coleman, J. (1986). Social theory, social research, and a theory of action. *American Journal of Sociology, 91,* 1309-1335.

Curran, J. (1987). *K2: Triumph and tragedy.* Boston: Houghton-Mifflin.

Duncan, G. (1984). *Years of poverty, years of plenty.* Ann Arbor, MI: University of Michigan Press.

Elster, J. (1979). *Ulysses and the sirens.* New York: Cambridge University Press.

Elster, J. (1986). Introduction. In J. Elster (Ed.), *Rational choice.* Oxford: Billings & Sons, Ltd.

Evans, L., & Wasielewski, P. (1983). Risky driving related to driver and vehicle characteristics. *Accident Analysis and Prevention, 15,* 121-136.

Finn, P., & Bragg, B. (1986). Perception of the risk of an accident by younger and older drivers. *Accident Analysis and Prevention, 18,* 289-298.

Fisher, I. (1930). *The theory of interest as determined by impatience to spend income and the opportunity to invest it.* New York: MacMillan.

Fuchs, V. (1986). *The health economy.* Cambridge, MA: Harvard University Press.

Furby, L., & Beyth-Marom, R. (in press). Risk taking in adolescence: A decision-making perspective. *Developmental Review.*

Gardner, W., & Herman, J. (1991). Adolescents: AIDS risk taking: A rational choice perspective. In W. Gardner, S. Mielstein, & B. Wilcox (Eds.), *Adolescents in the AIDS epidemic.* San Francisco: Jossey-Bass.

Gardner, W., Scherer, D., & Tester, M. (1989). Asserting scientific authority: Cognitive development and adolescent legal rights. *American Psychologist, 44,* 895-902.

Gottfredson, M., & Hirschi, T. (1990). *A general theory of crime.* Stanford, CA: Stanford University Press.

Grossman, M. (1972). On the concept of health capital and the demand for health. *Journal of Political Economy, 80,* 223-255.

Halperin, S., Bass, J., Mehta, K., & Betts, K. (1983). Unintentional injuries among adolescents and young adults: A review and analysis. *Journal of Adolescent Health Care, 4,* 275-281.

Hirschi, T., & Gottfredson, M. (1983). Age and the explanation of crime. *American Journal of Sociology, 89,* 552-584.

Ippolito, P. (1981). Information and the life cycle consumption of hazardous goods. *Economic Inquiry, 19,* 529-558.

Irwin, C., & Millstein, S. (in press). Correlates and predictors of risk-taking behavior during adolescence. In L. Lipsitt & L. Mitnick (Eds.), *Self-regulatory behavior and risk-taking: Causes and consequences.* Norwood, NJ: Ablex.

Jonah, B. (1986). Accident risk and risk-taking behavior among young drivers. *Accident Analysis and Prevention, 18,* 255-271.

Jonah, B., & Dawson, N. (1987). Youth and risk: Age differences in risky driving, risk perception, and risk utility. *Alcohol, drugs, and drinking, 3,* 13-27.

Kahneman, D., & Tversky, A. (1984). Choices, values, and frames. *American Psychologist, 39,* 341-350.

Kandel, D., & Logan, J. (1984). Patterns of drug use from adolescence to young adulthood: I. Periods of risk for initiation, continued use, and discontinuation. *American Journal of Public Health, 74,* 660-666.

Keegan, J. (1976). *The face of battle.* New York: Viking.

Land, K., McCall, P., & Cohen, L. (1990). Structural covariates of homicide rates: Are there any invariances across time and space? *American Journal of Sociology, 95,* 922-963.

Luce, D., & Raiffa, H. (1957). *Games and decisions: Introduction and critical survey.* New York: Wiley.

Maital, S., & Maital, S. (1977). Time preference, delay of gratification, and the intergenerational transmission of economic inequality: A behavioral theory of income distribution. In O. Ashenfelter & W. Oates (Eds.), *Essays in labor market analysis.* New York: Wiley.

Matthews, M., & Moran, A. (1986). Age differences in male drivers' perception of accident risk: The role of perceived driving ability. *Accident Analysis and Prevention, 18,* 299-313.

McNeill, B., Pauker, S., Sox, H., & Tversky, A. (1982). On the elicitation of preferences for alternative therapies. *The New England Journal of Medicine, 306,* 1259-1262.

McNeill, B., Weichselbaum, R., & Pauker, S. (1981). Speech and survival: Tradeoffs between the quality and quantity of life. *The New England Journal of Medicine, 305*, 982-987.

Melton, G. (1984). Developmental psychology and the law: The state of the art. *Journal of Family Law, 22*, 445-482.

Miyamoto, J., & Eraker, S. (1985). Parameter estimates for a QALY utility model. *Medical Decision Making, 2*, 191-213.

Miyamoto, J., & Eraker, S. (1988). A multiplicative model of the utility of survival duration and health quality. *Journal of Experimental Psychology: General, 117*, 3-20.

Millstein, S. (1989). Adolescent health: Challenges for behavioral scientists. *American Psychologist, 44*, 837-842.

Millstein, S. (1991). Risk factors for AIDS among adolescents. In W. Gardner, S. Millstein, & B. Wilcox (Eds.), *Adolescents in the AIDS epidemic.* San Francisco: Jossey-Bass.

Mischel, W., & Mischel, H. (1976). A cognitive-social learning approach to morality and self-regulation. In T. Lickona (Ed.), *Morality: theory, research, and social issues.* New York: Holt, Rinehart, & Winston.

Parham v. J. R. (1979). 442 U.S. 584, 603.

Peltzman, S. (1975). The effects of automobile safety regulation. *Journal of Political Economy, 83*, 677-725.

Pratt, J. (1964). Risk aversion in the small and the large. *Econometrica, 32*, 122-136.

Real, L. (1980). On uncertainty and diminishing returns in evolution and behavior. In J. Staddon (Ed.), *Limits to action: The allocation of individual behavior.* New York: Academic Press.

Reuter, P. (1983). *Disorganized crime.* Cambridge, MA: MIT Press.

Rubenstein, D. (1982). Risk, uncertainty, and evolutionary strategies. In King's College Sociobiology Group (Eds.), *Current problems in sociobiology.* New York: Cambridge University Press.

Schoemaker, P. (1982). The expected utility model: Its variants, purposes, evidence, and limitations. *Journal of Economic Literature, 20*, 529-563.

Shavit, Y., & Rattner, A. (1988). Age, crime, and the early life course. *American Journal of Sociology, 93*, 1457-1470.

Sørensen, A. (1975). The structure of intragenerational mobility. *American Sociological Review, 40*, 456-471.

Sørensen, A. (1977). The structure of inequality and the process of attainment. *American Sociological Review, 42*, 965-978.

Stearns, S. (1977). The evolution of life history traits: a critique of the theory and a review of the ideas. *Annual review of ecology and systematics, 8*, 145-171.

Strotz, R. (1956). Myopia and inconsistency in dynamic utility maximization. *Review of Economic Studies, 23*, 166-180.

Tester, M., Gardner, W., & Wilfong, E. (1987). *Experimental studies of decision making competence.* Presented at the Symposium "Children, decisions, and risks" at the meetings of the American Psychological Association, August, New York

Thaler, R., & Rosen, S. (1975). The value of saving a life: Evidence from the labor market. In N. Terleckyj (Ed.), *Household production and consumption.* New York: National Bureau of Economic Research.

Thaler, R., & Shefrin, H. (1981). An economic theory of self control. *Journal of Political Economy, 89*, 392-406.

Tooby, J., & Cosmides, L. (1989). Evolutionary psychology and the generation of culture, Part I. *Ethology and sociobiology, 10*, 29-49.

U.S. Department of Health & Human Services (1988). *Vital statistics of the United States:1986. Volume II—Mortality. Part A.* Hyattsville, MD: U.S. Department of Health & Human Services.

U.S. Department of Justice: Federal Bureau of Investigation (1988). *Uniform crime reporting program: Age-specific arrest rates and race-specific arrest rates for selected offenses.* Washington, DC: U.S. Department of Justice.

Wilson, J., & Herrnstein, R. (1985). *Crime and human nature.* New York: Simon & Schuster.

Wilson, M., & Daly, M. (1985). Competitiveness, risk taking, and violence: the young male syndrome. *Ethology and sociobiology, 6,* 59-73.

Zuckerman, M. (1979). *Sensation seeking: beyond the optimal level of arousal.* Hillsdale, NJ: Erlbaum.

LETHAL CONFRONTATIONAL VIOLENCE
AMONG YOUNG MEN

MARGO WILSON AND MARTIN DALY

What do American President Andrew Jackson and gangster kingpin Al Capone have in common? What unites legendary lawman Wyatt Earp and legendary outlaw Jesse James? They all shot antagonists dead in face-to-face encounters, and advanced their careers in the process. Men, both prominent and obscure, have killed one another for millennia, and if their lethal acts often have been deplored, they have been much admired, too. Lethality is more than just a tactic of personal advancement, though it has certainly been that for uncounted despots: In a world where mistreatment must be answered and deterred, lethality is a virtue. Jackson was a trained lawyer and elected head of state, but he was also an accomplished duelist who took to heart his mother's admonition that "the law affords no remedy that can satisfy the feelings of a true man" (Rogin, 1975, p.58). Cowardice is often a greater social stigma than violence, and honor is widely equated with the willingness to resort to risky violence when provoked.

Men are everywhere the more dangerous sex, both to others and to themselves. In every human society for which relevant information can be found, lethal interpersonal confrontations are vastly more frequent among men than among women (table 1). Why should this be so? Many scholars have remarked upon this sex difference and have blamed it upon culturally specific phenomena such as "the theme of masculinity in American culture" (Wolfgang, 1978, p.87), the "different social roles that contemporaries expected the sexes to play" in medieval England (Given 1977, pp.134-137), the fact that southeast Asian "cultures offer [women] behavioral alternatives which channel anger into nondestructive syndromes" (Westermeyer, 1973, p.875), and so forth. The problem with these accounts is that they invoke local peculiarities to explain global regularities. Cultural specifics can provide meaningful explanations of *differences* between human groups, but the fact that men are more violent than women transcends cultural variation, suggesting that this regularity requires explanation in terms of cross-culturally universal features of human existence.

TABLE 1.—*Numbers of same-sex non-relative homicides in various studies.*

	Male	Female	Reference
Chicago, 1965-1981	7439	195	Daly & Wilson, 1990
Detroit, 1972	316	11	Daly & Wilson, 1990
Miami, 1980	358	0	Wilbanks, 1984
Canada, 1974-1983	2387	59	Daly & Wilson, 1990
England & Wales, 1977-1986	2195	95	Daly & Wilson, 1990
Scotland, 1953-1974	143	5	Gillies, 1976
Iceland, 1946-1970	7	0	Hansen & Bjarnason, 1974
A Mayan village, 1938-1965	15	0	Nash, 1967
Bison-Horn Maria (India), 1920-1941	36	1[*]	Elwin, 1950
Munda (India)	34	0	Saran, 1974
Oraon (India)	26	0	Saran, 1974
Bhil (India), 1971-1975	50	1[*]	Varma, 1978
Tiv (Nigeria), 1931-1949	74	1	Bohannan, 1960b
BaSoga (Uganda), 1952-1954	38	0	Fallers & Fallers, 1960
Gisu (Uganda), 1948-1954	44	2	LaFontaine, 1960
BaLuyia (Kenya), 1949-1954	65	3[*]	Bohannan, 1960a
Banyoro (Uganda), 1936-1955	9	1[*]	Beattie, 1960
JoLuo (Kenya), c.1949	22	2[*]	Wilson, 1960
Alur (Uganda), 1945-1954	33	1[*]	Southall, 1960
!Kung San (Botswana), 1920-1955	12	0	Lee, 1979

[*]Victim and killer were unrelated co-wives of a polygynous man in the lone female-female case in each of the Maria, Bhil, Banyoro and Alur samples, as well as 1 of 3 BaLuyia cases and 1 of 2 JoLuo cases. We exempted co-wife cases from our criterion (see p. 87) excluding marital as well as genetic relatives because unrelated co-wives represent a female analogue of male-male rivalries.

Sexual selection theory (Bradbury & Andersson, 1987; Trivers 1972) offers a more promising answer. Among animal species generally, the sex that has a higher ceiling on potential offspring production and a higher variance in reproductive success has the most to gain in competition with same-sex rivals and the least to lose by escalating tactics of social competition when otherwise facing competitive failure. In Mammalia generally, and in *Homo sapiens* in particular, the high-ceiling, high-variance sex is the male. The relevance of this fact will be expanded upon in a subsequent section ("The adaptive logic of the sex difference in lethal risk-taking"), but first we must explain why we consider homicides a source of evidence about competition and risk.

THE LOGIC OF TREATING HOMICIDE AS A COMPETITION ASSAY

Competition refers to any conflict of interests in which one party's possession or use of a mutually desired resource precludes the other party's possession or use of the same. (Although many conflicts can be interpreted as competitive, not all can: If a woman spurns one suitor for another, for example, then she and the rejected man have a conflict of interests, but they are not competitors, whereas the rival suitors are.) Some limited resources are not worth risking one's life or even expending much time for, but others are crucial. As the variance in attained utility increases, the costs that competitors are willing to incur in the pursuit of victory increase as well, and competition can become deadly (see, e.g., Enquist & Leimar, 1990).

Competition is not necessarily confrontational, and the above considerations apply in any case. But confrontational conflict is one particularly clear case of a competitive situation in which an escalation of conflict tactics increases the danger both to one's antagonist and to oneself. Carrying a gun to rob a convenience store is likely to increase your take over what you could get by shop-lifting, but it will also earn you a stiffer penalty if apprehended and is probably likelier to get you shot, too.

Most homicides can be construed as the results of confrontational competition, especially when victim and killer are unrelated (which they usually are). Robbery homicides are unequivocal instances. More subtle examples are the "face" and "status" disputes among acquaintances which constitute a substantial proportion—perhaps as many as half—of all homicides in the United States; the social resources that are contested in these conflicts are limited means to the end of more tangible resources (Daly & Wilson, 1988, 1990; Wilson & Daly, 1985). Another substantial source of lethal competition is overt sexual rivalry.

Homicides provide a valuable assay of dangerous competitive conflict for comparisons among demographic or other groups, partly because they are unequivocal manifestations of severe interpersonal conflict, and also because homicide records avoid recording and other biases. Whereas archives of assaults, self-report surveys, and other sources of data on sublethal conflict are likely to suffer biases in relation to social class and other variables, there is no reason to believe that significant numbers of homicides escape detection, and a sample of all homicides known to police has at least some information on every single case. This chapter's analyses of the demography of homicide are based on four victim-based archives of all homicides known to police during a given period of time in a given city or country. Because the archives are victim-based, any killer of several victims is counted separately for each victim, a fact with no conspicuous impact upon demographic patterns. In multiple-offender cases, we attributed the killing to the first offender listed by police, this offender usually being the most clearly culpable (Daly & Wilson, 1990).

In this chapter, our focus is on those homicides in which victim and killer were of the same sex, and unrelated by birth or marriage. In general, competitive conflict is predominantly a same-sex affair because same-sex individuals are usually more similar in the resources they desire than are opposite-sex individuals; in particular, opposite-sex individuals are often the "resource" being competed for. An additional reason for excluding opposite-sex cases is that such cases often are ambiguous as regards the gender of the initial aggressor and/or the party responsible for the escalation to lethal danger; in a same-sex case, the initial aggressor's identity may be ambiguous but his or her sex is not. As for our rationale for eliminating cases in which victim and killer were related, the conflicts precipitating family homicides are often rather different from the competitive conflicts that are our focus: Killing one's infant, for example, is not a "competitive" act in any straightforward sense. Genetic and marital relationships entail an element of overlapping interests in the welfare of joint kin, so the exclusion of relatives permits a sharper focus on competitive conflict. Furthermore, killers of blood kin are frequently insane (whereas those who kill non-relatives hardly ever are), so that responsiveness to substantive conflicts of interest such as resource competition may be aberrant or absent (Daly & Wilson, 1988).

THE MOTIVE FOR KILLING

The concept of "motive" can be problematic (Daly & Wilson 1988). Attributions of motive by police officers entail considerable subjectivity and may be driven by concerns about implications of premeditation versus spontaneity which bear on whether the case can be prosecuted as a murder or a mere manslaughter. "Robbery" is probably the most reliably coded homicide motive category and constitutes a substantial minority of cases. In Detroit in 1972, for example, there were 305 solved same-sex nonrelative homicides, of which 83 (27.2%) occurred in the context of robbery; this includes cases in which robbers were slain as well as those in which they were the killers. In Chicago between 1965 and 1981, 20.4% of 6,999 cases were robberies or burglaries, as were 15.0% of 2,291 Canadian cases between 1974 and 1983, and 14.8% of 1,918 cases in England and Wales between 1977 and 1986.

In the North American samples, robbery homicides are even more strongly male-biased than other same-sex nonrelative cases (table 2). Indeed, robbery with threatened or actual violence is apparently a virtual male monopoly everywhere. This massive sex difference is not easily explained if one simply attributes desperate acts to desperate circumstances. Poor women are no less in need than poor men, but they are far less likely to employ violence to expropriate the resources of others.

TABLE 2.—*Numbers of male- and female-perpetrated robbery homicides* vs. *other homicides within four samples of same-sex, non-relative killings.*

		Robbery	Other	
Chicago	Male	1422	6017	ChiSquare$_{1df}$=28.1
1965-1981	Female	8	187	$p < .001$
Detroit	Male	83	233	Fisher Exact Test
1972	Female	0	11	$p = .038$
Canada	Male	343	2044	ChiSquare$_{1df}$=7.7
1974-1983	Female	1	58	$p < .01$
England/Wales	Male	271	1924	ChiSquare$_{1df}$=0.1
1977-1986	Female	13	82	p=ns

The majority of same-sex nonrelative homicides do not occur in the course of a robbery or felony, but rather, in the context of individualized interpersonal conflicts (Daly & Wilson, 1988; Wilson & Daly, 1985). Information available from police records is usually inadequate to make inferences about the sources of conflict between the participants because of between-sample variations in the definition of "motives" or "circumstances" and because of the extremely limited information conveyed by many motive codes. Some exemplary police-labelled motives in our four victim-based archives are "revenge", "jealousy", "anger", "argument", "verbal insult", "hatred", "money owed", "gambling", and "provocation". Other cases involving acquaintances may be attributed simply to "drinking", with no hint about the substance of conflict, and if the initial aggressor ends up dead, the "motive" may be recorded simply as "self-defense". In many cases, however, the statements of killers and witnesses recorded in the police department's investigative files can provide a rich descriptive account of the substance and progression of lethal conflicts; for some examples, see Wilson & Daly (1985) and Daly & Wilson (1988).

SEX-SPECIFIC LIFE-SPAN CHANGES IN KILLING

Figure 1 presents age- and sex-specific rates of killing unrelated persons of one's own sex in Canada, Chicago, Detroit, and England/Wales. Although homicide rates are markedly different, with the peak rate in Detroit exceeding that in England/Wales by more than 40-fold, age- and sex-specific patterns for these four samples are strikingly similar. This pattern of a steeply rising offense rate in late adolescence and early twenties with a steady decline thereafter has been noted by others with regard to both homicides and other crimes (Gardner, this volume; Hirschi & Gottfredson, 1983, 1986; Hollinger, 1987; Steffensmeier & Allen, 1988; Steffensmeier, Allan, Harer & Streifel, 1989).

The criminological literature on the age-crime curve is largely focused on a naive and unproductive debate, namely, whether this age pattern is invariant and impervious to circumstantial variations, as argued mainly by Hirschi and Gottfredson (1983, 1986), or is labile, as maintained by Steffensmeier et al.(1989), Tittle (1988) and others. In this debate, invariance of the age-crime relationship is widely considered evidence of "biological" influence, and variability is sought in order to rescue the pattern from biological explanation and return it to the sociological realm.

The remainder of this chapter is intended, in part, to expose the inadequate conceptual underpinnings of such debates. "Biological" explanation is not usefully contrasted with "social" explanation: Sociality is a feature of living things, and contingent social responsiveness has been shaped by natural and sexual selection. Far from warranting the expectation that age- and sex-related patterns of behavior will be impervious to circumstance and experience, evolutionary biological theories of social action are explicitly concerned with the questions of what sort of contingent social responsiveness has evolved. What social, demographic and

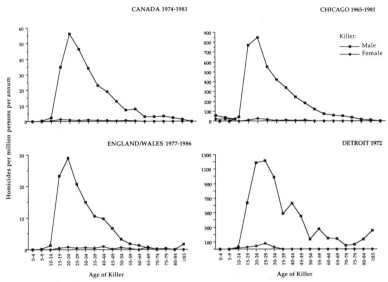

FIG. 1. Age- and sex-specific rates of killing nonrelatives of one's own sex: (a) Canada 1974-1983; (b) England/Wales 1977-1986; (c) Chicago 1965-1981; (d) Detroit 1972. (Modified from Daly & Wilson, 1990.)

ecological variables influence social action and social development, how, and why? We shall argue that the demographic variables of sex, age, marital status, and employment status are predictably associated with variable rates of killing. In *Homo sapiens,* sex, age, resource circumstance, and marital status have always been correlates of the statistical utility of dangerous competitive tactics, as compared to other tactics, in particular contexts during our evolutionary past, and hence potential cues for behavioral decision-making.

EVOLUTIONARY PSYCHOLOGY

We assume that behavioral control mechanisms—information processing mechanisms and motives and emotions—have been shaped by a history of natural and sexual selection so as to tend to produce adaptive outcomes in ancestral environments. The word "adaptive" in this context means that those outcomes contributed to the actor's expected fitness (genetic posterity). The quantity that selection tends to maximize is not simply longevity or happiness or health, but inclusive fitness (which is mainly achieved in animals like ourselves through personal reproduction). This insight is crucial to the explanation of risk-taking: A world in which organisms were designed to maximize mere longevity would be unimaginably different from the world we inhabit.

Consider feeding behavior. Physiological psychologists have analyzed "hunger" (the control of feeding) in terms of proximate goal states such as gut loads and glucostat readings. To capture the integrated functioning of these mechanisms, they may appeal to more distal and basic "objectives" such as energy balance. More distally still, animals must eat to live. But an evolutionary perspective tells us that "energy balance" or even "survival" is no more the animal's "purpose" than is a gut load, because all of these things are adaptive only insofar as they are convertible to reproductive gains, a consideration which is not superfluous to the analysis of motivational mechanisms. For example, animals exhibit "adaptive anorexias" such that the mechanisms determining inclination to feed are sensitive not just to internal energy reserves but also to the likely fitness costs of taking time out from other adaptive activities like incubation in order to feed (Mrosovsky & Sherry, 1980; Sherry, Mrosovsky & Hogan 1980).

Another illustration of the motivational psychologist's need for selection-mindedness, of obvious relevance to the issue of risk taking, is the contingent control of fearfulness. A stickleback fish guarding a nest full of eggs, for example, will stand his ground against an approaching predator longer, and dart at the predator more bravely, the more eggs he has in the nest (Pressley, 1981). In effect, the greater fitness value of a larger brood elevates the statistical probability of death that the little fish is prepared to accept. One correlate of brood size, which may be the cue modulating fear versus bravery in this case, is carbon dioxide production by the eggs, and if so, then it is likely that this cue will prove to mitigate fearfulness only in egg-guarding males. One could never understand, and would be unlikely even to discover, such contextual variation in the controls of fearfulness without the basic Darwinian insight that even personal survival is a subordinate objective to that of genetic posterity.

Few psychologists would quarrel with the claim that the psyche has evolved by selection, but until recently, too few have derived direction or inspiration from what evolutionary biologists know about the process of evolution by selection.

DANGEROUS CONFRONTATIONAL TACTICS CAN BE ADAPTIVE

Since organisms have evolved to value and seek whatever was predictive of fitness in evolutionary history, species-characteristic perceptions of self-interest reflect expected fitness consequences ("expected" in the statistical sense of average consequences in ancestral circumstances). This view of the basis of self-interest implies a theory of commonalities and conflicts of interest. You and I are likely to perceive our interests as consonant to the extent that the exigencies which promote your statistically expected fitness also promote mine—or would have done so in the environments in which we evolved—and we are likely to find ourselves at odds when circumstances are such that either party's avenues to expected fitness are detrimental to the other's.

Dangerous acts are adaptive choices if their fitness benefits are large enough and probable enough to offset possible fitness costs. Protection and defense of one's offspring is one obvious context in which dangerous acts can be adaptive choices. Another is confrontational competitive conflict. Imagine that two types of individuals exist in a population—one risk-prone and the other risk-averse in dangerous competitive situations. The risk-prone type escalates conflicts in such a way that he creates some mortal risk both to himself and to his antagonists, whereas the risk-averse type retreats from such escalations. The risk-averse type is likely to outlive the risk-prone type, but whenever they compete with one another, the risk-prone type is likelier to win. Well, if the resources being competed over are translatable into reproductive output, then the risk-prone type can easily outreproduce the risk-averse type—to the point of the risk-averse type going extinct—even if the risk-prone type consistently incurs higher mortality (see Box 8.1 in Daly & Wilson, 1988).

Again, the point is that selection favors those who reproduce, not merely those who survive, and that there were many situations in the environments in which we evolved in which some acceptance of risk was adaptive. The contingencies of those situations have shaped the designs of our evolved behavioral control mechanisms.

We find this framework valuable for the analysis of differential risks of killing, but we do not assume that killing today is adaptive. *Rather, we assume that a history of selection has shaped our psychologies such that there is an adaptive logic to the sort of information we attend to and the ways we process it in deciding whether and when we will take dangerous competitive risks.* Killings provide a window upon that decision-making process, regardless of whether they serve the killers' interests or are instead maladaptive slips in the brinkmanship of confrontational competition.

EVOLUTIONARY PSYCHOLOGY OF DANGEROUS
CONFRONTATIONAL RISK TAKING

Behavioral control mechanisms have been shaped by selection to be sensitive to cues of commonality or conflict of interest such that one's "perception" of conflict follows from processing relevant information about the statistically expected consequences of each's actions. The kinds of information that are likely to be attended to, remembered, and deemed salient, will be domain-specific, and, when characterized at the right level of abstraction will be cross-culturally and historically general. Dangerous risk-taking necessarily involves making inferences (at least implicit inferences) about the probability of uncertain events, but then there's also the question of whether you accept the gamble— whether you take the risk—given your perceptions of the probabilities of the various outcomes. If one person embraces a lethal risk that another rejects, they may or may not differ in their perceptions of the outcome likelihoods, because the difference in their choices might reflect different valuations of the payoffs instead. The money to be got from a risky robbery might be worth more to Bob than to Nancy, or Nancy might be more reluctant to risk her life than Bob, not because they perceive the probabilities differently, but simply because she values her life more than he values his.

Despite considerable research on risk perception, subjective probability, and the heuristics of decision-making (e.g., Gigerenzer & Murray, 1987; Kahneman, Slovic, & Tversky, 1982; Lopes, 1987, this volume; Nisbett & Ross, 1980; Slovic 1987), differences in response as a function of sex or age have hitherto been ignored. Decision theorists have yet to address the functional significance of domain-specific decision processes in any depth, presumably because they fail to appreciate the value of an evolutionary perspective from which to derive predictions about the utilities and subjective costs of alternative consequences of one's decisions. One might intuitively grasp, for example, that death will be a major cost and an appreciable risk thereof a major deterrent, without apprehending that psychological mechanisms may therefore evolve to treat death itself and the "genetic death" of nonreproduction as effectively equivalent outcomes.

It would be interesting to inquire what psychological mechanisms or processes mediate age- and gender-related variations in dangerous confrontational risk-taking of the sort illustrated in figure 1. Escalated risk-proneness in a given situation might be mediated by an intensified desire for the fruits of success, or by an intensified fear of the stigma of nonparticipation. Other possibilities are that there are age and sex differences in whether one finds the adrenaline rush of danger pleasurable in itself, or in the likelihood of underestimating objective dangers, or in the likelihood of overestimating one's competence. Any one of these sorts of psychological processes might mediate these demographic effects, or there might be some combination of them.

Age-specific sex differences similar to the homicidal patterns in figure 1 characterize other manifestations of risk-taking, too. For example, age-specific rates of driver fatalities per mile driven are maximally sexually differentiated in the late teens and early twenties (fig. 2). In this case, we know something about the psychological mediation of dangerousness: Young male drivers have been shown both to underestimate objective driving risks and to overestimate their own skills, as compared to older male drivers, and as compared to women (Brown & Groeger, 1988; Finn & Bragg, 1986; Matthews & Moran, 1986). Other age-related changes in things like the affect associated with thrills and near misses, and the strength of inclinations to impress others with skillful displays, are also of probable relevance to this change (Gove, 1985; Jonah, 1986; Jackson & Gray, 1976; Rothe, 1987). Certainly, the life-span changes underlying the homicide patterns in figure 1 are not peculiar to violent confrontations; instead, they appear to reflect changes in a more generalized "taste for risk", as might be expected if the relevant psychology evolved in response to age differentials in the intensity of sexual selection, demanding age-appropriate modulations of competitive effort in general.

THE ADAPTIVE LOGIC OF THE SEX DIFFERENCE IN LETHAL RISK TAKING

An obvious expectation to an evolution-minded scientist is that there would be a sex difference in dangerous competitive risk-taking. As noted earlier, this expectation is based on the fact that in animals generally, and in mammals in particular, males usually have a higher ceiling on their potential lifetime reproductive success than females and a higher likelihood of going to their graves with no descendants at all. Higher outcome variances select for higher-risk strategies (Gardner, this volume; Real & Caraco, 1986; Rubin & Paul, 1979). There are both theoretical and empirical reasons for concluding that hominids have been characterized by a sex difference in fitness variance throughout their evolution

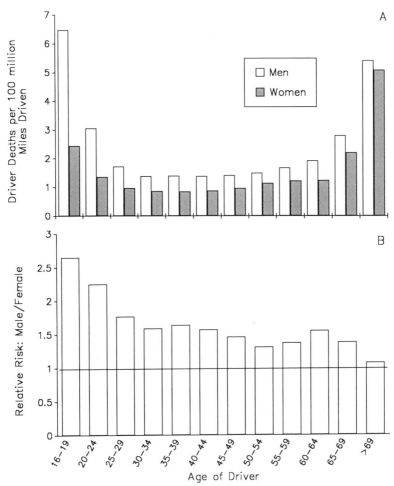

FIG. 2.   Driver deaths (excluding motorcycles) in the United States in 1970, by age and sex; (A) death rates on a per driving distance basis; and (B) the ratio of male mortality over female mortality. (Modified from Wilson & Daly, 1985.)

(Alexander, Hoogland, Howard, Noonan, & Sherman, 1979; Daly & Wilson 1983).

Polygynous marriage to two or more wives is available to some men in all hunting-and-gathering societies, and presumably characterized most of human prehistory. Polygyny is a major contributor to male fitness variance, as can be seen from contemporary studies of natural-fertility societies. In a survey of the Xavante people of Brazil (Salzano, Neel, & Mayberry-Lewis, 1967), for example, most married men had only one wife, but chiefs had up to five, and thus had many more children than same-age monogamists. Moreover, whereas just 1 of 195 women remained childless by the age of 20 years, 6% of the men were still childless at forty. So while the average number of surviving offspring in completed families was identical for men and women—namely, 3.6 children— the male variance was 12.1 and the female variance was 3.9.

So the more wives, the more children, and the more polygynists, the more bachelors. This situation is not sexually symmetrical: Male fertility is limited by access to women, but female fertility is not limited by access to men. Indeed, it is hardly possible for a woman to bear more than about 20 children in her lifetime, although the *Guiness Book of Records* (McWhirter, 1980) credits a 19th century Muscovite with 69 live births in 27 pregnancies. Astounding though that figure may be, the male record is much greater: 888 children were sired by the Sharifian emperor of Morocco, Moulay Ismail the Bloodthirsty, who maintained a harem of 500 young concubines in addition to his four wives and who was alleged to have earned his sobriquet by having slain 30,000 people with his own hand (Busnot, 1715).

The polygynous men in both tribal societies and despotic states were the socially successful men of their respective communities. Great disparities of status and power must be recent phenomena in human evolutionary history, for they are possible only where agricultural technology has permitted large-scale food storage, dense settlement, and extensive role specializations, all of which arose only within the last few thousand years. But even in relatively egalitarian societies where people occupy a foraging niche, much like that known to most of our human ancestors, still there is some differentiation of status, and it is still the most respected men who are able to maintain two or three wives (e.g., Balikci, 1970; Hart & Pilling, 1960; Hiatt, 1965; Howell, 1979). A sex difference in fitness variance has been demonstrated in some foraging societies (Hewlett, 1988; Howell, 1979), albeit a smaller sex difference than among horticulturalists like the Xavante and much smaller than in the Sharifian empire of Morocco.

Thus, the human psyche evolved in a social milieu in which the differential consequences of success versus failure in competition over resources and status were almost certainly greater for men than for women. If reproductive failure is evolutionarily equivalent to death, you can see why men might be especially likely to embrace high-risk tactics of social competition when they perceive themselves as otherwise predictably doomed to failure. Two evolution-minded economists put it quite succinctly: ". . . gambling and losing is equivalent to death. However, avoidance of the gamble will imply leaving no offspring, and thus will be (genetically) equivalent to death" (Rubin & Paul, 1979, p.592).

Though the direction of sex difference in interpersonal violence is thus predictable from sex differences in the historical intensity of intrasexual selection, the magnitude of difference in figure 1 and table 1 might be deemed surprisingly large for what is after all only a slightly dimorphic and effectively polygynous primate. One plausible hypothesis is that a hunting specialization has incidentally elevated men's violent capabilities so that the cost-benefit structure of male-male versus female-female conflict is more different than it would be if the sexes foraged similarly. There is much anthropological and historical evidence of male domination in both hunting and homicide/warfare, and it will not be easy to separate their roles in the evolution of men's violent capabilities and inclinations. A test of the relative merit of foraging versus social competition in accounting for these sex differences would require, among other things, specification of morphological, physiological and psychological design features that could be convincingly attributed to selection pressures in foraging versus combative contexts.

DOES HUMAN MALE RISK-TAKING EXHIBIT A SEXUALLY SELECTED LIFE-SPAN PATTERN?

By the same sort of evolutionary reasoning that we used with respect to sex differences in dangerous risk-taking, one may anticipate that there will be major differences between age groups: Variance in the fitness consequences of within-sex competitive success is likely to change over the lifespan, making relatively competitive, risk-prone inclinations adaptive in certain life stages and risk-aversion adaptive in others. Although competitive success or failure may be consequential even at immature life stages, its fitness effects become clearer and presumably are intensified when reproductive competition begins in earnest. The anthropological record on face-to-face non-state societies suggests that women in ancestral environments were unanimously married and reproducing as soon as they were fertile, whereas men exhibited greater delays and greater variance in attaining marriage and fatherhood. A major source of the variance in men's fitness must reside in variable post-pubertal progressions to reproductive status; estimation of this variability in contemporary hunter-gatherer studies would be feasible and worthwhile. Prowess in hunting, warfare, and other dangerous activities is evidently a major determinant of young men's marriageability and probably affects their opportunities for extra-marital reproduction, too (e.g., Chagnon, 1988; Kaplan & Hill, 1985).

Many authors have suggested that maturity evolves to occur later whenever younger animals cannot compete with older animals and would only damage their eventual fitness by trying (see Daly & Wilson, 1983). A main support for this argument comes from an observed cross-species correlation between the degree of polygyny of the mating system and the extent to which males mature at a later age than females ("sexual bimaturism"). Increased polygyny means increased male variance and male-male competition, and it seems sensible to interpret the associated delay in maturing as a response to that intensified competition. (The sexual bimaturism of *Homo sapiens* is one of our species' several attributes bespeaking a selective history in which fitness variance was greater for males than females.)

Several anatomical and physiological indicators support the idea that young men constitute a demographic class specialized by a history of selection for maximal competitive effort. Changes in muscle strength which are apparently unrelated to exercise show characteristic sex-specific patterns: Male strength increases abruptly at puberty and then continues to increase slightly over the next decade before declining (McComas, Sica, & Petito, 1973; Murray, Duthrie, Gambert, Sepic, & Mollinger, 1985; Thomas & French, 1985). Female strength also increases at puberty, but the sex difference is greatest in young adulthood. Aerobic capacity is similarly both maximal and maximally sexually differentiated in the teens and twenties (e.g., Shephard, 1986). Young men are thus the most physically formidable of human demographic classes, and we would suggest that the life-span development of their psyches is co-adapted: It is young men who are most psychologically "prepared" to embrace dangerous, competitive risk taking (e.g., Daly & Wilson 1990; Gardner, this volume; Gove, 1985; Holinger, 1987; Jonah, 1986; Kandel, 1980; Lyng, 1990, this volume; Sullivan, 1989; Tonkin, 1987; Wilson & Daly, 1985).

Human beings engage in competitions not just for the immediate spoils of present victories but for more subtle and enduring reputational consequences, too. Fierceness, hunting prowess, effective leadership, "coolness under fire" and other manifestations of competence in the face of risk are assumed to be at least partially persisting attributes of individuals. Young men are constantly being assessed as *prospects* by those who might select them as husbands or lovers, sons- or brothers-in-law, exchange partners, and war chiefs. Kaplan and Hill (1985) found that the better Ache hunters out-reproduce poorer ones, partly because their children survive better, but also in part because hunting prowess gains men extra-marital affairs with fertile women. Chagnon (1988) has evidence that among the Yanomamö, chronically involved in small-scale warfare, those men who have killed have more wives and children than other men. An established reputation for fierceness is an important social asset for a Yanomamö man and one that he needn't re-establish frequently. There is no reason to believe that the Yanomamö are unusual in this regard.

LIFE-SPAN SCHEDULE OR CORRELATED CIRCUMSTANCES?

An alternative to the hypothesis that men have evolved an adaptive life-span schedule of risk proneness is that age patterns are entirely the result of changes in relevant circumstances such as employment or marital status which happen to be correlated with age. Criminologists often present correlated circumstance hypotheses as the alternatives to "biological" accounts, but a sophisticated biology is a generator, not an abnegator, of such hypotheses. Selection-mindedness directs attention to the ways in which ecological and social variations have framed the diverse problems in response to which species-typical psyches have evolved their contingent responses (Daly & Wilson, 1990). If one's present status promises lifelong exclusion from mating opportunities, for example, then very different social tactics are warranted from those that are adaptive for a monogamously mated individual engaged in parental nurture. In the case of the dangerous confrontational competitiveness characteristic of young men, it is expectable that the underlying behavioral control mechanisms would be sensitive to variations in present circumstances, personal competitive capabilities, and anything else affecting the predictable costs and benefits of alternative social tactics.

Poor prospects favor risk-proneness. Bob Dylan (1965) sang it in *Like a Rolling Stone:* "When you got nothing, you got nothing to lose." And insofar as present poverty promises a dim future, as it surely does, it is a sign of adaptation, not pathology, for the disadvantaged to escalate their tactics of social competition. In the United States, it is the young men in urban ghettos who have the highest unemployment rates, the poorest prospects for supporting a family, and the shortest expected lifespans (e.g., Sampson, 1987; Sullivan, 1989; Wilson & Aponte, 1985). Little wonder that they also exhibit high rates of risky predatory crime and interpersonal violence.

So do poor circumstances and prospects explain age patterns? Probably not entirely. For example, unemployed men behave more dangerously than those with jobs, and unemployment rates are maximal in young adulthood. Wilson & Daly (1985) have shown that unemployed men in Detroit are much more likely than their employed counterparts to become involved in a homicidal altercation, both as victim and as killer. However, age effects remain conspicuous when employed and unemployed men are distinguished.

Similarly, unmarried men are far more likely to kill than are same-age married men, but homicide rates decline after young adulthood in both married and unmarried men (Daly & Wilson, 1990). Being married would be expected to inspire a reduction in dangerous behavior because access to mates is a principal issue inspiring competition and married men have more to lose than their single counterparts. The fact that married men are indeed the less lethal group does not warrant any conclusion about the direction of causality, however. It is possible that this difference does not reflect effects of marriage, but only that the kind of men who marry are more pacific and risk-averse than the kind who stay single. Evidence against this argument and in support of the pacifying effect of the married state comes from comparisons within the category of unmarried men: Both divorced and widowed men exhibit rates of killing similar to those of single men. While it might be argued that divorced men are more violence-prone— that their violent natures make them relatively likely both to divorce and to kill—that sort of argument seems less applicable to widowed men.

That unemployment and unmarried status are both related to the use of violence does not indicate whether or to what extent they are separately relevant. Government statistics show that men who have never married in the USA are significantly poorer than men who have, and that men who remarry after divorce or widowhood have significantly greater annual incomes than similar-aged men who do not remarry. We do not know whether effects of age could be completely abolished in a multivariate analysis incorporating unemployment, marital status, and other circumstantial correlates of age, such as fatherhood. No suitable data set presently exists to answer the question. However, the life-stage changes in physical prowess reviewed above, as well as the literature's indications of maturational changes in taste for risk, suggest to us that some age-associated variation in confrontational violence and other dangerous activity would persist even if all extrinsic circumstantial contributors to the pattern were accounted for.

CONCLUDING REMARKS

The earliest known lethal use of human weapons was not an act of interspecific predation. It was the fatal stabbing of a Neanderthal man in the chest by a right-handed antagonist more than 50,000 years ago (Trinkaus & Zimmerman, 1982).

Killing other people, both collaboratively and alone, is cross-culturally and historically universal, as documented in written records, archaeological artifacts, and fossil remains (Daly & Wilson, 1988). Killing is by no means universally deplored. It is justified in various contexts, and may even be deemed laudable when carried out in the defense of personal or familial honor or of the community that rewards it. Whereas killing members of one's lineage or in-group is considered tragic, stupid, wicked, or insane, killing foreigners or enemies or slaves or other non-persons may be no offense at all. And while homicide rates are enormously variable among human societies, they seem generally to have been much higher among foragers and other "self-help" societies than in state societies with judicial systems and central authorities that enforce the judges' decisions.

The ubiquity of killing bespeaks in part the universal utility of a credible threat of violence. Interests conflict, and effective deterrence is a matter of convincing our rivals that any attempt to advance their interests at our expense will lead to such severe costs that the competitive gambit will end up a net loss which should never have been undertaken. In face-to-face societies in which no ruler or bureaucracy can be counted upon to punish those who abuse their neighbors, wronged individuals and lineages must deter continued aggression and exploitation, or perish. The concept of blood vengeance is cross-culturally universal (Daly & Wilson, 1988), and the balance of terror that is chronic blood feud can be a major source of mortality (e.g., Chagnon, 1988). Even in modern nation states, homicides often entail elements of revenge or retaliation for prior insults and injuries; many others occur in defense of one's status, reputation or honor. Killing another in protecting one's unjustly violated interests is what renders homicide justifiable.

Homicide is widely considered to be primarily an act perpetrated by losers or outlaws. And so it is in societies in which the upper strata have recourse to police and courts when wronged while the disenfranchised underclasses rely on their personal deterrent and exploitive capabilities. But in most human societies through most of human history, the upper strata were often killers, too, and their lethality may have been part of what gained them power and respect. We have mentioned Chagnon's demonstration that Yanomamö men who have killed have more wives and children than other men. Although it is unclear in this case whether the killing *per se* contributed to their fitness or was merely a correlate of otherwise effective prowess, fierce men have elsewhere killed rivals, stolen women, and even established themselves as despots countless times. A socially recognized capacity for violence is a social asset.

There can be little doubt that human violence has been a sufficient cause of human mortality to have constituted an important selective force. Whether we exhibit adaptation *to* kill or not, it seems likely that our evolved psychological mechanisms and decision processes are in part adapted to recognizing and averting risk of lethal assaults upon us. If face-to-face conflict were not so dangerous, we might enter into competitive contests more frequently and carelessly and expend less attention and effort upon appeasement and the forging of compromise. Moreover, it is in part the lethality of human coalitions that ironically places a premium upon human cooperation (Alexander, 1971, 1987). In any event, whether there are any aspects of human nature which owe their existence (or parameter settings) to selection for homicidal efficacy is an open question.

An evolutionary psychological view of people does not imply that they are irrational automata, but rather that their behavior is the result of decision processes with a cost-benefit structure that incorporates age-, sex-, and circumstance-specific valuations of various material and social goods. Evolutionary models of the lifespan agendas of men and women indicate how behavioral control mechanisms must be functionally organized to have achieved adaptive ends in ancestral environments. By thinking about what the mind was designed by selection to do, we believe that psychologists can develop more conceptually coherent models of domain-specific decision processes.

The age-, sex-, and circumstance-specific patterns of killing an unrelated person of the same sex portrayed in this chapter need to be explained from several perspectives. We have argued that these demographic risk patterns are the kinds of epidemiological patterns of risk that are expected of a sexually-selected lifespan psychology of dangerous confrontational risk taking. We have suggested some of the sorts of information-processing mechanisms that could modulate such risk taking, including changed estimations of one's competence or of objective dangers, variable affect associated with the arousal caused by accepting a risk, and changes in the subjective utilities of the expected consequences of alternative courses of action. We have not discussed physiological or developmental explanations, nor have we addressed the issue of individual differences in willingness to embrace dangerous risk-taking. All of these kinds of explanations will, in the end, have to be complementary and conceptually integrated.

ACKNOWLEDGMENTS

Our research on homicide has been supported by The Harry Frank Guggenheim Foundation, the Social Sciences and Humanities Research Council of Canada, the North Atlantic Treaty Organization, and the Natural Sciences and Engineering Research Council of Canada. This chapter was completed while the authors were Fellows of the Center for Advanced Study in the Behavioral Sciences with financial support from the John D. and Catherine T. MacArthur Foundation, the National Science Foundation #BNS87-008, the Harry Frank Guggenheim Foundation, and the Gordon P. Getty Trust, and while M. Daly was a Fellow of the John Simon Guggenheim Foundation. We wish to thank Carolyn Rebecca Block and Richard Block (Chicago); James Bannon, Robert Hislop, and Marie Wilt Swanson (Detroit); Joanne Lacroix, Craig McKie, and Bryan Reingold (Canada); and Rosemary Gartner, Mary Tuck, L. Davidoff, Kathleen Shaw, and Michael O'Brien (England/Wales) for their help in creating and making available the homicide data files; and Jim Karr for his role in the number crunching. We are delighted that Nancy and Robert Bell organized such an interesting conference and wish to thank them for their hospitality.

NOTE

This chapter is largely derived from material in Wilson and Daly, 1985, Daly and Wilson, 1988, and Daly and Wilson, 1990.

REFERENCES

Alexander, R. D.(1971). The search for an evolutionary philosophy of man. *Proceedings of the Royal Society of Victoria, 84,* 99-120.

Alexander, R. D.(1987). *The biology of moral systems.* Hawthorne, NY: Aldine de Gruyter.

Alexander, R. D., Hoogland, J. L., Howard, R. D., Noonan, K. M., & Sherman, P. W. (1979). Sexual dimorphisms and breeding systems in pinnipeds, ungulates, primates and humans. In N. A. Chagnon & W. Irons (Eds.), *Evolutionary biology and human social behavior*. North Scituate, MA: Duxbury.

Balikci, A. (1970). *The Netsilik Eskimo*. Garden City, NY: The Natural History Press.

Beattie, J. H. M. (1960). Homicide and suicide in Bunyoro. In P. Bohannan (Ed.), *African homicide and suicide*. Princeton, NJ: Princeton University Press.

Bohannan, P. (1960a). Homicide and suicide in North Kavirondo. In P. Bohannan (Ed.), *African homicide and suicide*. Princeton, NJ: Princeton University Press.

Bohannan, P. (1960b). Homicide among the Tiv of central Nigeria. In P. Bohannan, (Ed.), *African homicide and suicide*. Princeton, NJ: Princeton University Pres.

Bradbury, J. W., & Andersson, M. (Eds.). (1987). *Sexual selection: Testing the alternatives*. Chichester: John Wiley.

Brown, I. D., & Groeger, J. A. (1988). Risk perception and decision taking during the transition between novice and experienced driver status. *Ergonomics, 31*, 585-597.

Busnot F. D. (1715). *The History of the reign of Muley Ismael, the present king of Morocco, Fez, Tafilet, Sous, & c.* (Translated from the original 1714). London: A. Bell.

Chagnon, N. A. (1988). Life histories, blood revenge, and warfare in a tribal population. *Science, 239*, 985-992.

Daly, M., & Wilson, M. (1983). *Sex, evolution and behavior*. Belmont, CA: Wadsworth.

Daly, M., & Wilson, M. (1988). *Homicide*. Hawthorne, NY: Aldine de Gruyter.

Daly, M., & Wilson, M. (1990). Killing the competition: Female/female and male/male homicide. *Human Nature, 1*, 81-107.

Dylan, B. (1965). Like a rolling stone. Warner Brothers Music.

Elwin, V. (1950). *Maria murder and suicide* (2nd edition). Bombay: Oxford University Press.

Enquist, M., & Leimar, O. (1990). The evolution of fatal fighting. *Animal Behaviour, 39*, 1-9.

Fallers, L. A., & Fallers, M. C. (1960). Homicide and suicide in Busoga. In P. Bohannan (Ed.), *African homicide and suicide*. Princeton, NJ: Princeton University Press.

Finn, P., & Bragg, B. W. E. (1986). Perception of the risk of an accident by young and older drivers. *Accident Analysis & Prevention, 18*, 289-298.

Gigerenzer G., & Murray D. J. (1987). *Cognition as intuitive statistics*. Hillsdale, NJ: Lawrence Erlbaum.

Gillies, H. (1976). Homicide in the west of Scotland. *British Journal of Psychiatry, 128*, 105-127.

Given, J. B. (1977). *Society and homicide in thirteenth-century England*. Stanford, CA: Stanford University Press.

Gove W. R. (1985). The effect of age and gender on deviant behavior: A biopsychological perspective. In A. S. Rossi (Ed.), *Gender and the life course*. New York: Aldine.

Hansen, J. P. H., & Bjarnason, O. (1974). Homicide in Iceland 1946-1970. *Forensic Science, 4*, 107-117.

Hart C. W. M., & Pilling, A. R. (1960). *The Tiwi of North Australia*. New York: Holt, Rinehart & Winston.

Hewlett, B. S. (1988). Sexual selection and paternal investment among Aka pygmies. In L. Betzig, M. Borgerhoff Mulder, & P. Turke (Eds.), *Human reproductive behavior.* Cambridge: Cambridge University Press.

Hiatt L. R. (1965). *Kinship and conflict: A study of an aboriginal community in northern Arnhem Land.* Canberra: Australia National University Press.

Hirschi, T., & Gottfredson, M. (1983). Age and the explanation of crime. *American Journal of Sociology, 89,* 552-584.

Hirschi, T., & Gottfredson, M. (1986). The distinction between crime and criminality. In T. F. Hartnagel & R. A. Silverman (Eds.), *Critique and explanation.* New Brunswick, NJ: Transaction Books.

Hollinger, P. C. (1987). *Violent deaths in the United States.* New York: Guilford Press.

Howell N. (1979). *Demography of the Dobe !Kung.* New York: Academic Press.

Jackson, T. T., & Gray, M. (1976). Field study of risk-taking behavior of automobile drivers. *Perceptual & Motor Skills, 43,* 471-474.

Jonah, B. A. (1986). Accident risk and risk-taking behaviour among young drivers. *Accident Analysis & Prevention, 18,* 155-271.

Kahneman, D., Slovic, P., & Tversky, A. (Eds.). (1982). *Judgment under uncertainty: Heuristics and biases.* New York: Cambridge University Press.

Kandel, D. B. (1980). Drug and drinking behavior among youth. *Annual Review of Sociology, 6,* 235-285.

Kaplan, H., & Hill, K. (1985). Hunting ability and reproductive success among male Ache foragers: Preliminary results. *Current Anthropology, 26,* 131- 133.

LaFontaine, J. S. (1960). Homicide and suicide among the Gisu. In P. Bohannan (Ed.), *African homicide and suicide.* Princeton, NJ: Princeton University Press.

Lee, R. B. (1979). *The !Kung San: Men, women, and work in a foraging society.* Cambridge: Cambridge University Press.

Lopes, L. L. (1987). Between hope and fear: The psychology of risk. *Advances in Experimental Social Psychology, 20,* 255-295.

Lyng, S. (1990). Edgework: A social psychological analysis of voluntary risk taking. *American Journal of Sociology, 95,* 851-886.

Matthews, M.L., & Moran, A. R. (1986). Age differences in male drivers' perception of accident risk: The role of perceived driving ability. *Accident Analysis & Prevention, 18,* 299-313.

McComas, A. J., Sica, R. E. P., & Petito, F. (1973). Muscle strength in boys of different ages. *Journal of Neurology, Neurosurgery & Psychiatry, 36,* 171-173.

McWhirter, N. (Ed.). (1980). *Guiness book of records.* Enfield, England: Guiness Superlatives Ltd.

Mrosovsky, N., & Sherry, D. F. (1980). Animal anorexias. *Science, 207,* 837-842.

Murray, M. P., Duthie, E. H., Gambert, S. R., Sepic, S. B., & Mollinger, L. A. (1985). Age-related differences in knee muscle strength in normal women. *Journal of Gerontology, 40,* 275-280.

Nash, J. (1967). Death as a way of life: The increasing resort to homicide in a Maya Indian community. *American Anthropologist, 69,* 455-470.

Nisbett, R., & Ross, L. (1980). *Human inference: Strategies and shortcomings of social judgment.* Englewood Cliffs, NJ: Prentice-Hall.

Pressley, P. H. (1981). Parental effort and the evolution of nest-guarding tactics in the threespine stickleback, *Gasterosteus aculeatus* L. *Evolution, 35,* 282-295.

Real, L., & Caraco, T. (1986). Risk and foraging in stochastic environments. *Annual Review of Ecology and Systematics, 17,* 371-390.

Rogin, M. P. (1975). *Fathers and children: Andrew Jackson and the subjugation of the American Indian.* New York: Vintage Books.

Rothe, J. P. (1987). *Rethinking young drivers.* North Vancouver, BC: Insurance Corporation of British Columbia.

Rubin, P. H., & Paul, C. W. (1979). An evolutionary model of taste for risk. *Economic Inquiry, 17,* 585-596.

Salzano, F. M., Neel, J. V., & Maybury-Lewis D. (1967). Further studies on the Xavante Indians. I. Demographic data on two additional villages: Genetic structure of the tribe. *American Journal of Human Genetics, 19,* 463-489.

Sampson, R. J. (1987). Urban black violence: The effect of male joblessness and family disruption. *American Journal of Sociology, 93,* 348-382.

Saran, A. B. (1974). *Murder and suicide among the Munda and the Oraon.* Delhi: National Publishing House.

Shephard, R. J. (1986). *Fitness of a nation.* Basel: Karger.

Sherry, D. F., Mrosovsky, N., & Hogan, J. A. (1980). Weight loss and anorexia during incubation in birds. *Journal of Comparative and Physiological Psychology, 94,* 89-98.

Slovic, P. (1987). Perception of risk. *Science, 236,* 280-285.

Southall, A. W. (1960). Homicide and suicide among the Alur. In P. Bohannan (Ed.), *African homicide and suicide.* Princeton, NJ: Princeton University Press.

Steffensmeier, D. J., & Allan, E. A. (1988). Sex disparities in arrests by residence, race, and age: An assessment of the gender convergence/crime hypothesis. *Justice Quarterly, 5,* 53-80.

Steffensmeier D. J., Allan, E. A., Harer, M. D., & Streifel, C. (1989). Age and the distribution of crime. *American Journal of Sociology, 94,* 803-831.

Sullivan, M. L. (1989). *"Getting paid": Youth crime and work in the inner city.* Ithaca, NY: Cornell University Press.

Thomas, J. R., & French, K. E. (1985). Gender differences across age in motor performance: A meta-analysis. *Psychological Bulletin, 98,* 260-282.

Tittle, C. R. (1988). Two empirical regularities (maybe) in search of an explanation: Commentary on the age/crime debate. *Criminology, 26,* 76-85.

Tonkin, R. S. (1987). Adolescent risk-taking behavior. *Journal of Adolescent Health Care, 8,* 213-220.

Trinkaus, E., & Zimmerman, M. R. (1982). Trauma among the Shanidar Neandertals. *American Journal of Physical Anthropology, 57,* 61-76.

Trivers, R. L. (1972). Parental investment and sexual selection. In B. Campbell (Ed.), *Sexual selection and the descent of man 1871-1971.* Chicago: Aldine.

Varma, S. C. (1978). *The Bhil kills.* Delhi: Kunj Publishing House.

Westermeyer, J. (1973). On the epidemiology of amok violence. *Archives of General Psychiatry, 28,* 873-876.

Wilbanks, W. (1984). *Murder in Miami.* Lanham, MD: University Press of America.

Wilson, G. M. (1960). Homicide and suicide among the Joluo of Kenya. In P. Bohannan (Ed.), *African homicide and suicide.* Princeton, NJ: Princeton University Press.

Wilson, M., & Daly, M. (1985). Competitiveness, risk-taking and violence: The young male syndrome. *Ethology & Sociobiology, 6,* 59-73.

Wilson, W. J., & Aponte, R. (1985). Urban poverty. *American Sociological Review, 11,* 231-258.

Wolfgang, M. E. (1978). Family violence and criminal behavior. In R.L. Sadoff, (Ed.), *Violence and responsibility.* New York: Spectrum.

DYSFUNCTIONAL RISK TAKING:
CRIMINAL BEHAVIOR AS EDGEWORK

STEPHEN LYNG

One of the more vibrant new areas of research in sociology to have emerged in recent years is the field of risk analysis. In the six years since a former president of the American Sociological Association used the occasion of his presidential address to call for a significant expansion of this field (Short, 1984), we have witnessed an explosion of books and articles dealing with a variety of concerns related to the assessment and management of risks at both the individual and collective levels (see Heimer, 1988). Fueling this expanding body of research is the realization that the problem of dealing with risks is a central concern of actors operating within many different domains of modern social life. The present paper builds on this insight by exploring the usefulness of risk analysis for understanding a problem area that has occupied center stage in the social and behavioral sciences for many decades—accounting for the prevalence and persistence of criminal behavior in modern postindustrial society.

Examining a wide range of literature dealing with crime (broadly defined), one finds scattered references to the possibility of a connection between risk taking and certain kinds of criminal behavior. For example, some researchers focusing on illegal drug use have posited that such behavior is motivated by a desire for "kicks" (Schuman and Polkowski, 1975), for the experience of an unusual thrill or the heightened sensations associated with a life and death struggle (Frederick, 1980). Additional references to the desire for taking risks as a motive force in other kinds of criminal behavior can be found in the literature (see Toch, 1980) but no one has yet provided a way to link the new developments in risk analysis to the study of any type of criminal activity. As I will presently show, the failure to establish systematic links between these two fields in the past can be traced to the limitations of the theoretical perspectives that have structured research in both areas of study. However, this state of affairs has been altered by recent theoretical advances in both fields. With the emergence of a phenomenological approach to the study of certain types of criminal behavior (Katz, 1988) and a micro-macro theory of voluntary risk taking (Lyng, 1990), new possibilities exist for an integration of ideas from both domains.

The primary goal of this paper is to conceptualize some forms of crime as voluntary risk taking behavior or "edgework" (Lyng, 1990). By applying the edgework model to criminal behavior, I hope to provide a more systematic and comprehensive explanation of the data that has been highlighted by the phenomenological account of crime (Katz, 1988). The edgework perspective offers an explanation of criminal behavior that not only emphasizes "the actor's own experience of the criminal act" (Katz, 1988) but also an understanding of the relationship between this experience and broader social structural conditions of modern American life.

CRIME AND RISK TAKING: DIFFERENT BEHAVIORS, COMMON EXPLANATIONS

Despite the absence of theories for linking crime and risk taking behavior, the types of explanations that have been offered for both problems have been very similar. In the study of crime, theorists have tended to adopt one of three basic approaches: First, crime is viewed as a rational effort to satisfy certain basic needs (either instrinsic—i.e., sex—or more socially structured—i.e., money) that cannot be satisfied through normal institutional channels. Second, some criminal behavior is treated as manifestations of irrational impulses associated either with particular personality predispositions or mental illness. Third, criminal acts are correlated with sociological variables such as age, gender, race, and class, which are then linked to more proximate variables in complex casual models.

In the small body of literature on voluntary risk taking, one finds variations on these same three approaches. Some analysts emphasize the rational pursuit of basic human needs and identify specific instrinsic desires that risk takers satisfy when they engage in this form of behavior. The needs in question run the gamut from the "need for arousal or stimulation" (Klausner, 1968, p. 139; Farberow, 1980, p. 21) to the need for competent control over environmental objects (Klausner, 1968, p. 156). Others focus on impulses arising from specific personality factors (Balint, 1959) or abnormal psychological functions such as depression and despair (Achte, 1980; Filstead, 1980; Litman, 1980). Finally, the standard sociological analysis of variations across social groups defined by age, sex, class, culture, etc. also is represented in the study of voluntary risk taking behavior (Bernard, 1968).

Thus, past research has tended to treat both forms of behavior as dependent variables to be explained by the three general categories of independent variables listed above, but no attempts have been made to explore, in any systematic way, the possible causal connections between the two forms of behavior. More importantly, data that would allow us to examine possible links between certain criminal behavior and voluntary risk taking have not been collected and analyzed. Traditional theoretical and methodological approaches in the social sciences have directed researchers away from the very things that common-sense suggests may be important for understanding crime and risk taking behavior—the subjective sense of the experience itself. However, with the emergence of phenomenologically-oriented studies of both criminal behavior (Katz, 1988) and voluntary risk taking (Lyng, 1990; Lyng & Snow, 1986; Mitchell, 1983), these data are now beginning to accumulate.

An examination of the phenomenological data in both areas of study reveals some strikingly similar themes. Data relating to actors' subjective interpretations of their experiences in committing criminal acts reveals a vocabulary for describing the emotional and sensual dimensions of the experience that is virtually indistinguishable from the experiential vocabulary employed by participants in high risk occupations (fire-fighting, police work, airplane test piloting, etc.) and leisure pursuits (skydiving, hang gliding, etc.). In both domains, actors often interpret their experiences as magical and sensual, as belonging to a special realm that transcends more conventional, institutional experience. While it long has been understood within some quarters that the line separating criminal behavior from more acceptable risk taking behavior (i.e., criminal work vs. police work) may be a fuzzy one, no one has undertaken a systematic effort to assay the similarities and differences between these two types of experience.

As an initial step in this direction, I will use some of the existing phenomenological data on crime and voluntary risk taking to identify elements of the "sensual dynamics" common to these two realms. This analysis is hampered by the limitations of the existing data, but it will be of sufficient scope to accomplish a second and, perhaps more important, goal. Demonstrating that certain forms of criminal behavior can be conceptualized as voluntary risk taking or "edgework," helps to resolve a difficult theoretical problem now confronting the phenomenological study of crime—the problem of linking experiential dimensions of crime to the macro-level, structural factors that correlate with criminal behavior.

EDGEWORK: A MODEL OF VOLUNTARY RISK TAKING

In introducing the concept of "edgework" into the social scientific study of voluntary risk taking, I have attempted to conceptualize this form of behavior in a way that highlights its most sociologically relevant features. The psychologically reductionist explanations and traditional sociological approaches identified above suffer from some significant shortcomings. On the other hand, the psychological models assume that the motives for risk taking are constant across time and space, an assumption that is in no way supported by cross-societal data. On the other hand the standard sociological account tends to ignore the internal causal processes that move actors between social structural influences and the actual risk taking behavior. By organizing a wide range of data on risk taking activities in terms of the edgework concept, it has been possible to develop a theoretical framework for analyzing this behavior that attends to both the micro and macro levels and that can account for the causal links between experiential and social structural dimensions.

As noted in a previous study (Lyng, 1990), edgework refers to activities that typically involve the process of negotiating the boundary line between life and death, consciousness and unconsciousness, sanity and insanity, or any other dramatic experiential expression of the line between order and disorder. The initial empirical base for the development of this concept consisted of data relating to high risk leisure sports such as skydiving, motorcycle racing, hang gliding and similar activities. While the boundary line of concern to participants in these sports is the line between life and death, an examination of data relating to other boundary negotiating activities reveals a common pattern of sensations. Individuals engaged in excessive alcohol or other drug use often traverse the line between consciousness and unconsciousness, while artists and business entrepreneurs may adopt work schedules that test the limits of psychological well being. The sensations associated with such activities are remarkably similar to the sensations produced by participation in many high risk sports. This suggests that all of these activities may be properly subsumed under a single concept, one that emphasizes the centrality of the boundary negotiating process in the experience. The concept of edgework was introduced with this goal in mind.

As a type of "experiential anarchy," edgework most typically involves an effort to define the performance limits of some form or object and, in the process, explore the line between form and formlessness. The variety of ways in which one may pursue such an experience, ranging from the exploration of the performance limits of technological forms like racecars and airplanes, to testing the limits of body and mind in athletic endeavors and creative activities, all possess a common requirement for the use of specific skills. This use of specially developed skills is one of the central features of edgework and edgeworkers typically place a high value on the opportunities that edgework holds for the development and use of complex skills. These skills belong to one of two general categories: (a) those specific to the activity in question, such as riding a motorcycle or flying one's body in freefall and (b) a special skill common to all forms of edgework—a capacity I have termed as the "survival skill" (Lyng, 1990, p. 859).

Participants in edgework activities generally believe that success in these endeavors depends on the special ability to maintain control over a situation that verges on complete chaos. Being able to exercise this type of control in situations that are almost completely novel and unpredictable is clearly a crucial requirement of edgework, especially considering that in many edgework circumstances one's survival is at stake. Although there are reasons to believe that the notion of a survival skill is largely a metaphysical construct of edgework participants (see Lyng, 1990), one's success in edgework is, in fact, dependent upon such capacities as the ability to focus one's attention on the crucial elements of experience, the ability to resist becoming paralyzed by fear and so forth. These more specific dimensions of the survival skill are measurable capacities that potentially apply to all forms of edgework.

The edgework concept also refers to a collection of sensations that typically are associated with a wide range of risk-taking activities. Edgeworkers uniformly experience feelings of "self-actualization" or "self-determination" in their confrontation with the edge. These feelings of a magnified, authentic sense of self are so powerful that participants are motivated to return again and again to the activities that produce such feelings. Hence, participants often report that edgework possesses an addictive quality. They also develop feelings of omnipotence and empowerment which sometimes contribute to an elitist orientation among some edgework groups. Certain perceptual changes may accompany these affective patterns, including such things as an alteration in one's ability to gauge the passage of time and feelings of enmeshment with essential objects in the environment. As a result of such perceptual changes, participants typically come to regard the edgework experience as a "hyperreality," an existential domain that is much more "real" than the circumstances of everyday social life. These sensations give rise to a common feeling among edgeworkers that the experience is ineffable—that to fully understand edgework, one must experience it directly because language simply cannot capture the essence of the phenomenon.

The principle value of the edgework conceptualization of voluntary risk taking is to shift the focus away from aspects of the phenomenon that have been of greatest concern to past researchers—i.e., the psychodynamics of fear and arousal or self-destructive impulses in risk taking—to a consideration of those phenomenological aspects of the activity that have the greatest sociological relevance—the spontaneous, anarchic, impulsive character of the experience. In highlighting these features the concept of edgework allows us to analyze voluntary risk taking within a socio-cultural context. Before we move to this level of analysis, however, I wish to show how the edgework concept can be applied to empirical data in an entirely new domain. This field, which seems to offer the greatest promise for a broader application of the concept, is the study of criminal behavior.

EDGEWORK AND THE PHENOMENOLOGY OF CRIME

The newest approach to the sociological study of criminal behavior relies on a body of empirical data that steadily has accumulated over the years but which largely has been ignored by criminologists in the past. Phenomenological data collected through participant observational studies, extensive open-ended interviews with criminals, first-hand accounts written by criminals themselves, ethnographies, journalistic reports, and the like, has recently been used by Jack Katz (1988) as a data base for a powerful new perspective on the criminal experience. Katz has challenged the existing theoretical explanations of crime by locating some of the most important motivations for criminal acts in the criminal experience itself. Katz's phenomenological data reveal that the attraction of crime has more to do with the rewards of the experience itself rather than what the criminal act will yield in the way of

material goods or other concrete goals. Some criminal acts are experienced as almost magical events that involve distinctive "sensual
dynamics." These criminal pursuits often take on a transcendent
appeal, offering the criminal an opportunity for a passionate, intensely authentic experience. In Katz's view, this dimension of the
criminal enterprise is the most important force impelling people
towards crime.

The similaritiy between Katz's study of the criminal experience
and the edgework conceptualization of voluntary risk taking are
apparent. Both analyses emphasize the appealing character of the
respective experiences and propose that participants seek out such
opportunities because the sensations and feelings they offer cannot be found in any other realm of life experience. The similarities
in the empirical and explanatory themes of both areas of study suggest that the two fields may be converging on a common phenomenon or, at least, a common subset of elements that constitute
two related but analytically distinct domains of human action. To
explore this possibility, I will now endeavor to theoretically organize some of the phenomenological data on the criminal experience in terms of the edgework model.

CHAOS AND ANARCHY IN THE CRIMINAL ACT

To conceptualize some forms of crime as edgework, we must
first attend to the defining feature of all varieties of edgework—the
process of negotiating the boundary between order and disorder.
On this point, there is little doubt that many criminal acts constitute particularly intense forms of edgework. A central theme in
Katz's descriptive data on crime is the inherent chaos and ambiguity of most criminal enterprises. Although criminal acts in
general involve a relatively high degree of unpredictability as compared with most noncriminal behavior, the uncertainty and chaos
of crimes such as robbery or "stickup" are so profound that this becomes the central feature of the action. As Katz notes, the offender
who engages in a stickup inevitably enters a state of suspense in
which he can never be sure about how things will develop: "First
there is the offender's uncertainty about how much he will have to
pressure the victim before he succeeds. When he victimizes
strangers, he comes suddenly and intimately into a subjective world
that he knows he does not know well. And when his victims are acquaintances, the stickup man can anticipate the possibility of a
response shaped by extraneous emotional themes" (1988, p. 187).

In addition to the ambiguities associated with possible resistance by victims, Katz documents other sources of uncertainty in robbery situations that range from the chance of bystander intervention to the offender's inability to know what undisclosed loot the victim may be holding. In general, the chaotic circumstance of the stickup subjects the robber to the "suspense of existing in alien worlds" (1988, p. 191). Even his efforts to control some sources of uncertainty—as, for example, when he relies on co-offenders to help quell potential resistance by victims or bystanders—places him in yet another alien world. "Colleagues in a stickup may not do enough to dominate their assigned part of the interaction or, what is perhaps more disconcerting, they may do too much" (1988, p. 191). By choosing to enter the alien worlds of victims, bystander interveners, and co-offenders, the robber places himself very close to the line that separates order from disorder. He must be prepared to deal with any contingency, to respond creatively and effectively to a unique sequence of events that cannot be fully anticipated or planned for in advance. Like the test pilot or firefighter, the offender doing stickup must have the capacity to formulate a non-routinized, ad hoc response to a constantly evolving, potentially out-of-control situation.

The distinguishing disposition of the edgeworker is to regard these marginal situations as seductively appealing. This attraction to uncertain circumstances is perhaps most clearly revealed by evidence of an inclination by some edgeworkers to actually *increase* the risks involved in the action, as when mountain climbers make ascents without oxygen tanks or when "career" robbers purposively choose to work with inexperienced co-offenders. Indeed, the data suggest that criminals may be especially interested in finding ways to increase the challenge by assuming greater risks. Referring to a low-level street criminal, Katz notes that, "The threat of chaos was characteristic of Henry's stickups, not only because he could not know what the victims would do, but because of his spur-of-the-moment method of beginning the crimes and because of his lack of knowledge of his colleagues—just because of the temporal and social network characteristics that enabled the action of stickups to become diffuse in his life. And the forms of action he favored created a great risk of chaos in the robberies themselves" (1988, p. 220).

Katz also cites evidence on high status criminals working within organized crime circles who seem to cultivate chaos as an integral feature of their everyday life. "There is something resembling a

death wish among some such villains. Not just in the lack of care
they take to cover their tracks, or in the reckless way in which
'profits' are gambled away, but in the self-dramatizing which they
bring to their roles. . . .[A]ctual robbers and con men and gang-
sters appear to go out of their way to increase their own visibility,
and thus their likelihood of detection, by trying to live up to [mass
media images of criminals.] . . . After a very short time, I found
them instantly recognizable in straight clubs and restaurants; as
though they were acting out a little stage version of the
'underworld' for the benefit of the patrons at adjoining tables"
(Taylor, 1985, pp. 180-81).

A central theme of Katz's analysis of robbery, as well as many
other forms of criminal behavior, is that the disorder and uncertainty of the criminal act reflect a general commitment to illicit,
noninstitutional behavior in every facet of the criminal's cultivated
lifestyle. Relying on Erving Goffman's concept of "action,"
(defined as behavior that is consequential for the individual and
that has unpredictable but clear-cut outcomes [Goffman, 1967, p.
185]), Katz notes that "more commonly, stickup is combined with
various other forms of action . . . as one state in an ongoing episode
of action" (1988, p. 197). The criminal is enmeshed in a lifestyle
pattern in a which he moves from one type of action to another,
from illicit sexual relations and heavy drug use to intense episodes
of gambling and stickups. Viewed within this context, it can be
seen that the criminal act does not differ in kind from the other
forms of action pursued by the offender. It represents just one
more way the individual can place himself close to the boundary
between order and chaos. Thus, robbing people is not unlike the
gaming involved in unconventional sexual relations which, according to Katz, "require as many quick-thinking tactics and tricky maneuvers" as does the criminal action (1988, p. 201). This analysis
also challenges the conventional wisdom about the relationship
between drug use and crime. Katz's subjects were not typically
"forced" into crime in order to support their drug addictions. Although there is a close association between drug use and robbery,
using drugs is not the organizing theme of these criminals' lives: "It
was only one of several seductive ways of staying in the action"
(1988, p. 205). The same can be said about most features of the
robber's lifestyle, from gambling to the "irrational" consumption
patterns of many criminals. Indeed, in some exceptional
instances, one finds "so many intensely lived themes of illicit

action [among robbers] that they depict a process of rampage" (1988, p. 197).

It is clear from this evidence that stickup and closely related criminal acts can be appropriately conceptualized as a special variety of edgework. The prominent place of chaotic, uncertain circumstances and the actors' spontaneous responses to such conditions in criminal action is a feature this activity has in common with all other behavior classified as edgework. Further support for this way of thinking about stickup can be found in an additional empirical theme of Katz's study—the problem of *controlling* the inherent chaos involved in the action. This problem is most directly relevant to the "survival skill" component of the edgework model.

THE SURVIVAL SKILL IN CRIMINAL ACTION

As noted above, edgeworkers of all stripes tend to believe that their success in negotiating the edge ultimately depends upon an innate "survival skill." The survival skill is constituted, in part, of some empirically demonstrable capacities, such as being able to focus one's attention, and controlling fear, but at its core, it seems to involve transcendental properties. Thus, edgeworkers in many different domains often describe the survival instinct in terms of a special form of "mental toughness" (Lyng, 1990, p. 859). The phenomenological perspective on crime offers a clear analogue to this way of thinking about the survival skill in the form of Katz's notion of the robber's "hardheadedness" or "competent immorality." "That a distinctive morally insensitive will, a true hardheadedness, is essential to stick with stickup has not been appreciated in the study of robbery, which has emphasized numerous striking patterns depicting offenders as flexibly rational. These patterns are not false or artificial, but they do not warrant the characterization of offenders as simply instrumental, morally sensitive, and basically rational in their use of violence. [We must appreciate] the hardheadedness and moral meanness that are required by the situational practicalities of the offense to make sense of persisting in a stickup" (Katz, 1988, p. 194).

The idea of competent immorality applies to a particularly important source of unpredictability in the stickup—the robber's uncertainty about his own potential behavior in the criminal act. As Katz notes, "the stickup is a process in which one's *own* capacities and inclinations may become features of an alien system" (1988, p. 192). Adopting the vocabulary of noncriminal edgeworkers, it could be said that one does not know for sure if one possesses the mental toughness to bring the action to a successful completion until one attempts actually to carry it out. For example, military test pilots rely on a peculiar tautology for determining who possesses the "right stuff" (i.e., the survival capacity): Pilots with the right stuff can handle any situation that might arise; therefore, a comrade who dies in the line of duty obviously did not possess the right stuff (Wolfe, 1979). For the robber, the true test of his status as an edgeworker is his willingness to "go to the limit" in suspending all normative constraints on his actions in bringing the stickup to a successful completion. And, like the test pilot who wonders if he has the right stuff, the robber cannot know if he is truly "bad" enough to do this kind of work until he actually places himself on the normative edge. "In stickups, as in other fields in which a difficult spiritual commitment must be made, many are called but few are chosen . . .[T]he practical constraints on making a career of stickups are such that one *cannot* simply adopt violence as an instrumental device, to be enacted or dropped as situational contingencies dictate. It is practically impossible to make a career of stickups just by making a calculated show of a disposition to be 'bad'; you must live the commitment to deviance. You must really mean it" (Katz, 1988, p. 193).

The confrontation with the normative edge is where the robber faces his ultimate challenge. A part of this challenge is to convince himself not to "give it up" (Katz, 1988, p. 194); but he also must draw on his "morally insensitive will" to exercise control over a situation that is normatively and experientially chaotic. This ability to "control the seemingly uncontrollable" is the essence of the survival instinct.

A preoccupation with one's ability to transcend or control chaos is perhaps the most important common characteristic of edgeworkers in both the criminal and noncriminal domains. In my analysis of members of high risk occupations and leisure groups, I have found that the opportunity for exercising the survival skill is what these individuals seem to value most about their risk taking pursuits (Lyng, 1990). Katz also finds the criminal "hardman's" desire to establish control over the anarchic situations he initiates to be the overriding feature of this way of life. Indeed, this mixture of chaos and control is the thing that ultimately accounts for the seductive appeal of a criminal act like robbery: "The chaos in the life of action lends a distinctive significance to those who respond by imposing a disciplined control through the force of their personality. This is the final, compelling appeal of the hardman—that he alone, in the face of chaos, embodies transcendence by sticking up for himself, literally and figuratively" (1988, p. 225). Thus, the robber, like other edgeworkers, does not recoil from the experience of disorder and uncertainty; he embraces this experience because it becomes "a provocation to manifest transcendent powers of control" (1988, p. 220).

By considering the importance of this commitment to willful control over chaos, we can better understand the unrelenting pursuit of edgework by both criminal and noncriminal risk takers. A belief in one's special ability to survive anarchic situations impels the actor to create the conditions for an encounter with the edge. The chaotic situation thus created can be transformed through the edgeworker's imposition of his own form and discipline—i.e., personal control over chaos—which reconfirms his identity as a member of the edgework elite. When the process involves the form and discipline of a stickup, the robber reconfirms his identity as a "triumphant hardman" (1988, p. 225). This status is different in content but identical in form to such statuses as pilots with the "right stuff," "skygods" (within the skydiver subculture), and the like.

Up to this point, I have emphasized the similarities between criminal and noncriminal forms of edgework, but it also is important to identify the crucial differences between the two domains. While this task can ultimately be accomplished only through systematic empirical research, it is possible to establish some conceptual parameters for differentiating the criminal edgework project from other varieties of edgework. One important difference is captured by the conceptual distinction between "ecological" and "interpersonal" edgework.

In light of the edgeworker's fascination with anarchic experience, it is tempting to posit that anyone attracted to high risk occupations or leisure activities also is predisposed to engage in violent criminal behavior. Although the available data on voluntary risk taking does not directly address this problem, none of the empirical patterns or themes within these data would suggest that such a correlation exists. Evidence from my (participant observational studies) indicate that these individuals focus most of their attention on the ecological environment: The locus of action for occupational and leisure sport edgeworkers is some aspect of the physical world—one's body (for athletes), a piece of technology (airplanes, motorcycles, etc.), a mountain or cliff, a burning building, the stock market, etc. While they enthusiastically embrace any opportunity for anarchic experience in these domains, ecological edgeworkers are not uniquely inclined to generate disorder in interpersonal relations. Like most nonedgeworkers in the general population, these individuals seem to respect normative proscriptions against "doing harm to others," particularly the middle-class proscriptions against inflicting physical injury on other people. However, for the violent criminal and some of his less violent brethren, this kind of normative constraint does not exist. Indeed, the realm of interpersonal relations is the preferred locus of action for many types of criminal edgeworkers.

The evidence for this claim emerges as another dominant theme in Katz's data. The criminal "hardman"—the career robber who commits the lion's share of violent crimes—posseses an unrestrained willingness to transcend any moral boundary in exploiting other people, not only the strangers he victimizes but friends and relatives as well. "[T]he thrust of life-history evidence is that the construction of a career as a heavy in stickups requires living as a hardman—a person who anticipates mobilizing violence at any moment. . . one who will appear ready to back his intentions violently and remorselessly, outside and independent of the situated interaction of robbery. The way of the hardman is a distinctive response to the chaos faced by virtually all who persist in common crimes" (1988, pp. 218, 219). Criminal offenders who pursue robbery, con games, mugging, gang violence, and similar activities as a way of life seek opportunities for experiential anarchy specifically within the realm of face-to-face interaction. The goal is to transport yourself and your victim to the limits of an ordered reality and then to use your transcendent power as a hardman to control the ensuing chaos. This commitment to realizing one's identity as a hardman is, of course, the driving force in all aspects of one's life, in managing *all* interpersonal exchanges. Katz notes that "the biographies of stickup men are rich with evidence of a gut- deep desire to impose this hard control on close personal relationships. . . . The point is not that one must regularly beat up one's lover and children to make sense of persisting in stickup. It is that persisting in stickup seems to make sense only as part of a larger project of transcending chaos in general, virtually wherever it may appear in one's life, through imposing a cold, hard, violent discipline" (1988, p. 228). In the final outcome, these forms of interpersonal edgework result in the offender gaining ascendancy over the victim. If surviving an instance of *ecological* edgework allows one to "thumb one's nose" at the determinant power of the natural world (beating the odds, as calculated by mother nature, so to speak), then prevailing in a case of *interpersonal* edgework allows one to humiliate, exploit, defile one's fellow man. To state it in crass terms, the end result of interpersonal edgework is that someone "gets fucked over." Whether this specific outcome is one of the things that gives interpersonal edgework its seductive appeal, or whether it is simply a consequence not directly intended by those engaging in this type of edgework, remains an open question.

Finally, in classifying some forms of criminal behavior as edgework, we must also consider the third dimension of the edgework phenomenon—the various sensations that accompany the experience. As noted above, edgeworkers of many different types report common sensations in their encounters with the edge: feelings of self-actualization, authenticity, and omnipotence; transformations in the perception of time and space; and the sense that these marginal situations constitute a hyperreality that cannot be described adequately in words (ineffability). Examination of the phenomenological data on crime reveals an unfortunate lack of evidence relating to the sensations of the criminal experience. One can certainly infer from Katz's study that many criminal actions produce these sorts of sensations, but the data needed to verify the claim that the criminal experience generates edgework sensations is not generally available. This is an important problem that should be addressed in future research.

THE MICRO-MACRO ANALYSIS OF ILLICIT EDGEWORK

Having demonstrated the empirical basis for conceptualizing certain forms of criminal behavior as edgework, it now remains to be shown how the application of the broader edgework framework to crime actually advances our understanding of this domain of human behavior. This is best accomplished by addressing one of the primary analytical concerns of Katz's study. Throughout the analysis, Katz returns repeatedly to the problem of establishing linkages between the factors that his study emphasizes—elements in the "foreground" of the criminal project (i.e., phenomenological factors)—and those variables that criminologists have traditionally emphasized, the "background" factors of age, sex, ethnicity, and class. In exploring the link between the foreground and background dimensions of crime, Katz seeks to address the fundamental challenge that his study raises—that is, fashioning an explanatory framework for understanding crime that not only considers the actor's lived experience of criminal activities but also connects this experience to the broad institutional patterns of the modern social order. Although the micro-level causal factors have been largely excluded from past analyses of crime, to focus exclusively on these factors would be as shortsighted as focusing only on the macro-level factors emphasized by previous research. Katz recognizes that real progress in the study of crime demands that we begin thinking in terms of micro-macro frameworks for explaining the criminal enterprise.

The primary thrust of this effort is to locate the most important causes of crime in the foreground of the criminal experience and treat the structural background factors as influences that may determine the *form* of the criminal project but not the *drive* toward this end (1988, p. 316). Consistent with his phenomenological interpretation, Katz defines the motive forces for criminal behavior in terms of the seductive appeal of the experience itself. In recognizing the "lived sensuality" of various types of criminal behavior, "we are compelled to acknowledge the power that still may be created in the modern world through the sensualities of defilement, spiritual chaos, and the apprehension of vengeance" (1988, p. 312). In Katz's view, not everyone is equally likely to discover the sensual attractions of crime but the experience holds an attraction that virtually anyone can appreciate. The primary task, then, for constructing a micro-macro explanation of criminal behavior is to understand how background factors put one in touch with the sensualities of the criminal project.

Katz addresses this latter problem by positing that being male, non-white, and poor predisposes an individual to a lifestyle characterized by a significant amount of "illicit action." A life world increasingly circumscribed by activities like low riding, gambling, gang banging, sports, street hustles and related pursuits, increasing one's sensitivity to the magical character of spontaneous action. Thus, Katz can claim that "the stickup is a form of illicit action that some men and few women find seductive—the kind of illicit action that may be represented equally by activities like low riding, gang banging, and sports that have no monetary overlay and by those like street hustles and gambling that do" (1988, p. 242).

If more extensive participation in illicit action predisposes males to a life of crime, the same also can be said about racial minorities and the poor. For members of these populations involvement in illicit action constitutes a slippery slope that easily can lead to the criminal project. Katz is careful to point out that other more specific dynamics operate besides the allure of action. African-Americans, like other distinctive ethnic groups, develop unique subcultural definitions of the criminal experience that also take on motivational relevance. These "vocabularies of motive" usually reflect the dominant subcultural themes of the groups that create them. For example, the overrepresentation of African-American males in robbery not only indicates the prevalence of illicit action within this population but also two other factors: one "is the distinctive shape given to the social role of criminal hardman in American black ghettoes, compared to the shaping of that role in the historical experience of other ethnic groups. [Another factor] is the emotionally powerful attraction of the 'bad nigger' identity as a transcendent response to the racial humiliation of ghetto blacks" (1988, p. 247).

This analysis poses a significant challenge to one of the most well established traditions in social science—the "materialist" sociological approach to the study of crime. While not denying the importance of the well known correlations between crime and such variables as ethnicity and class, Katz notes that his phenomenological data simply do not support the inference that has been drawn from these correlations—the idea that ethnic and class patterns in criminal behavior reflect the specific structural conditions that breed the motivation to deviance. All of the materialist perspectives, from Marx and Durkheim to the contemporary sociological materialism of Robert K. Merton, see social actors making use of a rational calculus to deal with the exigencies of their social-cultural environment. Within this framework, deviant behavior emerges as a rational response by some individuals to inevitable contradictions in the structure of modern society. What troubles Katz, however, is the lack of empirical support for the idea that rational considerations play any significant part in the decision to undertake the criminal project. In his own words, the materialist sentiment simply cannot appreciate "the many sensually explosive, diabolically creative, realities of crime" (1988, p. 314).

While Katz's critique of the materialist perspective is well founded, we must question his willingness to exclude all potential structural variables from the explanatory model simply because his phenomenological data is incompatible with *existing* structural theories of crime. Although "background" factors are included in his framework, these are merely descriptive of the social group characteristics of criminal offenders: As a matter of theoretical fiat, any structural forces that may be implicated by the background factors cannot operate as variables in the causal sequence. In his own words, the theory that emerges from this study "relates material conditions to the form or quality of deviance but not to its incidence or prevalence" (1988, p. 317).

To provide a thorough-going micro-macro theory of crime, it is necessary to identify a theoretical framework that establishes causal links between the types of phenomenological themes emphasized in Katz's study and broader structural forces operating in contemporary American society. The edgework model constitutes such a framework. I have demonstrated that there is a strong empirical basis for classifying most of the criminal activities discussed by Katz as forms of "illicit edgework." Consequently, it is possible that the same structural forces that give rise to varieties of edgework emphasized by my previous research (Lyng, 1990) also play a causal role in the emergence of illicit (or interpersonal) edgework.

In exploring this possibility I will discuss the edgework model only in broad terms (see Lyng, 1990 for a more detailed description of the model). Emerging from a new line of research in sociological theory that attempts a synthesis between the perspectives of Karl Marx and George H. Mead, the approach emphasizes the division of human experience into the categories of "spontaneous" and "constrained" action, conceptualized as two opposing poles of a common dialectical relation. Each theorist focuses on a different dimension of the social system, with Marx emphasizing the macro-level structural patterns of the socio-economic system and Mead dealing with the micro-level patterns of face-to-face interaction (making possible a micro-macro sociological theory). At the same time both see spontaneous and constrained action as constituting the two major dimensions of a unified self. This common view of the unified self serves as the primary reference point for analyzing modern society, for explanatory purposes as well as for the purpose of critically evaluating the existing social order.

The Marx-Mead synthetic framework focuses special attention on the problem of human creativity. Marx and Mead both posit that the individual typically assigns special significance to the spontaneous dimension of the self because it is the locus of creative action. Mead expresses this point best when he notes that the spontaneous self (the "I") involves "that which is actually going on, taking place, and it is in some sense the most fascinating part of our experience. It is there that novelty arises, and it is there that our most important values are located. It is the realization in some sense of this self that we are continually seeking" (Mead [1934] 1964, pp. 250-251).

Because Marx and Mead choose different but complementary frameworks for analyzing the social order, the phenomenal forms of spontaneous action differ for each theorist. For Marx, spontaneous action appears phenomenally as "conscious, purposive, concentrated, physically and mentally flexible, and skillful" (Ollman, 1971, p. 120). For Mead, such action is conceptualized in terms of the "I" portion of the self: Found at the "razor edge of the present," the "I" designates the creative, impulsive behavior of the individual and reflects all the uncertainty and uniqueness of the moment.

The most important thing to say about spontaneous action, however, is that it represents the "opposing but necessary" side of constrained action. In other words, as one pole of a dialectical relation, free action can emerge only within the context of certain types of constraining structures. Identifying the institutional (constraining) structures that make possible creative action is perhaps the most controversial aspect of both the Marxian and Meadian frameworks because each theorist is forced to define these structures in utopian terms, and each uses his respective utopia as a basis for critically assessing modern society (an explicit task for Marx, an implicit one for Mead).

The critical requirements for free action, in Marx's view, are institutional arrangements that allow work to become the principle means through which individuals develop their human capacities rather than merely serving the capitalist function of maximizing profit. In addition, both Marx and Mead place special emphasis on the need for an institutional system free of divisions and separations (divisions that in the modern era are associated with class conflict, alienation, and the consumptive imperative). Such a system would enhance the possibilities for community action rather than diminishing those possibilities. On this point, Mead is particularly instructive because his system describes the conceptual links between the community, the normative order, and the self. Thus, for Mead, free action requires the development of structural conditions facilitating the formation of a social self (a "me") that incorporates the attitude of the entire social community. This fully developed "me" creates the potential for free, spontaneous action by the "I."

By identifying the social structural conditions required for the emergence of free action and a unified definition of self, the Marx-Mead framework succeeds in establishing a reference point for the critical analysis of modern postindustrial society. In a social system in which people cannot realize their full human potential through material production and cannot live as part of a fully developed moral community, a unified definition of self (consisting of both the constrained and spontaneous components) is not possible. The failure of the self to fully develop under these conditions is manifested phenomenologically as an absence of ego. The individual's personal experience accords with the sociological notion of "oversocialization"—the feeling that one is being pushed through daily life by forces that are entirely opaque to individual understanding and action. Some who live under such structural conditions and confront the personal experience of oversocialization are likely to positively assess any experience that is ego-enhancing and that offers the phenomenal characteristics associated with free action as defined by the Marx-Mead framework. I have argued that edgework represents just such an experience.

I shall now recapitulate this argument, by focusing on the illicit forms of edgework of concern here rather than the ecological edgework emphasized in the previous research. It is clear that the pursuit of illicit edgework places one in an experiential realm that differs fundamentally from the realm of normal institutional routines. As Katz notes, the overriding feature of the criminal project is the chaotic, spontaneous nature of the experience. Moreover, this chaotic situation does not emerge accidentally; it is often *created* by the offender for a specific purpose. Immersing himself in the chaotic conditions of a criminal project, provides the offender with an opportunity for the use of his special skills, the most important of which is the "survival capacity"—the ability to exercise a hard discipline over the emerging disorder and bring the situation to a successful end. In the case of robbery, one imposes this transcendent control through the force of one's will and personality and, in the process, reaffirms one's status as a "hardman." The survival skill requires the use of some more specific skills as well, like focusing one's attention, concentrating on the essential elements of the situation, and dealing with the potentially paralyzing effects of fear. All of these actions contribute to a sense of "controlling the seemingly uncontrollable."

Those who practice illicit edgework value the opportunity for skillful performance—the use of the survival skill as well as the craft skills that are specific to the criminal action undertaken (cracking safes, running cons, etc.). One way to account for the attractive character of illicit edgework, then, is to emphasize the unique opportunity it affords for the development and use of skills, in the context of a broader socio-economic system in which most forms of work have become increasingly "deskilled" and subjected to bureaucratic standards (cf. Braverman,1974; Edwards,1979; Piore and Sabel 1984). But the thing that sets edgework apart from other types of skillful pursuits (such as home maintenance, leisure sports, etc.) is the requirement for survival capacities that involve a maximum degree of mental and physical flexibility, creativity and concentration. Recall that these are precisely the terms used to describe the phenomenological characteristics of Marx's concept of "free activity."

The use of the survival skill also reflects another important dimension of the relationship between the criminal project and the broader structural forces of modern society. In the earlier study of edgework, it was noted that all members of modern society confront significant threats to their well-being that seem to be largely beyond their control. Facing mental or physical threats such as toxic chemicals in the environment, nuclear war, financial instability, the instability of modern personal relations, disease and natural disaster, many people develop an overriding concern for their personal survival. At the same time, however, many sense that their survival possibilities have nothing at all to do with their own survival skills. This dilemma is particularly pronounced among people possessing some of the "background" social characteristics that are highly correlated with criminal behavior. Being poor in modern American society substantially increases the likelihood of mental or physical insults to one's well-being, from the threats of victimization and destitution to the high risks of marital and family breakup. Moreover, people of minority status confront additional threats arising from racial hatred and discrimination. What is most distinctive about these threats is their *institutional* character. Because they are rooted in the structure of poverty and discrimination in the U.S., they seem to be beyond the control of the people who confront them.

If personal survival skills seem to bear no relation to one's chances of surviving institutional threats, the opposite is true of the threats posed by edgework. In edgework, both in its ecological and illicit forms, participants perceive a direct link between survival capacities and survival outcome. When an offender manufactures an opportunity for illicit edgework, he senses that his fate rests in his own hands. If he succeeds in mobilizing his powers of control and criminal skills, he will survive the experience. In contrast, any failure of willpower or breakdown in one's skilled performance will result in disaster. In either case, the outcome of the effort becomes a signal event in the edgeworker's life because it clearly distinguishes the edgework elite from everyone else. Among robbers, for instance, it distinguishes the true "hardman" from those who must live with the insults of poverty, discrimination, and/or a failed criminal career.

Thus, another reason why illicit edgework may hold a special allure is because it offers a unique contrast to "normal" institutional life: While a person may never know for sure if s/he is successfully dealing with the institutional threats of modern life (are we free from environmentally produced disease, will we die tomorrow in a nuclear holocaust, is our marital and family life healthy and nourishing?), illicit edgework allows one to measure success in an unambiguous way. Every successful stickup, con game, shoplift, etc. is taken as proof that one possesses the basic survival instinct. And, most importantly, the evidence of this ability is revealed in an immediate and straightforward manner, with none of the ambiguity that attends one's efforts to deal with institutional threats. Living as a member of a dispossessed group within modern society may leave one with a profound sense of powerlessness, but to successfully negotiate the edge as a criminal offender time and time again is to experience a feeling of omnipotence and transcendence.

Finally, the synthetic framework also allows us to examine the links between the social structural dimension and the various sensations that may give illicit edgework its magical appeal. The Meadian elements of the framework are most relevant to this problem, in particular, Mead's analysis of the dynamic relationship between the "I" and "me" portions of the self. As noted above, the "I" and "me" designate the spontaneous and constrained dimensions of the self, respectively, and both dimensions must be present for a unified definition of self. A social order characterized by divisions and separations produced by class conflict and alienation inhibits the full development of the social self (the "me"), and true creative action by the "I" is not possible. The earlier treatment of ecological edgework suggests that under these conditions, any experience that mimics the spontaneity and freedom of the "I" portion of a unified self will be highly appealing to the individual. In modern society, such an experience is provided by actions that serve to "obliterate the social self" (the "me").

The inspiration for this proposition comes from Herbert Blumer's (1934/1969) work on crowd behavior, which focuses on how the "milling" process within crowds (aimless moving about) disrupts reflective consciousness and leads to spontaneous action by a residual nonsocial self. Just as milling within crowds suppresses the cognitive processes ("imaginative rehearsal") that sustain the social self, we may posit that the unique circumstances of illicit edgework also produces this effect. The criminal offender engaged in illicit edgework places himself in circumstances that demand immediate and instinctive responses to the emerging chaos of the encounter. As Katz stresses throughout his study, rational decision- making is an insignificant part of the criminal experience. It simply is not possible to anticipate the precise course of events in illicit edgework, nor does one have the luxury to casually reflect on the emerging situation. Thus, the demand for instinctive action combined with fear serve essentially to shut down the process of imaginative rehearsal. In this condition, the "voice of society" ceases to speak and the individual is left with a residual self—not a self that can be classified as the "I" but one that possesses many of the same characteristics.

As the earlier study suggests "edgework sensations" are associated with the absence of the "me" component of the self in edgework action. When the "me" is obliterated by the demands of the situation, action is no longer constrained by those social forces that take the form of internalized normative dictates. Consequently, the individual is left with a sense of self-determination or self-actualization (viewed here as the antithesis of social determination). Action directed by the nonsocial self also is experienced as more "authentic" than institutional action and seems to reflect the proclivities of the "true self." As the repository of such social elements as the attitudes of others, societal knowledge and language, the "me" and functions as the medium through which ongoing action can be made intelligible. Consequently, the absence of the "me" in illicit edgework makes the experience literally "indescribable" or ineffable. This seems to account as well for the alterations in the perception of time and space that often accompany the edgework experience, perceptual transformations that may account, in part, for the magical and seductive character of illicit edgework.

In short, the Marx-Mead framework makes it possible to move from Katz's basic insight about crime—the notion that the causes of criminal behavior can be found in the experience itself—to a level of analysis which allows us to understand how these causal factors relate to the broader structures of modern American society.

It is important to appreciate that the criminal experience possesses a seductive appeal that can pull some people toward this type of action; but it is also important to demonstrate the way in which the structural context of the experience shapes our sense of what is appealing in the first place. By drawing on the edgework model to both classify and explain certain types of criminal behavior, we may address this important problem.

REFERENCES

Achte, K. A. (1980). The psychopathology of indirect self-destruction. In N. L. Farberow (Ed.), *The many faces of suicide.* New York: McGraw- Hill.

Balint, M. (1959). *Thrills and regressions.* New York: International Universities Press.

Bernard, J. (1968). The eudaemonist. In S. Z. Klausner (Ed.), *Why men take chances.* Garden City, New York: Anchor Books.

Blumer, H. (1934/1969). Outline of collective behavior. In R. R. Evans (Ed.), *Readings in collective behavior.* Chicago: Rand McNally.

Braverman, H. (1974). *Labor and monopoly capitol: The degradation of work in the twentieth century.* New York: Monthly Review Press.

Edwards, R. (1979). *Contested terrain: The transformation of the workplace in the twentieth century.* New York: Basic Books.

Farberow, N. L. (1980). Indirect self-destructive behavior: Classification and characteristics. In N. L. Farberow (Ed.), *The many faces of suicide. New York: McGraw-Hill.*

Filstead, W. J. (1980). Dispair and its relationship to self-destructive behavior. In N. L. Farberow (Ed.), *The many faces of suicide.* New York: McGraw-Hill.

Frederick, C. J. (1980). Drug abuse as indirect self-destructive behavior. In N. L. Farberow (Ed.), *The many faces of suicide.* New York: McGraw Hill.

Goffman, E. (1967). In *Interaction ritual: Essays on face-to-face behavior.* New York: Anchor Books

Heimer, C. A. (1988). Social structure, psychology and the estimation of risk. *Annual Review of Sociology, 14,* 491-519.

Katz, J. (1988). *Seductions of crime: Moral and sensual attractions in doing evil.* New York: Basic Books.

Klausner, S. Z. (1968). The intermingling of pain and pleasure: the stress seeking personality in its social context. In S. Z. Klausner (Ed.), *Why men take chances.* Garden City, New York: Anchor Books.

Litman, R. E. (1980). Psychodynamics of indirect self-destructive behavior. In N. L. Farberow (Ed.), *The many faces of suicide.* New York: McGraw Hill.

Lyng, S. (1990). Edgework: a social psychological analysis of voluntary risk taking. *American Journal of Sociology, 95*(4), 851-856.

Lyng, S. G., & Snow, D. A. (1986). Vocabularies of motive and high risk behavior: the case of skydiving. In E. J. Lawler (Ed.), *Advances in group processes,* vol. 3. Greenwich, Conn.: JAI.

Mead, G. H. (1934/1964). In A. Strauss (Ed.), *George Herbert Mead on social psychology.* Chicago: University of Chicago Press.

Mitchell, R. G., Jr. (1983). *Mountain experience: The psychology and sociology of adventure.* Chicago: University of Chicago Press.

Ollman, B. (1971). *Alienation: Marx's conception of man in capitalist society.* Cambridge: Cambridge University Press.

Piore, M. J., & Sabel, C. F. (1984). *The second industrial divide: Possibilities for prosperity.* New York: Basic Books.

Schuman, S. H., & Polkowski, J. (1975). Drug and risk perceptions of ninth-grade students: Sex differences and similarities. *Community Mental Health Journal, 11,* 184-194.

Short, J. (1984). The social fabric at risk: Toward the social transformation of risk analysis. *American Sociological Review, 49,* 711-725.

Taylor, L. (1985). *In the underworld.* London: Umwin Paperbacks.

Toch, H. (1980). Self-destructiveness among offenders. In N. L. Farberow (Ed.), *The many faces of suicide.* New York: McGraw-Hill.

Wolfe, T. (1979). *The right stuff.* New York: Farrar, Straus, and Giroux.

COMMON COMPONENTS OF SUCCESSFUL
INTERVENTIONS WITH HIGH-RISK YOUTH

JOY G. DRYFOOS

Unlike my colleagues represented in this volume, I am not a primary researcher; and although I spend a lot of time visiting programs, I am not a practitioner. What I try to do is to make the bridge between research and practice by synthesizing knowledge that researchers generate and putting it into a form that program planners and developers might find useful. To this end, I present a summary of the results of the Adolescents-at-Risk Project, a six-year effort supported by the Carnegie Corporation that attempts to integrate information from four diverse fields that address the prevention of high-risk behaviors among adolescents: substance use, delinquency, teen pregnancy and school failure and dropout. In this paper, I will describe what I have learned about the common components of successful intervention programs, discuss a number of issues that are not resolved in this synthesis of program information, and suggest a program model that incorporates many of the concepts from effective programs.

WHO ARE HIGH-RISK YOUTH?

The title of this paper includes three phrases that require definition: high-risk youth, successful interventions and common components. The concept of risk, a part of every life insurance contract, fits well in appraising the actuarial chances that a child can grow into a responsible adult. We know enough now to calculate the probabilities that, given particular characteristics and social conditions, a certain individual will or will not be able to make it. My own estimates are that one in four children in the United States are at high risk of growing into adults who cannot effectively parent, can never be productive members of the labor force, and will not be able to participate as voters (Dryfoos, 1990).

This may sound like a pessimistic estimate, but other analysts have produced even higher figures. The Committee for Economic Development (1987), an organization that represents the nation's largest businesses, estimates that 30% of American youth will not be able to enter the labor force because of their inadequate preparation. Berlin and Sum (1988), in an insightful analysis of the effects of lack of basic educational skills on future opportunity, show that those high school students in the bottom 20% of their classes are nine times more likely to drop out of school, eight times more likely to become mothers out of wedlock, and four times more likely to go on welfare. Low school achievement and lack of basic skills always are included in analyses of the characteristics of high-risk youth, sometimes as antecedents or precursors, sometimes as consequences, and often as both.

Most descriptions of risky behavior center on one specific domain: drug and alcohol abuse, promiscuous sexual behavior, truancy, or other forms of delinquent behavior. Yet the young people who do one of these acts are very likely to do them all. The overlap between high risk behaviors is striking.

The variables that are presented in widely diverse literatures as antecedents or predictors of the separate behaviors are quite similar. My review of numerous behavioral studies of delinquency, substance use, teenage pregnancy, and school failure and dropout revealed many common characteristics of high-risk youth: low school achievement and low basic skills, lack of parental support, low resistance to peer influences, early "acting out" in any of the behavioral domains, and residence in poverty neighborhoods. High-risk behavior of varying kinds appeared to be associated with stress and depression (Dryfoos, 1990).

The definition of high-risk behavior used in this paper builds on the concept of the "problem behavior syndrome" which served as the cornerstone of much that has followed in trying to understand high risk behavior among young people (Jessor & Jessor, 1977). The Jessors' original research showed the clustering of adolescent risk behaviors and stimulated the proposal that prevention interventions should address simultaneously the common antecedents of problem behaviors. The concept of focusing on "risk factors" rather than "risk behaviors" has been furthered by Hawkins and Catalano (1989) who call for: "Interventions that target those children that seem to be most problem-prone, and address multiple risk factors across multiple domains—cultural, environmental, community, family, and individual" (p. 2).

WHAT ARE SUCCESSFUL INTERVENTIONS?

The term intervention is used here as a synonym for program (although the former is more pro-active than the latter). Both imply planned action and a sequence of operations to achieve a certain result. Programs aimed at a specific category of behavior, such as prevention of substance abuse or provision of compensatory education, are labeled "categorical." Most funding for youth-at-risk programs derives from federal categorical grants that pass through state categorical agencies on their way to communities. Comprehensive youth programs are those that include a package of services that may include several categorial programs.

A lot of hand-wringing goes on about what to do about high-risk youth. One hears repeatedly that we don't know what works and we certainly don't want to "throw good money after bad." We have not, as a society, gone about trying to answer the "what works" question in any kind of scientific way. Literally thousands of programs addressing to the problems of high-risk youth are operating without any particular evidence that they are accomplishing their goals. One need only look at the American public school "non-system" with its crazy mosaic of 16,000 different districts impacting in widely divergent ways on high risk children. In some districts, or even some schools within districts, children are succeeding. In others, they are failing. Despite the enormous output of educational research, only a few of these schools can document why they are doing better or worse than others.

Almost every high school student in America has been exposed to substance abuse prevention and sex education in the classroom, with little evidence that these curricula have made any difference on actual behaviors. School-based AIDS education is mandated currently in about half of the states, but we do not know whether it is reducing students' exposure to the HIV virus. While it is possible through curricular interventions to improve knowledge and modify attitudes, behavioral change does not necessarily follow (Basch, 1989).

All is not lost, however, because out of this giant pack of interventions to prevent high-risk behavior, models have begun to emerge that demand our attention. Fortunately, enough program evaluation has taken place so that we are not operating entirely in the dark. We have sufficient information now to design programs to help high risk children that could be much more effective (Kyle, 1987; Mueller & Higgins, 1988; Price, Cowen, Lorian, & Ramos-McKay, 1988; Schorr, 1988). I have identified 100 programs for which some form of documentation shows the behaviors of participants changed from negative to positive behavioral outcomes (Dryfoos, 1990). Desirable outcomes include: (a) reduction in misbehavior in school and home, (b) reduction in truancy, improvement in school attendance, (c) lower arrest rates, (d) delay in initiation of alcohol, (e) delay in initiation of smoking, (f) reduction in amount and frequency of drinking, (g) delay in initiation of sexual intercourse, (h) increase in use of contraception if sexually active, (i) reduction in the rate of pregnancy, (j) reduction in the rate of childbearing, (k) improvement in school grades, (l) higher expectations for school completion, (m) improved promotion rate, and (n) improved high school graduation rate.

Almost all of the successful programs identified (Dryfoos, 1990) were directed at changing behaviors within only one domain (e.g., substance use, pregnancy prevention, school remediation). Therefore, it is not surprising that most of these interventions reported changing at the most one or two of these outcomes. It is possible that the participants changed in other ways, but the evaluation protocol did not include those other outcomes. Typically, categorical programs only measure categorical outcomes.

A few programs stand out because the quality of evaluation meets most of the tests for scientific reliability. The Perry Preschool/ High Scope Foundation effort in Ypsilanti, Michigan is the most frequently cited prime example (Berreuta-Clement, Schweinhart, Barnett, Epstein, & Weikhart, 1984). Participants were enrolled in a two-year intervention for three and four year olds that included early childhood education and parental home visiting. They were followed longitudinally until adulthood along with a randomly selected comparison group. Recipients of the preschool services were found to have higher achievement and graduation rates and lower delinquency and teen pregnancy rates. Much of the current advocacy for Head Start programs is based on the findings from this research. The findings substantiate the importance of early childhood education in bolstering early school experiences; success in early grades acts as a deterrent to high risk behaviors throughout the school years.

WHAT ARE COMMON COMPONENTS?

We don't know from the Perry Preschool model which component was more important: early childhood enrichment in a nursery school setting or home visiting with the parents. Most successful programs directed at changing behaviors among high-risk youth are made up of more than one piece of action, for example, remediation by a teacher in a classroom plus individual counseling by a volunteer mentor plus after-school recreation. The 100 successful programs represent 100 different combinations of program components. My analysis of these programs (based largely on secondary data and reports) revealed that certain components stood out. These components were implemented in many different kinds of settings such as classrooms, community centers, or clinics and were addressed to a wide range of behavioral objectives. Yet the behavioral domain was less of an issue than the intensity and quality of the program. In other words, successful interventions may have focused on preventing different behaviors (e.g., drug abuse, delinquency, unprotected intercourse, school failure), but they employed similar techniques.

Ten common components of successful interventions were identified through this program review. These components might be compared to the ingredients of a cake which when put together provide a satisfactory culinary experience, but taken separately might not be so satisfactory (Dryfoos, 1990).

COMMON COMPONENTS
OF SUCCESSFUL PREVENTION PROGRAMS

If one undertook the creation of an inventory of effective program concepts without making the effort to review hundreds of programs, the list would probably be similar to what follows. There are very few surprises. All of the concepts fit into an intuitive understanding of what high risk-children need if they are to survive and flourish.

Intensive individual attention. First of all, successful programs of all kinds provide intensive individual attention to disadvantaged children. Programs use mentors, counselors, teachers, social workers, case managers, psychologists, community aides, older peers, senior citizens—all kinds of individuals who are willing to spend time with one or more children either within the school setting, after school in the community, or in the child's home. This component emerges so significantly because today's high-risk children are often high risk because of absent or non-supportive parents. In order for a child to make it, someone else has to provide "surrogate parenting," help with school work, friendship, and counseling. (I like to think of this role as a "sherpa," a Himalayan guide who helps people climb high mountains.)

Early intervention. The earlier that interventions take place, the more likely they are to be successful. It follows that if the nurturing that normally comes from parents is lacking, this need must be filled as soon as possible. As pointed out above, programs such as Perry Preschool served as the model. There are other contemporary preschool program models that involve families in creative ways (Price et al., 1988).

Focus on schools. School as an *experience* and school as a *site* are both very important components of successful interventions of all kinds. It is obvious that academic remediation takes place in the school. Some very interesting new classroom approaches to enhanced learning are emerging from the vast educational establishment. Cooperative learning in groups and team teaching are two examples that have been well-documented. But the improvement of educational outcomes is definitely not all that goes on within the school plant. Many other kinds of prevention programs take place there including those directed at substance abuse, teen pregnancy, and delinquency.

In some instances, the principal component of prevention of high-risk behavior *is* the remediation of the lack of basic skills. Of equal importance, individual and group counseling within the school premises also have been shown to reduce rates of substance abuse, teen pregnancy and delinquency. The utilization of school teams and the creation of a healthy school climate both have been shown to have effects on the different kinds of behaviors. School-based clinics have assisted high-risk youth learn to deal with many kinds of problems in their lives, particularly with acute mental health issues related to sexual abuse, substance abuse, and depression.

Services provided in schools by outside organizations. The focus of a wide array of prevention programs is on schools because that is where the high-risk children are found, at least until they drop out. A very significant finding from this review is that these successful non-educational programs are *not* operated by the schools in which they are located. Typically, an outside organization brings services into schools including the staff, the curricula, the equipment, and most importantly, the funding.

In each of the fields, agencies or organizations outside of the schools carried the major responsibility for exemplary programs that were implemented within the schools. Four types of arrangements were exemplified among the models:

1. The program was designed by a university-based researcher who obtained a grant to implement the program and conducted evaluation research in the school or community agency (Comer, 1988).

2. The model was designed by a non-profit youth services and research organization in schools or communities with support

from foundations or government agencies (Sipe, Grossman, & Milliner, 1988).

3.   A model was initiated by a foundation [9](such as Robert Wood Johnson or Annie Casey) or a government agency (such as the Office of Substance Abuse Prevention in Washington or the New Jersey Department of Human Services) which issued a Request for Proposals calling for comprehensive collaborative programs in schools.

4.   A program was developed by a local health or youth service agency in collaboration with a school with funding from a state health agency and from foundations (Adolescent Resources Corporation, 1987).

In these types of interventions, project staff may work for the outside agency, or agency staff may be responsible for training and supervising on-site staff. Curriculum materials usually are created by the program developers who also are available to provide technical assistance. In all cases, research is conducted by the outside agency. Schools typically provide space, maintenance, and coordination between outside agency staff and school personnel. The building principal is described as the key figure in these collaborations, acting as the gatekeeper to the school, the facilitator, and the negotiator.

Comprehensive multi-agency community-wide programs. I have mentioned four types of "outside" interventions that take place in schools. All of these programs involve several agencies with the schools in collaborative arrangements. This collaborative concept has been effectively applied in broader community-wide efforts.

The operating hypotheses of these community-wide programs is that, in order to change the behavior of young people, a number of different kinds of programs and services have to be in place. This theme is exemplified in the substance abuse prevention field by a community-wide health promotion campaign that used local media and community education to involve parents and community leaders in conjunction with the implementation of substance abuse prevention curricula in the local schools (Pentz, Cormack, Flay, Hansen, & Johnson, 1986). In the delinquency prevention field, a neighborhood development program involved local residents in neighborhood councils working with the schools, police, courts, gang leaders, and the media (Fagan, 1987). A successful model in pregnancy prevention concentrated on community education through media and a speaker's bureau, training of parents, clergy and other community leaders, and development and implementation of a comprehensive sex and family life education curriculum in the schools (Vincent, Clearie, & Schluchter, 1987). The problem of school dropout was addressed by an all out community effort involving the schools with local businesses, local government agencies, and universities in planning, teacher training, and training and job placement of students (Committee for Economic Development, 1987).

The multi-component methodology builds on significant successes in the early 1980s with community programs for heart disease prevention (Johnson & Solis, 1985). Partners in the more recent models for preventing high risk behavior among youth have included schools, community health and social agencies, businesses, media, church groups, universities, police and courts, parent groups, and youth groups. Typically, successful multi-agency efforts have representative advisory councils and use volunteers from the community for various tasks (e.g., planning, community information, seeking funds, personal mentoring). Cooperation with local media generally is used for gaining access to channels for community education and consciousness-raising. Local businesses offer mentors, equipment, incentives, act as role models for career education, and help with job training and job placement.

Parents have a defined role. We have seen how school and community personnel impact on high-risk children in a variety of collaborative efforts. Where do the parents fit in? Every program for high-risk children places the involvement of parents at the top of the list of program objectives but very few programs report success. However, several specific interventions were identified through which parents became participants and the outcomes for their children improved. Programs that organized regular home visits with the parents showed good results, not only for pre-schoolers but for pre-delinquent adolescents as well. Other successful programs assigned parents specific roles, such as paid classroom aides or as voting members of school reorganization committees and school teams. Invitations to parent meetings and workshops produced little positive response among these parents. The common component of success in regard to involving parents appeared to be giving them a *real* role and responding to their perceived needs rather than "talking at" them.

Peers have a defined role. We all know that high-risk children are heavily influenced by their peers, and every program prospectus calls for "peer involvement" as a method for changing behavior. Documentation of success in this area is limited. However, programs that identify older high-risk children and employ them to act as mentors and teachers for younger children have documented success both for the high-risk mentors and for their tutees. Using trained students as instructors in social skills programs has been proven to have a positive effect. In some cases, the peers who are selected to be teen counselors or to be in teen theater groups receive benefits, but no evidence could be found that they had an impact on changing the high-risk behaviors of their "clients" or their audiences. It may be that the common component of success in peer programs is the individual attention and training that young people receive.

Social skills training. High-risk children often lack the social competency necessary to deal with peers, family, teachers and the demands of the community. New curricula are emerging that teach high-risk children about their own risky behavior, give them the skills to cope with and, if necessary, resist the influences of their peers in social situations, and help them to make healthy decisions about their futures. Techniques such as role-playing, rehearsal, peer instruction, and media analysis typically are employed. While much of the impetus for these curricula emerged from successes in smoking prevention, curricula currently in use are designed to promote a range of positive behaviors such as delaying initiation of alcohol and marijuana use, delaying initiation of sexual intercourse, improving use of contraception, and improving behavior in school. The research has documented significant changes among participants that are maintained over a few years if they are exposed to booster (repeat) sessions in subsequent years of school. It should be pointed out that most of the social skills research to date has been carried out in suburban school districts where the incidence of high-risk behavior is considerably lower than in central cities or remote rural areas.

Arrangements for training. Many of the successful programs support training efforts with funding and released time. They employ special kinds of staff, professional or non-professional, who require particular training to implement a program, for example, to use a certain protocol (behavioral therapy) or a new curriculum (social skills). The implementation of school reorganization entails complex concepts such as school-based management, team teaching, and cooperative learning. These approaches require extensive in-service training and on-going supervision. A number of the model programs have established school teams, generally made up of the support personnel (social worker, psychologist, counselor), principal, in some instances parents, and occasionally students. These teams also require training and orientation to carry out the mandates of the intervention. Several model programs employ full-time staff to coordinate teams, curriculum development, treatment services, referrals and/or to expedite research protocols.

Link to the world of work. It generally is agreed that high-risk youth need to be better prepared to enter the labor force. In addition to educational remediation, they need exposure to the working world. Programs in a variety of settings use innovative approaches to introduce career planning, introduce youngsters to work experiences and prepare them to enter the labor force. Successful models offered various components: combining life planning curricula with school remediation and summer job placement; creating opportunities for volunteer community service; and paying high-risk youth to become tutors for younger children. These components were most often combined with group counseling and seminars to help students interpret and integrate the experience.

UNRESOLVED ISSUES

My review of research on interventions to prevent high risk behaviors resulted in the identification of 100 diverse programs that appeared to be making a difference in the lives of participants (Dryfoos, 1990). The ten components described above clearly are important concepts for designing effective prevention programs. However, it should be well understood that no "magic bullets" were discovered in this undertaking. No one program of any description was found that could perform miracles. Each program moved a defined target population in aggregate in a positive direction. However, a number of issues were not resolved by this program analysis.

Evaluation. It is true that we don't know as much as we should about effective programs. The amount of scientific program evaluation that takes place in this country represents a miniscule proportion of the amount of activity. It is surprising how many programs aimed at behavioral change go to the trouble of conducting pre- and post-test surveys of participants but fail to gather any information on behavioral outcomes. It is depressing to find programs that do determine behavioral outcomes but have neither baseline data nor control groups for the purposes of comparisons. One of the reasons for this lack of program evaluation is that researchers are not interested in this subject. Another reason is that program operators do not want researchers interfering in their programs. True, program evaluation is difficult, costly, and time-consuming. And, even for those who are interested, it is hard to find funding for evaluating large-scale, long term interventions from either government or foundation sources.

Categorical exigencies. The finding that larger collaborative school and community efforts appear to have more effect than single purpose programs is very important for program developers. The latest wave of interventions have multiple goals, for example, the Annie Casey Foundation has given large grants to five cities to build comprehensive youth service delivery systems that will simultaneously prevent school dropout, enhance employment opportunities, and prevent teen pregnancy. The 29 New Jersey School-based Comprehensive Centers focus on dropout prevention, mental health, substance use, employment opportunities, recreation, and, if the community approves, family planning.

Preliminary experience with these new programs suggests that, as the packaging of components becomes more complex, certain controversial elements may be eliminated. The most obvious example is in the area of pregnancy prevention. It generally is believed that sexually active teenagers must be ensured access to contraceptive services (Hayes, 1987). Yet even the school-based clinics set up for the expressed purpose of preventing pregnancy generally do not include family planning services on site (Kirby & Waszak, 1989). State funding may prohibit the use of public funds for the provision of birth control to adolescents. A protest from a vocal minority (not the parents) in a community may scare off program operators. Or the staff may never implement the family planning component because of imagined controversy.

Another very controversial area involves dealing with dysfunctional parents. Increasingly, the only solution for a youngster is to be removed temporarily from a situation where there are substance addicted parents or where there is evidence of sexual abuse, physical abuse, and other forms of neglect. Such drastic situations are encompassed in a few program models such as in shelters for runaway and homeless youth, yet evidence is mounting that the demand for foster care is growing faster than the supply (Select Committee on Children, Youth, and Families, 1989).

Replicating what doesn't work. The review of programs revealed a consensus not only on what works to prevent high-risk behavior but also on what doesn't work. Particularly in the area of substance abuse, there have been repeated syntheses of the state of the art, evaluating new approaches as they came on scene and disposing of old ones as they are discredited (Goodstadt, 1986). Unfortunately, the evaluation research does not seem to influence the market place so that some of the interventions that have long since been found *not* to have any effects are still being heavily utilized in the field. Consensus is strong across domains that prevention programs that use curricula that only provide information (without more interactive components such as social skills) have no impact on behaviors. No evidence was found to demonstrate the validity of "Saying No" approaches to behavioral modification. Programs that attempt to scare young people have been shown to lead to an increase in marijuana use and delinquent behavior. Programs for high-risk children that isolate them from the main stream are not successful. Placing delinquent boys in with other delinquent boys results in increased delinquency. School tracking and ability grouping (adherence to segregated achievement groups) are prime examples of techniques that are detrimental to disadvantaged children. (However, alternative schools and schools within schools that utilize the common principles cited above are more successful with young people who may be too "turned off" to attend "regular" school.)

Special cultural considerations. Some of the rhetoric in the growing literature on youth-at-risk focuses on the need for unique interventions for specific target populations. Recent initiatives have centered on young Black males, Native-American youth, and Hispanic youth. It has been proposed that unless attention is given to specific cultural traditions, language differences and social mores, the program will be ineffective. The same principle has been applied to seeking same gender, race, and ethnic-group staffing for youth programs. A recent proposal in Milwaukee called for special schools for young black males ("Milwaukee task force," 1990). Little evidence could be found from which one could conclude that these considerations are fundamental to success. The counter-argument is that all staff members, no matter what their demographic characteristics, should be sensitive to differences between individuals, whether they are culturally or psychologically or socially derived.

Stigmatizing high-risk children. Our understanding of the successful program models leads to the conclusion that identifying children at early ages who are at high risk of failure and helping them get on to the achievement track is a significant concept.

Teachers have reported that they can pick out children in the very early grades who will never make it without intensive interventions. New assessment techniques can facilitate this identification procedure, leading to the implementation of organized case management procedures. The problem with this rational response to case-finding is that the children who are identified may be stigmatized as "failures." The Chapter 1 program, our nation's most fully funded educational response to high-risk children, recently has changed its mode of operation from requiring "pull out" programs (taking failing students out of their classroom for a period for remediation) to allowing school districts to use program funds for school-wide improvements in schools where a large majority of the students are eligible. It is probable that the children's risk status reflects the social environment in which they live, their family situations, and the quality of their schooling. Therefore, it would seem like a better approach to identify high-risk communities, and within them, high risk school populations, and assume that everyone needs assistance.

Cloning charismatic leaders. Personal observations of many of the successful programs leads to the conclusion that the most effective programs have the most effective leaders. Fully half of the 100 models were implemented by the people who designed them, people who often were motivated by their concern for disadvantaged children and their families. Those who have visited exciting classrooms or dynamic community-based youth programs may share this impression of the group leader or teacher: a warm human being who walks into a roomful of children, knows who they are, cares about what they need and goes about getting those needs filled. It is improbable that many of the existing training institutions (graduate programs in education, psychology, social work, public health) currently are producing these kinds of people. Yet the programs of the future will need charismatic, concerned leadership who can both envision and manage large-scale multi-component comprehensive approaches.

Policy changes. Programs can make incremental changes in the lives of children by helping them to improve their behaviors. School programs are, of course, fundamental; acquisition of basic skills is the proverbial bottom line for preventing high risk behavior and helping disadvantaged youth to gain access to the opportunity structure in this modern industrial society. As we all know too well, what has to change is not the child or the child's family, but the school. The overlap between the school reform movement and the initiatives to prevent high-risk behavior is substantial. Intense battles are being fought in most state legislatures and within many community school boards over what policies to change in order to upgrade the quality of education. Issues such as school reorganization, tenure, testing, and above all, financing, are in the daily headlines.

But educational achievement is not the only behavioral outcome that may depend on policy changes. The evidence is very strong that adolescent substance abuse may best be curtailed through implementation of policies and laws such as regulations of the sale of cigarettes and alcohol, raising the age for legal use, increasing prices through the passage of "sin taxes" and strict enforcement regarding drunk driving (Ginzberg, Berliner, & Ostow, 1988). Cutting down on the incidence of teen childbearing may depend on policies that promote access to contraception and abortion services (Hayes, 1987).

Broad social changes. We have reviewed ten precepts that, if applied at the community level, could make incremental changes in the lives of high-risk children. It has been pointed out that many issues in youth development programming remain unresolved. Perhaps the most overwhelming barrier to success is the degree of disadvantage in which high-risk children live. The gap between the achievers and the non-achievers is widening dramatically as a small group, fall further and further behind. In some communities, community-wide interventions to prevent high-risk behavior will have to extend to issues of homelessness, poverty, racism, employment opportunities, and welfare. It is not the purpose of this paper to present solutions to those problems, but it is important to understand that the current social environment presents enormous barriers to changing the life course for disadvantaged children.

IMPLICATIONS

The programs that work to help high-risk youngsters lead more productive lives probably work because they are directed toward remediating the actual risk factors rather than the categorical high-risk behaviors. Successful models have been identified that: make up for deficits in basic skills and academic achievement; act as "surrogate parents" for those who lack the necessary nurturing and attention; counter the negative influences of peers; compensate for the social limitations and isolation of poverty neighborhoods; and, in some instances, address mental health issues such as feeling depressed or being "stressed out."

These findings strongly suggest the design of a new institution: community-schools with a kind of built-in "parallel thrust." On one side, there is the requirement for the reorganization of the school to make it a secure and creative place where children can learn. It is an unequivocal fact that without the acquisition of basic skills, few of the other interventions will have the desired effect. On the other side is "everything else" —all the services that are required to help children and families function well enough to take advantage of the upgraded education. Depending on the community needs, these services could include comprehensive health and family planning, mental health counseling, case-management, substance abuse treatment, job preparation and placement, after-school mentoring, parenting education, continuing education, and cultural and recreational events. I would like to see the welfare office located in the community-school to draw in the parents of high-risk children and offer enrichment to welfare mothers. The community-school would be open after school, weekends and summers—a friendly place where neighborhood children and their families would feel welcome.

In order to provide the "everything else" on school sites, community agencies would enter into collaborative and contractual arrangements with school systems. Some of the requisite program components which could be provided by either kind of institution (school or community agency), include health education and promotion; life planning; family life, sexuality and AIDS education; safety education and violence prevention programs; social skills and competency training; and volunteer community service programs.

The Community-School concept already is being implemented in selected communities (Pires, 1989). Driving this new initiative is the recognition on the part of school administrators that they can no longer attend to the social needs of their school populations. As the seriousness of the crisis among high-risk families deepens, schools are looking for more and more outside help to minister to the battered and deprived children arriving on their doorsteps in search of an education, or even of food and shelter. Community agencies are quick to rise to the challenge because everyone is frustrated with the current fragmented non-system of serving high-risk families. Health departments, medical schools, community mental health centers, Girls Clubs and Boys Clubs, Youth Bureaus, 4Hs—a profusion of community-based groups . . . are eager to be invited into schools where they know they are needed.

People in the private business sector are jumping on the youth development bandwagon, partly because they fear the absence of a qualified labor force in the near future. Social and psychological researchers also have a lot to contribute to the welfare of this generation of high-risk children. Enough has been documented from the practice in schools and youth-serving agencies to develop a framework for new institutional arrangements. Scientific program evaluation could refine these models. Hopefully a coordinated effort among schools, service providers in the community, business, researchers, and funding agencies will emerge from these concerns about high-risk youth and the future quality of life for the society as a whole.

REFERENCES

Adolescent Resources Corporation (1987). *Annual Report.* Kansas City: Adolescent Resources Corporation.

Basch, C. (1989). Preventing AIDS through education: Concepts, strategies, and research priorities. *Journal of School Health, 59,* 296-300.

Berlin, G., & Sum, A. (1988). *Toward a more perfect union: Basic skills, poor families, and our economic future.* New York: Ford Foundation.

Berrueta-Clement, J., Schweinhart, L., Barnett, S., Epstein, A., & Weikart, D. (1984). *Changed lives: The effects of the Perry Preschool Program on youths through age 19.* Ypsilanti, Michigan: The High Scope Press.

Comer, J. (1988). Educating poor minority children. *Scientific American, 259,* 42-48.

Committee for Economic Development (1987). *Children in need: Investment strategies for the educationally disadvantaged.* New York: Committee for Economic Development.

Dryfoos, J. (1990). *Adolescents-at-risk: Prevalence and prevention.* New York: Oxford.

Fagan, J. (1987). Neighborhood education, mobilization and organization for juvenile crime prevention. *Annals of American Academy of Political and Social Science, 494,* 54-70.

Ginzberg, E., Berliner, H., & Ostow, M. (1988). *Young people at risk: Is prevention possible?* Boulder, Colorado: Westview Press.

Goodstadt, M. (1986). School-based drug education in North America: What is wrong? What can be done? *Journal of School Health, 56,* 278-281, 1986.

Hawkins, J., & Catalano, R. (1989). Risk-focused prevention: From research to practical strategies. *OSAP High Risk Youth Update, 2,* 2-4.

Hayes, C. (1987) *Risking the future.* Washington: National Academy Press.

Jessor, R., & Jessor, S. (1977). *Problem behavior and psychosocial development: A longitudinal study of youth.* New York: Academic Press.

Johnson A., & Solis, J. (1985). Comprehensive community programs for drug abuse: Implications of the community heart disease prevention programs for future research. In T. Glynn (Ed.), *Preventing adolescent drug abuse: Intervention strategies,* Washington: Department of Health and Human Services, National Institute Drug Abuse, Research Monograph 47.

Kirby, D., & Waszak, C. (1989). *An assessment of six school-based clinics: Services, impact and potential.* Washington: Center for Population Options.

Kyle, J. (Ed.). (1987). *Children, families and cities: Programs that work at the local level.* Washington: National League of Cities.

Milwaukee task force to urge separate schools for black males. (1990, April 4). *Education Week*, p. 3.

Mueller, D., & Higgins, P. (1988). *Funders' guide manual: A guide to prevention programs in human services.* St.Paul, Minnesota: Amherst H. Wilder Foundation.

Pentz, M., Cormack, C., Flay, B., Hansen, W., & Johnson, C. (1986). Balancing program and research integrity in community drug abuse prevention: Project STAR approach. *Journal of School Health, 56.*, 389-393.

Pires, L. (1989). *New York State community schools pilot project: Summary update.* New York: Edwin Gould Foundation for Children.

Price, R., Cowen E., Lorian, R., & Ramos-McKay, J. (1988). *14 ounces of prevention: A casebook for practitioners.* Washington: American Psychological Association.

Schorr, L. (1988). *Within our reach.* New York: Doubleday.

Select Committee on Children, Youth, and Families (1989). *No place to call home: Discarded children in America.* Washington: United States Government Printing Office.

Sipe, C., Grossman, J., & Milliner, F. (1988). *Summer training and education program (STEP): Report on the 1987 experience.* Philadelphia: Public Private Ventures Inc.

Vincent, M., Clearie, A., & Schluchter, M. (1987). Reducing adolescent pregnancy through school and community-based education. *Journal of American Medical Association, 257 (24)*, 3382-3386.

DETERRING RISKY BEHAVIOR: POLICY PERSPECTIVES ON ADOLESCENT RISK TAKING

BRIAN L. WILCOX

Adolescent risk taking, besides being a topic of study for psychologists, sociologists, and other social scientists, is of immense concern to policymakers and public health officials. Many of the leading threats to adolescents' lives and health stem from behavioral factors, including risk taking. Motor vehicle accidents, drug abuse, unprotected sexual activity, alcohol abuse, tobacco use, and interpersonal violence all represent genuine public health threats within the adolescent population.

In this chapter I will examine the effectiveness of public policy decisions in altering risky behavior. The framework for this analysis is based in part on the work of Bonnie (1986), though the focus here will be exclusively on adolescent behavior and policy. I will begin with a few caveats. First, this chapter will address the effectiveness of public policy, that is, policy enacted by our legislatures and shaped by our courts. It will not address policy actions taken by private actors such as employers or service providers. Such actions are important but are beyond the scope of this chapter. Second, I will not attempt to address all types of policy "effects." I will not, for example, discuss the social norm enhancement function of policy actions, nor will I discuss policy actions designed to provide incentives for lowering risk taking. Instead, this chapter will be organized around three classes of policy actions intended to prevent or reduce risk taking: (1) risk deterrence and reduction through legal proscription and threats; (2) risk deterrence and reduction through economic regulation; and (3) risk deterrence and reduction through information dissemination and control. In each case I will give several examples of government actions intended to prevent and/or reduce risky behavior. To the extent possible, I will summarize what is known about the effectiveness of such actions. As you shall see, all too often there is little to summarize. Finally, I will examine barriers to and possibilities for conducting research on the effects of policy on adolescent risk taking.

LEGAL PROSCRIPTION AND THREATS

When most observers consider the likely effects of public policy on risky behavior, they think of this function: legal prohibition and the threat of punishment. The intent of the policies which I will be describing is to coerce persons into either behaving or not behaving in certain ways. This is what most people call the deterrence effect of law. General deterrence theory postulates that a deterrent effect is dependent upon both the objective and perceived characteristics of legal threats and punishments. These properties include certainty of punishment, severity of statutory and actual punishments, and swiftness of punishment, among others (Gibbs, 1986). This characterization actually represents a significant oversimplification of deterrence (Carroll, 1978).

A review of the general research literature on deterrence theory is striking for the paucity of studies involving adolescents and the virtual neglect of possible developmental effects. This is problematic for a variety of reasons, but one is particularly noteworthy. I would not be at all surprised to find that certain sanctions, fines for example, are less salient for adolescents than adults (Mecham, 1968). Adolescents frequently shift the burden of that sanction to others, namely parents. Sanctions which restrict the freedom of the adolescent, such as community service, may be more potent even though such punishment typically is judged by adults (and the courts) as less severe than fines. If developmental differences exist with respect to the potency of legal sanctions, deterrence would be reinforced by laws reflecting those differences.

This section will examine research and "educated speculation" regarding the deterrent effects of legal prohibitions and threatened sanctions in two behavioral risk contexts: underage tobacco and alcohol use, and unwed adolescent parenting.

Adolescent tobacco and alcohol use. Research describing the prevalence of adolescent tobacco and alcohol use indicates that both of these products are widely available to and easily obtained by adolescents, this despite the fact that all 50 states have complied with federal incentives and raised the legal drinking age to 21 and, with respect to tobacco, 44 states prohibit the sale of tobacco to minors. Note, however, that state definitions of minors vary when referencing tobacco sales restrictions—from ages 16 to 19. Six states place no prohibitions on tobacco sales to minors (Office on Smoking and Health, 1990).

It also must be noted that these laws all refer to the sale of tobacco or alcohol to adolescents. Some states also provide penalties for the purchase, possession or use of these products, though there are no studies of the effect of such proscriptions on adolescent alcohol and tobacco use. Indeed, there is virtually no data on the numbers of adolescents prosecuted for violations of these state statutes, though it appears that prosecutions are rare (Bonnie, 1986). Law enforcement officers are especially lax in enforcing tobacco restrictions (Kirn, 1987) and are much more likely to enforce "driving while under the influence" laws than alcohol purchase, possession, and use regulations. Given the centrality of the certainty of punishment to the deterrence effect, it seems unlikely that these purchase, possession and use proscriptions have any preventive impact beyond that ascribable to the restrictions on sales.

Unwed adolescent parenting. Neither the federal government nor any state government directly proscribes through statute unwed adolescent parenting for reasons that are probably obvious. Instead, in recent years the federal government has considered various means of enforcing disincentives to unwed adolescent childbearing. This federal interest has been motivated largely by two factors. First, the federal costs associated with unwed adolescent parenting, specifically, and more generally to adolescent parenting are extremely high. It is estimated that nearly half of Aid to Families With Dependent Children (AFDC) dollars are spent on women who were (or are still) adolescent mothers (Moore & Burt, 1982). A recent estimate suggests that in 1985 combined federal and state spending on public welfare programs attributable to adolescent childbearing was $16.65 billion (Burt & Levy, 1987). Second, critics of federal welfare programs (Murray, 1984) have argued that these programs actually provide incentives for adolescents to bear children out of wedlock, sending legislators scurrying to reduce such incentives and to put in place disincentives to such behavior. It should be noted that studies by Bane and her colleagues (Bane, 1986; Ellwood & Bane, 1984) indicate that the relationship between AFDC policy and adolescent unwed childbearing is quite small and, from a policy perspective, trivial. Nonetheless, legislators have generally accepted this premise and have searched for policy means of discouraging unwed adolescent parenting (Wilcox & O'Keeffe, 1990).

One federal program intended to serve as a disincentive to unwed childbearing among adolescents is the child support enforcement program. Prevention of fathering of children by adolescent males is actually a secondary goal of this program, which is designed principally to insure that fathers who are either unwed, separated, or divorced contribute to the financial support of their child(ren). This program recently was amended by the Family Support Act of 1988 (P.L. 100-485). The Act's original sponsor, Senator Daniel Patrick Moynihan, claimed that it was intended to send out a clear signal that no one can (or should) escape the economic responsibility of parenthood. Put another way, the message is "be ready to pay, or don't have children."

More concretely, the revised child support enforcement program takes several steps towards increasing the probability that an adolescent father will participate in the program. A number of changes strengthen the probability of paternity determination. States now are required to collect the Social Security numbers of both parents at the time of the child's birth. The federal government then will provide 90% of the cost of tests necessary to legally establish paternity (blood and/or genetic screening). States also must develop uniform guidelines for establishing child support awards and, following the determination of paternity and the establishment of an award, require that child support payments be automatically withheld from the absent parents' pay.

Because of the recency of these changes, their effects remain unclear. Historically, states have not pursued vigorously either the establishment of paternity or the collection of child support from adolescent parents because of the belief that these parents are unlikely to be in a position to provide significant financial support, at least over the near future. While the Family Support Act would allow states to require in-kind or token payments from those unable to meet the states' higher uniform support guideline, thus increasing the probability that low-income adolescent parents might be brought into the system, the fact that states are not being required to significantly increase the rate of paternity establishments mitigates against a major increase in paternity determinations for adolescent fathers. These aspects of the Family Support Act will be evaluated over the next several years, but at present there are no plans to assess the deterrence effect of these provisions on adolescent childbearing. Since "rational man" would wish to avoid these disincentives, policymakers assume that there will be a deterrence effect.

Policies intended to serve as a disincentive to childbearing by adolescent females (and more generally, to unwed mothers) differ from those just described. Again, partly in reaction to claims that "welfare rewards adolescent childbearing," the U.S. Congress made numerous changes to the federal welfare programs as part of the Family Support Act. The most significant "disincentive" involves a requirement that states, to the extent resources permit, require AFDC recipients with no children under age three (states have the option of lowering this to age one) to participate in a Job Opportunities and Basic Skills (JOBS) program. This program requires that most high school dropouts under age 20 return to school before a job placement will be made. Since neither states nor the federal government possess the resources to fund JOBS program participation for all AFDC recipients, the Family Support Act targets several groups, including custodial parents under age 24 who are not high school graduates or who have a poor work history.

A second component of the Family Support Act intended to discourage teen parenting would disallow the AFDC cash payment for unmarried minor mothers unless they live with a parent. While both the U.S. House of Representatives and Senate approved this provision, the bill as finally passed gives states the option of enforcing this provision.

There are no evaluations of the effects of these policies since they have recently been implemented. It would seem unwise to expect significant effects, however. Research on deterrence indicates that sanctions should be temporally proximal to the act being discouraged. Since most states are not requiring adolescent mothers to participate in the JOBS employment program until their children are age three, this condition would seem to be violated. The provision regarding minor mothers living with a parent in order to receive AFDC cash benefits also is unlikely to prove especially efficacious in light of the fact that few states have opted to enforce this provision.

When one examines the literature on the likely causal antecedents of adolescent childbearing (Hayes, 1987) it is not at all surprising that policies putting in place disincentives which are small, uncertain, distant, and poorly communicated would have small effects. Problems such as adolescent pregnancy and parenting are far too complex to be amenable to significant alteration by relatively weak policy tools (Bane & Jargowsky, 1988; Wilcox & O'Keeffe, 1990).

Summary. Many forms of adolescent risk taking occur in private—out of public view. This is true of adolescent sexual activity, drug use, alcohol and tobacco use, among others. Non-public actions of these types are unlikely to be detected until the damage is done. Since certainty of punishment is diminished in situations where individuals perceive the probability of detection to be low, deterrence will be limited, regardless of the severity of sanction to be imposed. Certainly laws with stiffer and more certain sanctions can and do have a deterrence effect, but such is not the case for the examples discussed here. What is most surprising, though, is the fact that research on deterrence effects on adolescents is virtually nonexistent.

MARKET REGULATION

A second broad category of policy interventions involve actions which increase the literal costs (price) of risk taking behavior or which reduce the opportunity for risk taking behavior via market intervention. An example of each type follows.

Increasing the price of tobacco use. Presently, the Federal government taxes cigarettes at the rate of 16 cents per pack. The federal excise tax dates back to 1864 and was imposed as a revenue generating measure, not as a means of reducing demand for the product. The 1864 excise tax was eight cents per pack. That rate decreased to one cent per pack at the turn of the century and did not reach its initial rate of eight cents again until 1951. The rate was temporarily increased to 16 cents in 1983, and the temporary increase was made permanent in 1986 (U.S. Department of Health and Human Services, 1989). On several occasions since then Congress has considered raising the excise tax even higher. For example, in 1986 the Senate approved an increase to 24 cents. This proposal was not acted upon by the House of Representatives and thus was not enacted. Proposals to increase the cigarette excise remain popular, though, and at present there are twelve such proposals pending before the 102nd Congress.

One reason for the widespread popularity of these excise tax proposals is the belief that by increasing the costs of cigarettes, demand will be lessened. Studies of changes in smoking behavior resulting from price variations confirm this assumption generally, but especially for adolescents (Warner, 1986a; Warner & Murt, 1984). Adolescents and young adults are more "price sensitive" than older adults, largely because of the differences in their economic resources. Consequently, one study (Lewit, Coate, & Grossman, 1981) estimates that for adolescents between the ages of 12 and 17, the price elasticity of demand is -1.2. In other words, a 10% price increase should result in a 12% decrease in cigarette demand. The vast majority of the demand reduction stems from decisions not to begin smoking; price has a more limited effect on quantity of cigarettes smoked (Lewit et al., 1981). A study of young adults (Lewit & Coate, 1982) found them to be substantially less price-sensitive than younger adolescents.

These findings are particularly important when one considers that age at onset of smoking is highly predictive of continued smoking; those that begin smoking in their early teens (or younger) are much more likely to continue smoking than those who first smoke during late adolescence (Blakeman, 1989; Coalition on Smoking and Health, 1989). Since price elasticity of demand is greater for younger than older adolescents, increasing the excise tax (or increasing the final price of cigarettes through any mechanism) would appear to be a strong intervention for reducing this form of risky behavior. Indeed, Warner (1986a) estimates that a doubling of the excise tax to 32 cents, annually adjusted for inflation and with no concomitant increase or decrease in other costs, would avert approximately 860,000 premature deaths and reduce the number of adolescent smokers by 800,000 (cf. Harris, 1987). While this estimate may be a little optimistic (General Accounting Office, 1989a), there is no doubt that raising the price of cigarettes through the excise tax will decrease demand by adolescents. Indeed, recent empirical analysis based on a rational model of addiction (Becker & Murphy, 1988) suggests that current price elasticity estimates underestimate longer term responses to price increases (Becker, Grossman, & Murphy, 1987; Chaloupka, 1988, cited in General Accounting Office, 1989a). However, over time inflation will reduce the value of any fixed increase in the cost of cigarettes. As noted in a recent study by U.S. General Accounting Office (1989a), the real value of the excise tax has fallen (in 1988 dollars) from 31 cents per pack in 1964 to 15 cents per pack in 1988, despite the doubling of the tax in 1983. Consequently, some policymakers are proposing that the excise tax be increased and then adjusted annually by an inflation index to preserve its value.

Decreasing the availability of alcohol. I have noted earlier that all 50 states have raised their minimum drinking age to 21; that while some of these laws impose criminal sanctions against adolescents who purchase, possess, or consume alcoholic beverages, many do not; and that it is unclear whether the addition of sanctions reduces adolescent alcohol use beyond the reduction presumably brought about by the decreased availability resulting from the sales restrictions.

In recent years studies have examined the impact of the sales ban on consumption and such high-risk behavior as driving under the influence of alcohol. I should mention before proceeding, though, that one of the effects of decreasing the availability of alcohol is to increase its effective price. Thus, the separation of market regulation according the mechanisms that increase price versus those that decrease availability is somewhat artificial. I am unaware of any studies jointly examining these two issues.

Early studies, such as one conducted in Michigan (Douglass & Freedman, 1977), found significant increases in the amount of on-premise beer consumption following the lowering of the minimum drinking age; and more recent studies have found decreases in beer consumption following the raising of the minimum drinking age (see General Accounting Office, 1987). These fluctuations are presumed to be a function of corresponding changes in consumption by adolescents. Other studies have examined directly consumption behavior of adolescents. One study found that college students consumed alcohol significantly less frequently in states with higher compared with lower drinking ages (McFadden & Wechsler, 1980). Bonnie (1985) suggests that changes in the minimum age have not significantly increased the number of adolescents who abstain from drinking but, rather, the frequency and circumstances of consumption. The weight of evidence indicates that the impact of minimum age laws on frequency of consumption is statistically significant, but the actual magnitude of the effect is not clear.

Other studies have examined the effect of the minimum age laws on drunk driving violations and on alcohol-related driving accidents and mortality. Age-related arrests and mortality data played a significant role in Congress' debate on raising the minimum drinking age to 21. Arrests for driving under the influence (DUI) have fluctuated with changes in the legal age of drinking. DUI rates (arrests per 100,000 drivers) for adolescents between 18 and 20 increased substantially following state decreases in the minimum drinking age. For example, between 1975 and 1983 DUI rates for this group increased by roughly 100 percent. Arrest rates peaked for 18-19-year-olds in 1982 and for 20-year-olds in 1983. As states began raising their minimum drinking age, arrest rates for DUI dropped. Between 1982 and 1986 the DUI arrest rates decreased by 17 percent for 18-20 year olds. Over the same period, rates decreased only slightly or increased slightly for 21-24 year olds (Greenfeld, 1988).

The U.S. General Accounting Office (GAO) conducted a meta-analysis of studies examining the effects of raising the legal drinking age on highway safety (General Accounting Office, 1987). The studies reviewed included multi- and single-state studies of the effects of raising the drinking age on traffic fatalities, injuries and accidents. Nineteen studies met the rigorous methodological threshold set by the GAO research team. The researchers concluded that "the evidence is persuasive that raising the minimum drinking age has had significant effects on reducing alcohol-related traffic accidents for the age group affected by the law" (General Accounting Office, 1987, p. 39). Multiple state studies of accidents involving driver fatalities all found significant reductions in fatalities ranging between 5% and 28%. Likewise, all studies of driving accidents for those between the ages of 18 and 21 found statistically significant reductions ranging between 9% and 22% following the raising of the minimum drinking age. This analysis is supported by other studies (Office of the Surgeon General, 1988), including a recent Department of Transportation study estimate that raising the age limit has reduced fatalities among 18 to 21 year olds by 12 to 13% (Segal, 1990).

Summary. Marketplace mechanisms appear to provide a significant means of regulating some forms of adolescent risk taking. Not all forms of risk-taking behaviors lend themselves so easily to market regulation. Price elasticity is less for alcohol than tobacco, though probably large enough to warrant policy action (National Alcohol Tax Coalition, 1989), and is minimal for illicit drugs. Other forms of market regulation remain to be explored. For example, some have argued that adolescent tobacco consumption might be reduced by banning the distribution of free samples (Davis & Jason, 1988) and by banning vending machine sales of cigarettes (Altman, Foster, Rasenick-Douss, & Tye, 1989). Since regulation along these lines is being implemented at the local level, the opportunity exists to study the impact of such changes.

INFORMATION DISSEMINATION AND CONTROL

One of the most commonly adopted mechanisms by which government attempts to influence the behavior of its citizens is information dissemination and control. By disseminating certain information, governments hope to inform consumers of the risks and benefits of specific courses of action and fairly often, to persuade citizens to make certain choices (eat healthy foods) and to dissuade them from making others (using illicit drugs). Not surprisingly, this governmental role is occasionally associated with controversy grounded both in differences in political philosophy and in disagreements about the appropriate messages to be communicated.

The government also regulates information dissemination by restricting certain types of speech (alcohol advertising on television) and requiring other forms (alcohol warning labels). I will give examples from tobacco control policy illustrating each of these approaches: the Surgeon Generals' reports and the accompanying anti-smoking messages, required warning labels on cigarettes, required "equal time" anti-smoking messages broadcast on television, and the ban on television advertising of cigarettes. These policy actions were not exclusively or primarily targeted toward adolescents. There is no research evidence of the effects of these policy actions on adolescent tobacco use. Nonetheless, data on the general effectiveness of these approaches suggest that they are likely to have substantially similar effects on adolescents as on adults.

The anti-smoking campaign. Most analysts mark 1964 as the beginning of what has become known as the anti-smoking campaign. That year saw the publication of the initial Surgeon General's Report on Smoking and Health which concluded that cigarette smoking causes lung cancer and emphysema. This report began an annual series of such reports describing the threats to health and well-being caused by smoking. Along with the information appearing in these reports, the federal government established the National Clearinghouse on Smoking and Health (later changed to the Office on Smoking and Health). This office conducts small-scale media campaigns on the health effects of smoking and disseminates information to both the public and scientific communities. Funding for the office and its functions has always been limited and has decreased substantially over time.

The second component of the anti-smoking campaign commenced in 1965, when Congress passed legislation requiring that all cigarette packages sold in the U.S. contain the warning: "Caution: Cigarette Smoking May Be Hazardous To Your Health." In passing this legislation, Congress actually preempted a stronger warning that the Federal Trade Commission (FTC) intended to require on all cigarette packages and advertisements. The warning was amended in 1969 to read: "Warning: The Surgeon General Has Determined That Cigarette Smoking Is Hazardous To Your Health." Again, Congress preempted a stronger warning

proposed by the FTC. In 1971 the FTC initiated regulatory action
resulting in a 1972 requirement that cigarette advertisements carry
the same warning as required on cigarette packages. The issue was
not revisited until 1981, when the FTC conducted a study evaluating the effectiveness of the existing warning label. In 1982 Congress passed legislation requiring that a set of four rotating health
warnings be included on all cigarette packages and advertisements.

The third component of this campaign consisted of a Federal
Communications Commission ruling requiring that broadcasters
give anti-smoking advocates "a significant amount of time" to air
messages countering the claims made by cigarette advertisements
on television and radio. The policy justification for this action was
found in the "Fairness Doctrine" which required broadcasters to
fairly address competing perspectives in controversial areas.

The fourth component of the campaign occurred when Congress passed legislation banning radio and television advertisements for cigarettes as of January 1971. This ban remains in effect
and was subsequently extended to smokeless tobacco products.
When the ban was instituted, the anti-smoking advertisements previously required by the Fairness Doctrine were no longer justified
by that policy. These "counter-ads" slowed to a trickle.

Estimating the impact of the individual components of the campaign is complicated by the fact that they temporally overlap with
one another. Most observers agree, however, that the early versions of the tobacco warning labels were ineffectual. This was the
conclusion of a study conducted by the Federal Trade Commission
(1981) which found that, despite a decade and a half of warning
labels, smokers dramatically underestimated the risks associated
with smoking. Substantial portions of the public failed to recognize the relations between cigarette smoking and a variety of diseases, including heart disease and emphysema. Studies of the
impact of the new warning labels are just appearing, and the
evidence does not at this point suggest that the effect is other than
minor (Federal Trade Commission, 1988). One of the few studies
examining adolescents and warning labels in magazine advertisements found that over 40% of the subjects did not even see the
warning labels and another 20% scanned but did not read them
(Fischer, Richards, Berman, & Krugman, 1989). Another study examining the readability of warning labels on billboards found the
warnings unreadable in the vast majority of instances, while the

brand names of the cigarettes were easily read (Davis & Kendrick, 1989).

The question of whether warning labels can (as opposed to do) have an effect on consumption was examined in a research review conducted by the office of the Assistant Secretary for Health (U.S. Department of Health and Human Services, 1987). This analysis concluded that health warning labels can be effective if properly designed. Effective warning labels must be visible, provide specific information with a clear and unambiguous message, and take into account factors influencing the consumer's response to warning labels, such as previous knowledge of risk associated with smoking.

At least one study has attempted to evaluate the effectiveness of two of the other components of the anti-smoking campaign. Warner (1977) utilized econometric methods to assess the impact of the release of the Surgeon General's first Report on Smoking and Health and the broadcasting of anti-smoking television and radio advertisements. Warner concludes that the "Surgeon General's Report induced a 5 percent decrease in 1964 cigarette consumption, with slightly smaller annual effects realized for the 1968-70 anti-smoking ads" (1977, p. 649).

Warner (1979, 1986b) also has examined the effect of the advertising ban on tobacco consumption. This has proven to be the most controversial provision in the anti-smoking campaign. When the advertising ban was proposed, it was embraced by the tobacco industry (though not by the advertising industry) because it ended the requirement for broadcasting anti-smoking advertisements. Warner (1979) argues that the tobacco industry's decision was a wise one. He found that cigarette consumption decreased by 7.2% during the period that anti-smoking ads were aired and that, following the advertising ban and the cessation of the anti-smoking ads, per capita consumption increased by 4.5% over the next three years. Hamilton (1972) concurred, his analyses indicating that pro-smoking advertisements had a small positive effect on cigarette consumption while the anti-smoking ads had a substantial negative effect on consumption. Evans (1976) has argued that the anti-smoking ads had little or no impact on adolescent cigarette consumption, although Lewit et al. (1981) suggest that these ads had a relatively small, short-lived downward impact on adolescent consumption.

Recent analyses indicate that while advertising does encourage smoking by young non-smokers, the greatest effect of advertising is on brand preference by smokers (Warner, 1986b). Thus Warner

(1979, 1986b) questions the wisdom of the ad ban. Interestingly, six years after the ban was instituted, a federal task force called for its recision, hoping that the reappearance of ads would trigger the Fairness Doctrine requirement for opposing ads. Unfortunately, the Reagan administration later repealed the Fairness Doctrine. A reinstatement of ads would no longer result in the requirement for opposing ads.

Summary. The dissemination and regulation of information represents a potentially powerful and broad mechanism through which government can influence adolescent risk-taking behavior (Warner & Murt, 1984). Surprisingly little research has been conducted on the effects of various broad, governmentally-sponsored public information campaigns, and most of these studies have focused on knowledge and attitude changes. These types of policy actions continue to be favored by policymakers. The first warning labels on alcoholic beverages appeared in early 1990, and numerous states now require that establishments selling alcoholic beverages post "point of sale" warning signs. Though it is too soon to tell, some observers believe these warning labels may prove ineffective, suffering from some of the same problems faced by the cigarette warning labels (General Accounting Office, 1989b).

DETERRING RISKY BEHAVIOR: BRIDGING THE GAPS BETWEEN THEORY, RESEARCH AND POLICY

One limitation involved in reviews of this sort is that they make artificial or arbitrary distinctions among classes of policy actions and effects. When individual policy actions are examined, their effects often appear minimal. What is missing from the foregoing analysis is the general effect of policy actions on social and cultural norms, or what Bonnie calls the "declarative aspects of legal regulation" (1986, p. 183). As Melton aptly notes, "to the extent that the law affects behavior, the process may be based more frequently on the cues the law provides about socially and morally appropriate behavior and the resulting internalization of legal norms" (1986, p. 255). When the government taxes cigarettes, bans advertising, limits smoking in public places, and sponsors anti-smoking information campaigns, it sends a powerful message to the public about changing social norms. This "declarative" function is perhaps the most powerful of the policy effects on behavior.

One of the most striking aspects of these policies designed to deter adolescent risk-taking is the degree to which they ignore the relevance of information concerning adolescent cognitive, emotional and social development. Given the nature of the decision-making process within the policy environment, this is not particularly surprising. Policymakers appear to embrace what Simon (1987) calls a substantive theory of rationality, in which actors always make decisions which are substantively (or objectively) best in terms of the given utility function. This classical economic model of rational choice, with its assumptions of risk aversion and rational expectations, has been seriously challenged in recent years (Simon, 1982, 1987; Tversky & Kahneman, 1981, 1987) and may be an especially poor model to be used in predicting or accounting for the behavior of adolescents. One challenge before us is to find ways of communicating the theoretical perspectives described by Gardner, Lopes, Millstein, Wilson, and Lyng (this volume) to policymakers. A second challenge will be to draw out the implications of these differing theoretical perspectives for policies addressing adolescent risk taking.

Policymakers have until recently shown little interest in the problems of adolescents. Discussions of "youth policy" (as opposed to child or family policy) are unheard of. There is reason to believe that this situation is changing. The Office of Technology Assessment recently completed a congressionally mandated study of adolescent health issues, policies, and programs (Office of Technology Assessment, 1991). Congressional interest in the problems of "youth" (as opposed to children) is reflected in an increasing number of hearings addressing the problems of adolescents, including drug use, suicide, AIDS, alcohol and tobacco use, and unplanned pregnancy. The congressionally-mandated National Commission on Children has devoted one of its hearings to the topic of risk taking among adolescents.

As policymakers examine these problems, many of the "solutions" being proposed fit into the categories examined here, i.e., restricting alcohol advertising, raising alcohol excise taxes, banning vending machine sales of cigarettes, expanding public service announcements regarding AIDS and adolescents, etc.

Given the paucity of research in some of these areas, the federal government would do well to support evaluations of these policy actions. As this review has made clear, all too often, little is known about the consequences of policy actions intended to improve adolescent health and well-being. Some policy actions are exceptionally difficult to evaluate. Rarely are policy decisions implemented in a fashion facilitating outcome evaluation; those that are represent the exceptional case.

If policy actions are to be better informed by basic knowledge about adolescent development and risk taking, policy makers must increase support for basic and applied developmental research addressing these issues. While large quantities of funds are being channeled into studies of specific problems such as drug abuse and AIDS, funding of longitudinal studies examining risk taking across multiple risk behaviors remains limited, as is support for more basic research on risk perception and risk communication with adolescents.

The behavioral underpinnings of most adolescent risk taking provide social scientists with great opportunities to contribute to our understanding of the problems confronting adolescents and the policies being proposed to prevent or remediate those problems.

REFERENCES

Altman, D. G., Foster, V., Rasenick-Douss, L., & Tye, J. B. (1989). Reducing the illegal sale of cigarettes to minors. *Journal of the American Medical Association, 261*, 80-83.

Bane, M. J. (1986). Household composition and poverty. In S. H. Danziger & D. H. Weinberg (Eds.), *Fighting poverty: What works and what doesn't.* Cambridge, MA: Harvard University Press.

Bane, M. J., & Jargowsky, P. A. (1988). The links between government policy and family structure: What matters and what doesn't. In A. J. Cherlin (Ed.), *The changing American family and public policy.* Washington, DC: Urban Institute Press.

Becker, G., Grossman, M., & Murphy, K. M. (1987). *An empirical analysis of cigarette addiction* (Working paper). Chicago: National Bureau of Economic Research.

Becker, G., & Murphy, K .M. (1988). A theory of rational addiction. *Journal of Political Economy, 96*, 657-700.

Blakeman, E. Mc. (Ed.). (1989). *Final report: Tobacco use in America conference.* Washington, DC: American Medical Association.

Bonnie, R. J. (1985). Regulating conditions of alcohol availability: Possible effects on highway safety. *Journal of Studies on Alcohol, 10* (Supplement), 129-143.

Bonnie, R. J. (1986). The efficacy of law as a paternalistic instrument. In G. B. Melton (Ed.), *The law as a behavioral instrument: Nebraska Symposium on Motivation, 1985.* Lincoln: University of Nebraska Press.

Burt, M. R., & Levy, F. (1987). Measuring program costs. In C. D. Hayes (Ed.), *Risking the future, Vol. 2: Working papers.* Washington, DC: National Academy Press.

Carroll, J. M. (1978). Psychological approach to deterrence. *Journal of Personality and Social Psychology, 36*, 1512-1520.

Chaloupka, F. (1988). *An economic analysis of addiction: The case of cigarette smoking* (Working paper). Chicago: National Bureau of Economic Research.

Coalition on Smoking or Health (1989). *Coalition agenda for 1989-1990.* Washington, DC: Author.

Davis, R. M., & Jason, L. A. (1988). The distribution of free cigarette samples to minors. *American Journal of Preventive Medicine, 4(1)*, 21-26.

Davis, R. M., & Kendrick, J. S. (1989). The Surgeon General's warnings in outdoor cigarette advertising: Are they readable? *Journal of the American Medical Association, 261,* 90-94.

Douglass, R. L., & Freedman, J. A. (1977). *Alcohol-related casualties and alcohol beverage market response to alcohol beverage availability policies in Michigan, Vol. 1.* Ann Arbor, MI: University of Michigan Highway Safety Research Institute.

Ellwood, D. T., & Bane, M. J. (1984). *The impact of AFDC on family structure and living arrangements* (Contract No. 92A-82). Washington, DC: U.S. Department of Health and Human Services.

Evans, R. I. (1976). Smoking in children: Developing a social psychological strategy of deterrence. *Preventive Medicine, 5,* 122-127.

Family Support Act of 1988, 102 U.S.C. Sec. 2343 (1989).

Federal Trade Commission (1981, May). *Staff report on the cigarette advertising investigation.* Washington, DC: Federal Trade Commission.

Federal Trade Commission (1988, May). *Report to the Congress pursuant to the Federal Cigarette Labeling and Advertising Act, 1986.* Washington, DC: Federal Trade Commission.

Fischer, P. M., Richards, J. W., Berman, E. J., & Krugman, D. M. (1989). Recall and eye tracking study of adolescents viewing tobacco advertisements. *Journal of the American Medical Association, 261,* 84-89.

General Accounting Office (1987). *Drinking-age laws: An evaluation synthesis of their impact on highway safety.* Washington, DC: General Accounting Office.

General Accounting Office (1989a, June). *Teenage smoking: Higher excise tax should significantly reduce the number of smokers.* Washington, DC: General Accounting Office.

General Accounting Office (1989b, June). *Alcohol warning labels: Current rules may allow health warnings to go unnoticed.* Washington, DC: General Accounting Office.

Gibbs, J. P. (1986). Deterrence theory and research. In G. B. Melton (Ed.), *The law as a behavioral instrument: Nebraska Symposium on Motivation, 1985.* Lincoln: University of Nebraska Press.

Greenfeld, L. A. (1988, February). *Bureau of Justice Statistics special report: Drunk driving.* Washington, DC: U.S. Department of Justice.

Hamilton, J. L. (1972). The demand for cigarettes: Advertising, the health scare, and the cigarette advertising ban. *Review of Economics and Statistics, 54,* 401-411.

Harris, J. E. (1987). The 1983 increase in the Federal Cigarette Excise Tax. In L. H. Summers (Ed.), *Tax policy and the economy.* Cambridge, MA: MIT Press.

Hayes, C. D. (Ed.). (1987). *Risking the future, Vol. 1: Adolescent sexuality, pregnancy, and childbearing.* Washington, DC: National Academy Press.

Kirn, T. F. (1987). Laws ban minors' tobacco purchases, but enforcement is another matter. *Journal of the American Medical Association, 257,* 3323-3324.

Lewit, E. M., & Coate, D. (1982). The potential for using excise taxes to reduce smoking. *Journal of Health Economics, 1,* 121-145.

Lewit, E. M., Coate, D., & Grossman, M. (1981). The effects of government regulation on teenage smoking. *Journal of Law and Economics, 25,* 545-569.

McFadden, M., & Wechsler, H. (1980). Minimum drinking age laws and teenage drinking. *Psychiatric Opinion, 16,* 22-28.

Mecham, G. D. (1968). Proceed with caution: Which penalties slow down the juvenile traffic offender. *Crime and Delinquency, 14,* 142-150.

Melton, G. M. (1986). The law as an instrument of socialization and social structure. In G. M. Melton (Ed.), *The law as a behavioral instrument: Nebraska Symposium on Motivation, 1985.* Lincoln: University of Nebraska Press.

Moore, K. A., & Burt, M. R. (1982). *Private crisis, public cost: Policy perspectives on teenage childbearing.* Washington, DC: Urban Institute.

Murray, C. (1984). *Losing ground.* New York: Basic Books.

National Alcohol Tax Coalition (1989, February). *Impact of alcohol excise tax increases on federal revenues, alcohol consumption and alcohol problems.* Washington, DC: Center for Science in the Public Interest.

Office of Technology Assessment (1991, April). *Adolescent Health—Volume 1: Summary and policy options.* Washington, DC: Government Printing Office.

Office of the Surgeon General (1988). *Surgeon General's workshop on drunk driving: proceedings.* Washington, DC: U.S. Department of Health and Human Services.

Office on Smoking and Health (1990). State laws restricting access to tobacco by minors. *Morbidity and Mortality Weekly Review, 39,* 349-353.

Segal, T. (1990). *Alcohol fatality reductions following the raising of the minimum drinking age.* Washington, DC: Department of Transportation

Simon, H. A. (1982). *Models of bounded rationality.* Cambridge, MA: MIT Press.

Simon, H. A. (1987). Rationality in psychology and economics. In R. M. Hogarth & M. W. Reder (Eds.), *Rational choice: The contrast between economics and psychology.* Chicago: University of Chicago Press.

Tversky, A., & Kahneman, D. (1981). The framing of decisions and the psychology of choice. *Science, 211,* 453-458.

Tversky, A., & Kahneman, D. (1987). Rational choice and the framing of decisions. In R. M. Hogarth & M. W. Reder (Eds.), *Rational choice: The contrast between economics and psychology.* Chicago: University of Chicago Press.

U.S. Department of Health and Human Services (1987, June). *Review of the research literature on the effects of health label warnings: A report to the United States Congress.* Washington, DC: U.S. Department of Health and Human Services.

U.S. Department of Health and Human Services (1989). *Reducing the health consequences of smoking: 25 years of progress. A report of the Surgeon General.* Washington, DC: Office on Smoking and Health.

Warner, K. E. (1977). The effects of the anti-smoking campaign on cigarette consumption. *American Journal of Public Health, 67,* 645-650.

Warner, K. E. (1979). Clearing the airwaves: The cigarette ad ban revisited. *Policy Analysis, 5,* 435-450.

Warner, K. E. (1986a). Smoking and health implications of a change in the federal cigarette excise tax. *Journal of the American Medical Association, 255,* 1032.

Warner, K. E. (1986b). *Selling smoke: Cigarette advertising and public health.* Washington, DC: American Public Health Association.

Warner, K. E., & Murt, H. A. (1984). Economic incentives for health. *Annual Review of Public Health, 5,* 107-133.

Wilcox, B. L., & O'Keeffe, J. E. (1990). Families, policy, and family support policies. *Prevention in Human Services, 9,* 109-126.

APPLYING A RISK-TAKING PERSPECTIVE

EDWARD R. ANDERSON, NANCY J. BELL, JUDITH L. FISCHER,
JOYCE MUNSCH, CHARLES W. PEEK, AND
GWENDOLYN T. SORELL

Several potential advantages of applying a risk-taking perspective to the study of self- and socially-destructive behaviors of youth were mentioned in the Introduction to this volume. We now review these points as they have been addressed in the previous chapters, suggest additional conceptual and methodological issues, and throughout, attempt to identify priorities for future research on adolescent and young adult risk taking. Finally, we discuss the implications of this research for intervention and for policy.

COMMON THEME HYPOTHESIS

The lack of independence between the "problem" behaviors of youth has been acknowledged for some time (c.f., Irwin, this volume). In recent years, evidence has accumulated indicating that deviant behaviors constitute a single general factor—unconventionality (Donovan & Jessor, 1985), or criminality (Hirschi, 1984). According to these investigators, individual behaviors do not have any important unique components beyond the variance shared with the underlying factor.

Osgood, Johnston, O'Malley, and Bachman (1988) reached a somewhat different conclusion in their causal modeling analysis of longitudinal data on 18-22 year olds which included measures of criminal behavior, alcohol, marijuana and other drug use, and dangerous driving. Examining the relationships between these behaviors cross-sectionally and over time, they found substantial components of the reliable variance attributable to not only a general factor but also to factors specific to the behaviors. With one exception (criminal behavior), the percent of reliable unique variance exceeded the percent of variance associated with the general factor. They conclude ". . . a theory that addresses only the general construct can never fully account for the separate behaviors, though it might account for much of each of them" (p. 91).

Unlike the conclusions of earlier studies, the Osgood et al. (1988) results imply that the unique characteristics of behaviors may be as important as their commonalities in explaining deviance. Thus, it would not be sufficient to study a sampling or subset of deviant behaviors, assuming that these are simply multiple indicators of a single latent construct. Their findings highlight the need for an adequate definition of the domain of behavior under consideration and a comprehensive inclusion of this domain in research studies.

We argue that an important implication of adopting a risk-taking perspective is that the domain of behaviors extends beyond that addressed by the deviance literature. Although many authors in the present volume did focus upon problem behaviors, their discussions in most cases were not intended to be restricted to this class of behaviors. The decision-making and perceptual bias issues raised by Lopes, Gardner, and Millstein apply to any situation involving risk. Wilson and Daly focus on homicide data but suggest that their conclusions may apply to other forms of risk taking. Lyng explicitly draws parallels between "voluntary" risk taking and criminal behavior.

In what ways might an expansion of the domain of risk-taking behaviors contribute to an understanding of the dysfunctional behaviors of youth? Lyng's edgework analysis provides one illustration of the potential advantages of this approach. Lyng (this volume) invites a reconsideration of the forces motivating criminal behavior, based upon an earlier analysis of voluntary (non-criminal) types of risk taking (Lyng, 1990). By conceptualizing both voluntary and criminal behaviors as "edgework", ". . . it is possible that the same structural forces that give rise to varieties of edgework emphasized by my previous research (Lyng, 1990) also play a causal role in the emergence of illicit (or interpersonal) edgework" (this volume, p. 123). If, as Lyng suggests, we view criminal behavior as well as voluntary risk taking largely as an attempt to gain personal control and increase feelings of instrumentality, then this has very different implications than viewing criminal behavior as a "rational" response to socio-cultural circumstances. That is, the disadvantaged may be more likely than the wealthy to commit robberies, but the goal is not so much to acquire resources as to maintain some sense of "self-determination and self-actualization" (this volume, p. 128). The context of the behavior remains important, but in a different way than in other theoretical explanations of the link between poverty and crime.

A specific implication of Lyng's work for the study of dysfunctional risk taking during adolescence is the suggestion that risk taking may be primarily motivated by an attempt to gain a feeling of personal control over an environment viewed as largely controlled by adults. There may, of course, be other important kinds of motivations for adolescents. But, identifying commonalities as well as differences among types of risk taking requires that we expand our studies beyond an exclusive focus on deviant behaviors.

Summary

Recent research suggests that there are both common and unique components among adolescent problem behaviors. This finding strongly implies that future studies must not be restricted to a limited set of behaviors with the assumption that these are sampling a single, underlying construct. A risk-taking perspective further implies extending the domain of behaviors beyond those defined as problem, or deviant, behaviors. This extension may shed new light on the factors motivating risk taking. However, the risk-taking domain has not been well-defined, and we now turn to a consideration of this issue.

CONCEPTUALIZATION AND DEFINITION OF RISK TAKING

Risk taking in formal tests of decision-making theory is evaluated in hypothetical situations with known probabilities and clear outcomes (e.g., there is a specified chance of winning X amount of money). As pointed out by Lopes (this volume), real-life decision making generally is not of this type. Not only are the probabilities associated with certain outcomes often unknown, but the outcomes may not be well understood. This poses problems not only for the decision maker but also for the scientist attempting to study risk taking outside of a laboratory setting. Although most decisions in life may involve some degree of risk, in many cases the perceived probability of loss is so low, or the consequences of loss so slight, that the decision would not be classified by most as risky. In the following we discuss this issue and suggest other distinctions that may be useful in defining the risk taking domain.

How Much Risk Is "Risky?"

Behaviors cited as examples of risk taking by authors in this volume include alcohol and drug use, unprotected sexual activity, reckless motor vehicle driving, homicide, and other criminal behavior. Several authors also make reference to risky leisure activities such as skydiving and mountain climbing. Each of these is regarded as risky because it can substantially endanger the health or safety of the individual. Other types of risks may involve the potential of different sorts of losses—money, jobs, relationships, and so forth.

In some of the activities regarded as risk taking, the actual risk to health may be minor. For example, the probability of a pregnancy resulting from a single act of unprotected intercourse is relatively low—some estimate the probability at around .04 (Bongaarts, 1976)—and the actual risk of contracting HIV from a single sexual act also remains low (although certain behaviors and situations will increase that risk). For many types of risk taking, there is no way of calculating the actual risks. Although it is agreed that risky behavior must involve some potential for loss, the perceived loss in a given situation may vary widely across individuals.

Yet, behaviors defined as risky must be judged to some extent on this basis. As we strive to define this domain, we will need to identify both the type and degree of loss associated with various behaviors. Normative data on perceptions of risk associated with a wide variety of behaviors from different subgroups of the population would be helpful, to be used as a supplement to health-related statistics.

Perception of Risk

In addition to gathering data on adolescent perceptions of risk, as mentioned above, we must be clear about the *bases* for the risk assessment from the youth's perspective. For example, although adolescents perceive less risk in cigarette smoking as they grow older (Irwin, this volume), this risk may not in fact be associated with health outcomes, at least those associated with the smoking itself. A much more salient risk might be that of parental punishment which likely declines as adolescents grow older.

Brooks-Gunn and Furstenberg (1989) report that many adolescents express surprise at becoming pregnant because they didn't expect "to get caught." That is, the risk involved in unprotected sexual activity from the adolescent's viewpoint lay not in getting pregnant, but in whether other people would find out about their sexual activities.

Differences or similarities between types of risk-taking behaviors that would not occur to adults studying risk taking may come from the perceptions of those being studied. The advantages of finding out what people are thinking in making decisions about their risk taking are demonstrated in the work of Lopes (this volume) and

Lyng (this volume). This point also is made by Furby and Beyth-Marom (in press) in their discussion of adolescent decision making. This seems an essential component to include in future studies of risk taking.

Reactive Versus Active Risks

Irwin (this volume) is interested in risk taking defined as "volitional behaviors in which the outcomes remain uncertain with the possibility of an identifiable negative health outcome" (p. 11). He excludes criminal behaviors such as homicide on the grounds that these may be less voluntary and more the result of environmental circumstances.

Rather than excluding certain categories of criminal behaviors on this basis, it may be useful to retain them within a definition of risk taking but to propose distinctions among risk-taking behaviors on a reactive—active dimension. The violent behavior directed toward others described in this volume by Wilson and Daly might be regarded as a response to the stressful conditions to which these individuals are exposed. However, some of the self-directed risky behavior also may result from stressful environmental conditions. For example, reckless driving among adolescent males may represent a flight from stress as well as an aggressive act, and may thus be less "voluntary" than supposed. According to Berkowitz (1983), stressful situations elicit "flight" responses as well as violent and aggressive behavior.

This reactive type of behavior seems to stand in contrast to the more active risk taking described by Lyng (1990, this volume). Active risk taking might be associated with positive adaptations, successes, and resourcefulness rather than simply being a reaction to stressful circumstances, even though it may put the individual at substantial personal risk to health and safety. This distinction is not the same as one between societally-defined deviant and non-deviant behavior (although this is an obvious additional distinction to be made): either type could potentially be classified as reactive or active.

Differentiating reactive from active risk taking will not be an easy task. It will require a consideration not only of the context but the individual's perception of and reaction to that context.

Gender and the Definition of Risk Taking

In addition to the above considerations, the domain of risk taking should include an adequate representation of the types of risk taking engaged in by all segments of the population of interest. Although we focus on gender here, similar points might be made with respect to age, race, ethnicity, and the like.

Much of the literature discusses risky choices and behaviors as though they were gender-neutral (e.g., Baumrind, 1987; Tonkin, 1987). In this volume, the chapter by Wilson and Daly is the only one offering an analysis and explanation of behaviors that differ for women and men in frequency, and, according to their model, in meaning and motivation. The failure to incorporate gender considerations in models is particularly notable, given the frequently-reported gender differences in many of these behaviors.

Almost all of the behaviors typically chosen for study in the research on adolescent risk taking, with the exception of cigarette smoking, have higher prevalence rates for men than for women. This gender difference in rates can lead to the conclusion that risk taking is inherently masculine or is inherent in masculine roles (e.g., Lemle & Mishkind, 1989). The case of alcoholism casts some doubt on this conclusion: Women who rate themselves as high in stereotypically masculine personal attributes or who pursue occupational roles traditionally reserved for men are less likely to have drinking problems than are those who see themselves as low in masculinity or who adopt traditional female roles (Wilsnack, Wilsnack, & Klassen, 1986). Noteworthy too are data on certain crimes. Female rates for prostitution, running away from home (juveniles), drug use, minor theft, forgery, counterfeiting, and fraud are close to and sometimes surpass male rates for these behaviors (Federal Bureau of Investigation, 1989; Jamieson & Flanagan, 1989).

Further, women may engage in risky behaviors other than those typically included in research. Because women's place in the social structure and their consciousness differ markedly from those of men (Gates, 1978; O'Kelly, 1980; Sanday, 1973, 1981; Schlegel, 1977; Stacey & Thorne, 1985), many behaviors which appear to be simple and routine for men may be risky for women. The propensity of men to engage in higher levels of aggression than women, combined with women's lower status and power, may make certain types of male-female affiliation risky for women. One example concerns women involved in battering relationships choosing to stay in these relationships (Walker, 1979), which is surely a form of risk taking. Females are much more likely than males to be victims of sexual abuse and incest (Herman, 1981). It is estimated that 25-50% of current cohorts of female children and adolescents will experience some form of sexual abuse before they are 19 years old (Badgely, 1984; Bagley & Young, 1990). Further, decisions regarding disclosure of sexual maltreatment may be risky choices for women. Adolescent victims of abuse often choose not to reveal their situations because in doing so, they risk social stigmatization and rejection by significant others (Bagley & Young, 1990).

Finally, women often are advised to (and do) restrict their behavior in ways that men are not in order to avoid sexual assault and rape (Sapiro, 1990). Women are cautioned not to be on the streets late at night, not to walk alone in parks, parking lots, and other deserted areas, not to go into certain establishments unless they are accompanied by men, to keep the doors to their homes locked to strangers, and to be constantly aware of the potential for assault in cross-sex relationships.

If situations such as those described above were defined as risk taking, it could be that the incidence of risky choices would not differ between women and men to the extent suggested by existing data. The considerable focus in the criminological literature on the risk of criminal victimization (e.g., LaGrange & Ferraro, 1989; Stafford & Galle, 1984) has yet to connect with the risk taking tradition this volume illustrates. If behaviors associated with victimization are included in studies of risk taking, the generalizability to women of currently proposed conceptual models focusing on men, such as Lyng's (this volume), could be tested. This expansion of the definition of risk taking also would permit more adequate tests of additional gender-related questions—whether men and women engage in risk taking for the same reasons, and whether the consequences for both are the same.

Some data suggest that there are few gender differences in reasons for taking risks (Johnston & O'Malley, 1986). Others (Ensminger, Brown, & Kellam, 1982) have reported different associations between close relationships and drug use for men and women, and positive relationships between levels of childhood characteristics (aggressiveness, shyness) and adolescent substance use for men, but not for women. In studies of sexual behavior, women are more likely than men to say they are sexually active because they are in love, whereas men are more likely to give pleasure as the primary motivation (Hatfield, 1983; Peplau, Rubin, & Hill, 1977). The crime of embezzlement may, for women, be motivated largely by unexpected financial problems impacting their families (Daly, 1989; Zietz, 1981). For men, embezzlement is more likely to occur as a result of their own behaviors, e.g., gambling losses (Cressey, 1971). And the "feminization of poverty" has been linked with women's increasing participation in property crimes (Box, 1987).

Sexual behavior provides a prime example of the different consequences of risk taking for women and men. When men impregnate women unintentionally, they do encounter certain psychological and social consequences from unplanned fatherhood (Elster & Lamb, 1986). However, men do not endure the physical sequela of pregnancy, abortion, miscarriage, or childbirth. Often they are not involved in decisions to terminate or continue pregnancies or decisions to retain custody of children or place them in adoptive homes. Neither do men encounter the same psychological and social consequences and responsibilities as do women who become mothers, especially unmarried mothers (Chilman, 1983; Klerman, 1986).

Thus, there is some basis in the existing literature to suggest that the meanings, motivations, and consequences of risk taking differ for women and men. If these kinds of differences are substantiated in the future, they will have to be taken into consideration in models and theories of risk taking. An essential first step, however, is an expansion of the risk-taking domain to include the types of risk-taking decisions more often encountered by women than by men in our society.

Risk Taking as Coping Behavior

Risk taking, in some form or to some degree, characterizes not only professionally successful adults but also developmentally "successful" adolescents. Making the distinction between developmentally-enhancing versus developmentally-detrimental risks is one of the important tasks facing those engaged in the study of risk taking. Risk taking as coping is illustrated by Lyng's conceptualization (this volume) of edgework as a way of coping with perceived lack of personal control.

In the third section of this chapter, we explore the advantages of considering risk taking as coping within a general model of adjustment and adaptation. This perspective impacts the domain of behaviors to be included in studies, and it also influences the questions being asked. There has been much debate about why adolescents engage in behaviors harmful to their health. The underlying assumption in many of these discussions is that risk taking signifies a deficit—some form of adolescent immaturity and inadequacy. One of the notable themes of many chapters in this volume is that we should begin to question this assumption (Gardner,

Lyng, Millstein, Wilson, & Daly). In their review of the decision-making literature, Furby and Beyth-Marom (in press) emphasize the current lack of sufficient research to support assumptions that adolescents are less competent decision makers than are adults. Perhaps the time has come to begin asking a different question—how does risk taking, even when it involves significant threats to physical health and well-being, play a positive role in development and in the mental health of the individual?

Summary

For research on risk taking to advance, a clear definition of what constitutes risky behavior is necessary. In defining this domain, we must give consideration to the types of loss and degree of risk as perceived by our samples as well as to risk reflected in health statistics.

Distinctions between active and reactive risk taking may be useful, as well as an examination of the reasons why adolescents view behaviors as risky. A review of gender issues in this research underscores the importance of including behaviors that may have been slighted because they are risks generally encountered by women rather than by men. A consideration of risk taking as coping behavior may expand not only the domain of behaviors to be included but the types of questions being asked in future research.

MULTIDISCIPLINARY EMPHASIS

The previous chapters in this volume exemplify the insights to be gained about adolescent risk taking from different disciplines and theoretical perspectives. In this section, we describe the way in which three additional areas of research—criminology, family science, and development—speak to the study of adolescent risk taking.

Criminology and the Measurement of Risk Taking

Papers in this volume suggest two ways in which experience in measuring crime may be useful to measuring risk taking. If much crime is a form of risk taking, experience in measuring crime can provide helpful direction in measuring other types of risk taking; and it can certainly aid in measuring *crime* as risk taking.

Measurement of risk taking. Considerable efforts toward measuring criminal behavior point to two strategies of measuring risky behavior: *prevalence*—the proportion of a population that participates in the behavior—and *incidence*—the number of times that behavior occurs in a population, usually expressed as a mean or median. Nearly all measures of risky behavior reported in this volume are prevalence measures. Although there is some discussion about the merits of prevalence versus incidence measures (Blumstein, Cohen, & Farrington, 1988a & b; Gottfredson & Hirschi, 1988), incidence measures generally are regarded as preferable. They provide not only the prevalence information about how many individuals have participated in a behavior, but as well the recurrence rate of the behaviors, a concern critical to differentiating and explaining levels of risk taking.

Prevalence measures frequently produce different, and sometimes misleading, results compared to incidence measures. For example, prevalence measures produce no statistically significant differences by social class or race in overall level of self-reported crime in a national sample of youth. Incidence data, however, show that both lower class and Black youth have higher overall levels of criminal behavior (Elliott & Huizinga, 1983). The potential for similar misleading results exists in connection with the covariation among risk-taking behaviors. To illustrate, think about a sample of three youth, all of whom have had experience with alcohol, marijauna, and sexual intercourse in a year, but each of whom participates in one behavior 50 times, one behavior 10 times, and the other behavior once. A prevalence measure of risk taking would exhibit perfect co-occurrence whereas a measure of actual incidence would show little association. To the extent that prevalence measures pervade research on the interrelationships of risk taking behaviors, we may be overestimating these connections.

Lifetime prevalence measures have even greater potential for producing different and misleading results, especially when applied over time in a developmental framework. As individuals move from earlier to later life stages, their previous behavior moves with them. Persons who have participated in a risky act during their early adolescent years are still going to be among those who have participated in this behavior when they are older adolescents or adults, even though incidence measures show they are no longer engaging in such behavior.

Not only are incidence measures of risk taking more informative and less likely to produce misleading results, they also are more in tune with what seems to be the central question of researchers: Why do some people take a greater number of risks than others? Pervading this volume is the idea that adolescents take more risks than adults, which certainly seems to be more about the total amount of adolescent risks (incidence) than about the range of risks.

Measurement of crime as risk taking. If the criminological literature provides direction in measuring risk taking in general, then it surely gives useful information about measuring crime itself as risk taking. Most research in the risk-taking genre virtually ignores several relevant and key data sets on crime (see Inter-university Consortium for Political and Social Research, 1989). For example, two longitudinal studies of self-reported crime, based on representative samples of U.S. youth, began in the mid 1970s. Since 1975 the Institute of Social Research at the University of Michigan has gathered data on a large national sample of high school seniors each year in its "Monitoring the Future" project (Johnston, Bachman, & O'Malley, 1989). These data, to which Irwin (this volume) briefly refers, contain a wide range of information on many sociological and psychological variables including risk taking: fourteen items on specific criminal acts other than drug and alcohol use as well as questions about dangerous driving, marijauna use, alcohol use, and use of several other illicit drugs. This study also has a panel design, obtaining these data from follow-up samples of youth initially interviewed as high school seniors. The other self-report survey of youthful crime comes from the University of Colorado's Institute of Behavioral Research (Elliott, Huizinga, & Ageton, 1985). It is a panel investigation of 2,365 youth aged 11-17 when first interviewed in 1976, and subsequently interviewed seven times by 1986. It has the most extensive information on self-reported crime available. Research has shown validity problems with this self-report data to be relatively minimal (Elliott & Ageton, 1980; Hindelang, Hirschi, & Weiss, 1981; O'Malley, Bachman, & Johnston, 1983).

The National Crime Surveys provide another important set of data on crime (Bureau of Justice Statistics, 1989). Beginning in 1973, a 49,000-59,000 representative sample of persons ages 12 and over in the U.S. have been asked every six months if they were victims during that period of six crimes: rape, robbery, assault, larceny (personal and household), burglary, and motor vehicle theft. These data contain social and demographic information about each respondent and considerable information about each victimization including characteristics of offenders and the victim-offender relationship for rape, robbery and assault victimizations. There are some accuracy problems, especially in respondent reporting of rape (Russell & Howell, 1983). However, these problems pale when compared to the huge inaccuracies built into police data on these crimes (Beirne & Messerschmidt, 1990).

Supplementary Homicide Reports, a part of the FBI's Uniform Crime Reporting Program, are a third set of data from which risk-taking research might profit. Started in 1961, these national data include details for each year on victim and offender characteristics and circumstances surrounding nearly all U.S. homicides—crimes on which there is no information from self-report or victimization surveys (Maxfield, 1989). Wilson and Daly (this volume) use these supplementary data from two cities.

Finally, in-depth ethnographic descriptions of all kinds of crime are available to researchers investigating risk taking. Lyng (this volume) calls attention to one such source, Katz's (1988) descriptions of robbery, property crime, urban gang membership, and assaultive behavior. Additional ethnographic work tends to place rape (Scully & Marolla, 1985), drug use (Carpenter, Glassner, Johnson, & Laughlin, 1988), and drug dealing (Adler, 1985) in a risk-taking framework.

When researchers are interested in crime as risk taking, these sources may be more useful than some others currently being cited because of the range of behaviors included, the nationally representative samples, or the insights potentially to be gained from ethnographic studies.

Risk Taking as Coping Behavior

A widely used model for family research is the Typology Model of Adjustment and Adaptation (McCubbin & McCubbin, 1989) presented with slight modification in figure l. Briefly, a stressor (A) and/or pile -up of stressors (AA) impacts a family. Different styles of family functioning are symbolized as T. Within the family, the individuals make appraisal of the stress (C), appraisal of the situation (CC), and invoke their own world view (CCC). These perceptual and cognitive activities are combined with utilization of resources to meet the stress (B), resources to meet the crisis situation (BB), and community and social support (BBB). The resultant activity is coping or problem solving (PSC) which, when it refers to a chance of loss, could be termed risky behavior. A feedback loop allows for the possibility that the risky behaviors themselves may constitute stressors that could pile-up and precipitate a crisis. The outcome of the entire process is adjustment and adaptation. By including such a component, the results of risky behavior may be seen to vary from negative to positive.

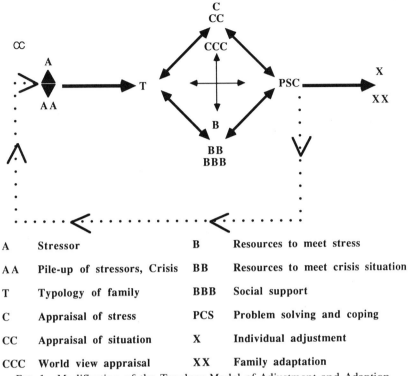

A	Stressor	B	Resources to meet stress
AA	Pile-up of stressors, Crisis	BB	Resources to meet crisis situation
T	Typology of family	BBB	Social support
C	Appraisal of stress	PCS	Problem solving and coping
CC	Appraisal of situation	X	Individual adjustment
CCC	World view appraisal	XX	Family adaptation

FIG. 1. Modification of the Typology Model of Adjustment and Adaption (McCubbin & McCubbin, 1989).

In applying this model to risk taking, one of the key implications is that risky behavior does not occur in a vacuum, but rather occurs as a result of stressors (A). What are some of these stressors? In the previous chapters within this volume, Wilson and Daly identify poor prospects in a biological evolutionary sense; Irwin describes early physiological maturity as a possible source of stress for the adolescent. From Lyng's work, we might guess that a lack of sense of efficacy creates a stressor which can be relieved by engaging in "edgework." Dryfoos identifies the following with stress and depression: lack of school achievement, low basic skills, lack of parental support, low resistance to peers, early acting out, and poverty.

A family style (T) which downplays family support, sometimes described as low cohesiveness, was pinpointed by Dryfoos as a risk factor. Furby and Beyth-Marom (in press) cited research showing a positive correlation between sexual abuse and drug abuse among adolescents. A family style which allowed sexual abuse of children would be one with boundary problems (Boss, 1987). This style may create intolerable stressors relievable by self-medication with illicit drugs.

The perceptual/cognitive domain of the model (CC and CCC) as applied to risk taking is illustrated by Millstein, Gardner, and Lopes (this volume). Millstein discussed perceptual and cognitive biases as they may affect adolescents' risk assessment strategies. Gardner's rational decision-making approach focuses on world view, such as future uncertainty, and identifies risk taking as a rational response to this uncertainty. In Lopes SP/A theory risk attitudes are addressed. The differential valuing of security versus potential again taps into world view issues, whereas aspiration level reflects choices about immediate needs and goals.

In the realm of resources (B), Dryfoos (this volume) identified several risk factors, mentioned earlier, which might be considered as inadequate resources. Many of the interventions she suggests concern supplementing and strengthening the resources of adolescents so that their coping can be deterred from destructive risk taking to more growth-promoting behaviors. Wilcox (this volume) similarly points to interventions at the community and national levels which affect resources. For example, the rationale for increasing prices of alcohol and cigarettes as a deterrent is based upon an assumption that limited resources are available, particularly for adolescents, to be used on these products.

With respect to the problem solving and coping part of the model (PSC), delineating the nature of the risky behaviors is important, as discussed in the first two sections of this chapter. Expanding our consideration of the outcomes of risky behaviors (X and XX) also is important. For many of these behaviors the outcomes are considered to be negative: indeed, they are the focus of research for this reason. On the other hand, as pointed out by Irwin (this volume) and others, enhancing outcomes also should be considered. Lyng's (this volume) work highlights a way in which we might begin such a consideration in his description of edgework.

In sum, the application of this model to risk taking reveals some challenges for future research. The family context requires additional attention as do the functional outcomes of risky behaviors. Integration of all components of the model, particularly the work on perceptual/cognitive factors with work on resources including a variety of risk-taking behaviors would be desirable. It would also seem worthwhile to attend to levels of analysis in this research, identifying and then investigating these in a systematic manner with respect to each factor in the Adjustment and Adaptation Model.

Risk Taking and Development

By specifying a particular age-defined group of interest, the topic "adolescent risk taking" implies a developmental approach. Based upon the chapters in this volume and the related literature, adolescence and young adulthood has been singled out because there is evidence that more risk taking occurs during these ages than is true earlier or later in development. Yet, while this evidence has resulted in many studies employing adolescent samples and generating data on age differences in certain types of risk taking, there does not seem to be much emphasis on risk taking as a developmental phenomenon.

Baumrind (1987) points out that many of the adolescent characteristics specified in the literature as indicative of a deviant pattern (because they are associated with problem behaviors) also describe normal and healthy functioning during adolescence. Further, adolescence is a time for experimentation: Avoiding all risk taking may bode less well for the individual, long term, than does the inclination to try new things, even if some of these new things pose a threat to health.

There is no disagreement that, from an adult perspective, the potential health consequences of some behaviors are not worth the risk, and it would be beneficial to be able to direct some of the adolescent experimentation along other, less dangerous avenues. The high levels of dangerous risk taking observed among certain segments of the adolescent population also may be qualitatively different from normal adolescent experimentation. But the main point here is that answers to these questions will require studies designed from developmental as well as from social-psychological and sociological perspectives.

A developmental emphasis in risk-taking research could be manifested in a variety of ways. One of these ways is the examination of developmental correlates of risk taking. Irwin and Millstein (1986) are moving in this direction by including in their model of adolescent risk taking such variables as biological maturation (e.g., puberty status) and adolescent egocentrism. In addition, it would be useful to explore risk-taking behaviors and the way adolescents think about risk in relationship to measures of cognitive development, identity development, and role-taking ability.

Second, in conjunction with the above measures of cognitive and social-cognitive development, more attention could be given to comparing correlates of risk taking at different developmental periods. Do the reasons adolescents give for taking risks change as they mature, and does this have implications for intervention with various age groups? One might speculate that adolescents in different stages of identity development, even if taking the same risks, might be doing so for quite different reasons. Also, societal standards and expectations change as adolescents grow older. Relevant to this point are the findings of Osgood et al. (1988) on the shifting associations between individual behaviors and the general underlying deviance factor over time. For example, heavy alcohol use was less strongly associated with "general deviance" for young adults in their early 20s than for those in their late teens. Once respondents reached the legal drinking age, alcohol use, unlike the use of illicit drugs, was less representative of a general tendency to violate the laws and norms of society.

Adolescents' attachments to particular social structures also change as they age. Thornberry (1987) shows that as youth move from early through middle to late adolescence, bonds to family, friends, school, youth culture, and work change. Correlated with these changing bonds are changes in the rate of delinquency which is highest during middle adolescence when ties to friends and youth culture are strongest. Sampson and Laub (1990) reach a similar conclusion. While deviant tendencies from early adolescence continued into adulthood, these tendencies were systematically altered by social bonds to adult institutions of work and family.

Third, we might ask whether the nature of risk taking—of the behaviors themselves—changes with development. As pointed out earlier in this chapter, incidence rather than prevalence rates address this type of question. With an expansion of the domain of risk behaviors included in studies, investigators may be able to identify shifting patterns of risk incidence over time that could be significant in distinguishing adaptive from dysfunctional tendencies. For example, among adolescents identified as engaging in dangerous risk taking during early adolescence, some may maintain or increase their involvement over time, while others might shift to less pathogenic forms of risk taking. Developmental changes in the behaviors also could occur in ways not detectable through incidence rates. Two adolescents who report similar amounts of alcohol use over time are not necessarily engaging in the same degree of risk if one has learned to monitor the alcohol's effects and adjust intake accordingly while the other has not.

Finally, it may be important to incorporate into models of risk taking not only the context of the behavior, but the developmental history of person-environment transactions. In the primate work of Suomi (1990), initial individual differences in reactivity (a trait describing anxiousness in the face of new situations) serves as a catalyst for growth, providing a wide variation in outcome. Under certain conditions, such as when the initial rearing environment is relatively deprived, the individuals described as highly reactive suffer sustained developmental delays when they later encounter stress. However, these same reactive individuals, when faced with more positive initial circumstances, excel under stress in comparison to non-reactive individuals. Stressful conditions are thus viewed as challenges to be mastered, and the trait which otherwise would serve to put the individual at risk now activates the individual to modify the environment in a positive manner. As investigators explore the relationships between individual characteristics, such as sensation seeking (Zuckerman, 1979), and risk taking, they would be well advised to give some consideration to these kinds of findings from the developmental literature.

Summary

Research on adolescent risk taking can benefit from the theories, methods, and findings of many disciplines, as demonstrated throughout this volume. We have suggested additional interfaces between risk-taking research and the literatures of criminology, family science, and developmental studies.

IMPLICATIONS FOR INTERVENTION

Authors throughout this volume have noted the significant implications that both the theory development and the findings of research on risk taking have for public policy. While a tremendous potential exists for using this information to inform policy, the translation will not be easy. As the content of this volume shows, at this time the field has a number of conflicting findings, its models have weak explanatory power (Furby & Beyth-Marom, in press) and the solutions that we call for require multilevel, multitarget interventions that will run up against the fiscal realities of the 1990s. Those engaged in risk-taking research point to the need for more and even better studies addressing a number of urgent issues.

Given the substantial stake that our society has in finding effective policies to reduce the costs to individuals and to society of a variety of risk-taking behaviors, policy makers have the obligation to help find the support necessary for this continued work.

However, legislators and policy makers do not just listen to the recommendations of social scientists, and the urgency of many of these issues means that policy cannot, and will not, wait for definitive answers from the scientific community. The level of societal concern and the costs to our society of the behaviors discussed in this volume will compel legislators and policy makers to move ahead. Wilcox (this volume) suggests that the alternatives at the disposal of legislators (e.g., the power to prohibit, to tax, and to regulate) may not be the mechanisms most likely to effect behavioral change. In fact, he describes the disincentives contained in our current legislation as often "small, uncertain, distant, and poorly communicated" (p. 152). Dryfoos' (this volume) efforts to identify common components in successful programs are very important. Knowing what works and what doesn't provides basic information for future program design.

As much as we need additional research that can inform policy, we also need more research that evaluates the effects of policy. There is little rigorous evaluation research on the consequences of legislative actions (Wilcox, this volume). Little effort or money goes into testing whether existing legislation brings about the changes for which it was designed. Dryfoos (this volume) also speaks to the lack of rigorous evaluation for the programs which implement social policy decisions. Such evaluation research is not a luxury or an "add-on" to programs. It is essential and serves multiple purposes. It not only can lead to improvement in the content of the programs themselves, but it can contribute to basic research efforts by providing additional tests of the theory used as a basis for designing the program.

The integrative and comprehensive programs advocated by Dryfoos (this volume) are the exception rather than the rule. Yet, these are likely the only types of programs that can hope to have any significant impact upon the dysfunctional risk taking of youth. It is a challenge for the field to find ways to make legislators and policy makers recognize that complex societal problems that fall under the rubric of "risk taking" will not lend themselves to simple solutions.

NOTE

The contributors to this chapter are listed in alphabetical order.

REFERENCES

Adler, P. (1985). *Wheeling and dealing: An ethnography of an upper-level drug dealing and smuggling community.* New York: Columbia University Press.

Badgely, R. (1984). *Several offenses against children.* Ottawa: Government of Canada, Ministry of Supply and Services.

Bagley, C. R., & Young, L. (1990). Depression, self-esteem, and suicidal behavior as sequels of sexual abuse in childhood: Research and therapy. In M. Rothery & G. Cameron (Eds.), *Child maltreatment: Expanding our concepts of helping.* Hillsdale, New Jersey: Erlbaum.

Baumrind, D. (1987). A developmental perspective on adolescent risk taking in contemporary America. In C. E. Irwin, Jr. (Ed.), *Adolescent social behavior and health. New directions for child development, No. 37.* San Francisco: Jossey-Bass.

Beirne, P., & Messerschmidt, J. (1990). *Criminology.* New York: Harcourt Brace Jovanovich.

Berkowitz, L. (1983). Aversively stimulated aggression: Some parallels and differences in research with animals and humans. *American Psychologist, 38,* 1135-1144.

Blumstein, A., Cohen, J., & Farrington, D. P. (1988a). Criminal career research: Its value for criminology. *Criminology, 26,* 1-35.

Blumstein, A., Cohen, J., & Farrington, D. P. (1988b). Longitudinal and criminal career research: Further clarifications. *Criminology, 26,* 57-74.

Bongaarts, J. (1976). Intermediate fertility variables and marital fertility rates. *Population Studies, 30,* 227-241.

Boss, P. (1987). Family stress. In M. B. Sussman & S. K. Steinmetz (Eds.), *Handbook of marriage and the family,* New York: Plenum.

Box, S. (1987). *Recession, crime and punishment.* London: Macmillan.

Brooks-Gunn, J., & Furstenberg, F. F., Jr. (1989). Adolescent sexual behavior. *American Psychologist, 44,* 249-257.

Bureau of Justice Statistics. (1989). *Criminal victimization in the United States, 1987.* Washington, D.C.: U.S. Department of Justice.

Carpenter, C., Glassner, B., Johnson, B. D., & Loughlin, J. (1988). *Kids, drugs, and crime.* Lexington, Mass.: D. C. Heath and Company.

Chilman, C. S. (1983). *Adolescent sexuality in a changing American society.* New York: Wiley.

Cressey, D. (1971). *Other people's money.* New York: Free Press.

Daly, K. (1989). Gender and varieties of white collar crime. *Criminology, 27,* 769-793.

Donovan, J. E., & Jessor, R. (1985). Structure of problem behavior in adolescence and young adulthood. *Journal of Consulting and Clinical Psychology, 53,* 890-904.

Elliott, D. S., & Ageton, S. S. (1980). Reconciling race and class differences in self-reported and official estimates of delinquency. *American Sociological Review, 45,* 95-110.

Elliott, D. S., & Huizinga, D. (1983). Social class and delinquent behavior in a national youth panel. *Criminology, 21,* 149-177.

Elliott, D. S., Huizinga, D., & Ageton, S. S. (1985). *Explaining delinquency and drug use.* Beverly Hills, CA: Sage.

Elster, A. B., & Lamb, M. E. (1986). Adolescent fathers: The under studied side of adolescent pregnancy. In J. B. Lancaster & B. A. Hamburg (Eds.), *School-age pregnancy and parenthood.* New York: Aldine deGruyter.

Ensminger, M. E., Brown, C. H., & Kellam, S. G. (1982). Sex differences in antecedents of substance use among adolescents. *Journal of Social Issues, 38,* 25-42.

Federal Bureau of Investigation. (1989). *Uniform crime reports: Crime in the United States 1987.* Washington, D.C.: U. S. Department of Justice.

Furby, L., & Beyth-Marom, R. (in press). Risk taking in adolescence: A decision-making perspective. *Developmental Review.*

Gates, M. (1978). Introduction. In J. R. Chapman & M. Gates (Eds.), *The victimization of women.* Beverly Hills, CA: Sage.

Gottfredson, M., & Hirschi, T. (1988). Science, public policy and the career paradigm. *Criminology, 26,* 37-55.

Hatfield, E. (1983). What do women and men want from love and sex? In E. R. Allgeiers & N. B. McCormick (Eds.), *Changing boundaries: Gender roles and sexual behavior.* Palo Alto, CA: Mayfield.

Herman, J. L. (1981). *Father-daughter incest.* Cambridge, Mass.: Harvard University Press.

Hindelang, M., Hirschi, T., & Weis, J. G. (1981). *Measuring delinquency.* Beverly Hills, CA: Sage.

Hirschi, T. (1984). A brief commentary on Akers "Delinquent behavior, drugs, and alcohol: What is the relationship?" *Today's Delinquent, 3,* 49-52.

Inter-university Consortium for Political and Social Research. (1989). *Data available form the national archive of criminal justice.* Ann Arbor, Mich: Inter-university Consortium for Political and Social Research, University of Michigan.

Irwin, C. E., Jr., & Milstein, S. G. (1986). Biopsychosocial correlates of risk-taking behaviors during adolescence. *Journal of Adolescent Health Care, 7,* 82S-96S.

Jamieson, K. M., & Flanagan, T. J, (Eds.). (1989). *Sourcebook of criminal justice statistics—1988.* Washington, D.C.: U.S. Department of Justice, Bureau of Justice Statistics.

Johnston, L. D., & O'Malley, P. M. (1986). Why do the nation's students use drugs and alcohol? Self-reported reasons from nine national surveys. *Journal of Drug Issues, 16,* 29-66.

Johnston, L. D., Bachman, J. G., & O'Malley, P. M. (1989). *Monitoring the future: Questionnaire responses from the nation's high school seniors, 1988.* Ann Arbor, Mich: Institute for Social Research.

Katz, J. (1988). *Seductions of crime: Moral and sensual attractions in doing evil.* New York: Basic Books.

Klerman, L. V. (1986). The economic impact of school-age child rearing. In J. B. Lancaster & B. A. Hamburg (Eds.), *School-age pregnancy and parenthood.* New York: Aldine DeGruyter.

LaGrange, R. L., & Ferraro, K. F. (1989). Assessing age and gender differences in perceived risk and fear of crime. *Criminology, 27,* 697-719.

Lemle, R., & Mishkind, M. E. (1989). Alcohol and masculinity. *Journal of Substance Abuse Treatment, 6,* 213-222.

Lyng, S. (1990). Edgework: A social psychological analysis of voluntary risk taking. *American Journal of Sociology, 95,* 851-886.

Maxfield, M. G. (1989). Circumstances in supplementary homicide reports: Variety and validity. *Criminology, 27,* 671-695.

McCubbin, M., & McCubbin, H. I. (1989). Theoretical orientations to family stress and coping. In C. R. Figley (Ed.), *Treating stress in families.* New York: Brunner/Mazel.

O'Kelly, C. G. (1980). *Women and men in society.* New York: Van Nostrand.

O'Malley, P. M., Bachman, J. G., & Johnston, L. D. (1983). Reliability and consistency in self-reports of drug use. *International Journal of the Addictions, 18,* 805-824.

Osgood, D. W., Johnston, L. D., O'Malley, P. M., & Bachman, J. G. (1988). The generality of deviance in late adolescence and early adulthood. *American Sociological Review, 53,* 81-93.

Peplau, L. A., Rubin, Z., & Hill, C. (1977). Sex intimacy in dating relationships. *Journal of Social Issues, 33,* 96-109.

Russell, D. E. H., & Howell, N. (1983). The prevalence of rape in the United States revisited. *Signs, 8,* 688-695.

Sampson, R. J., & Laub, J. H. (1990). Crime and deviance over the life course: The salience of adult social bonds. *American Sociological Review, 55,* 609-627.

Sanday, P. R. (1973). Toward a theory of the status of women. *American Anthropologist, 75,* 1682-1700.

Sanday, P. R. (1981). *Female power and male dominance: On the origins of sexual inequality.* Cambridge: Cambridge University Press.

Sapiro, V. (1990). *Women in American society* (2nd ed.). Mountain View CA: Mayfield.

Schlegel, A. (Ed.). (1977). *Sexual stratification: A cross-cultural view.* New York: Columbia University Press.

Scully, D., & Marolla, J. (1985). Riding the bull at Gilley's. Convicted rapists describe the rewards of rape. *Social Problems, 32,* 251-263.

Stacey, J., & Thorne, B. (1985). The missing feminist revolution in sociology. *Social Problems, 32,* 301-316.

Stafford, M., & Galle, O. (1984). Victimization rates, exposure to risk, and fear of crime. *Criminology, 22,* 173-185.

Suomi, S. J. (1990, March). *Primate models of hormonal-behavioral changes in adolescents.* Presented at the meetings of the Society for Research on Adolescence, Atlanta, GA.

Thornberry, T. P. (1987). Toward an interactional theory of delinquency. *Criminology, 25,* 863-891.

Tonkin, R. S. (1987). Adolescent risk-taking behavior. *Journal of Adolescent Health Care, 8,* 213-220.

Walker, L. E. (1979). *The battered woman.* New York: Harper & Row.

Wilsnack, S. C., Wilsnack, R. W., & Klassen, A. D. (1986). Epidemiological research on women's drinking, 1978-1984. In *Women and alcohol: Health related issues.* (DHHS Publication No. ADM 86-1139). Washington, D.C.: U.S. Government Printing Office.

Zietz, D. (1981). *Women who embezzle or defraud: A study of convicted felons.* New York: Praeger.

Zuckerman, M. (1979). *Sensation seeking: Beyond the optimal level of arousal.* Hillsdale, N.J.: Erlbaum.

ABOUT THE CONTRIBUTORS

Nancy J. Bell is a professor and chair of the Department of Human Development and Family Studies, Texas Tech University. She received her doctorate in psychology from Northwestern University in 1973. She coordinates the Institute of Multidisciplinary Research on Adolescent and Adult Risk Taking Behavior and the interdisciplinary graduate minor in risk taking at Texas Tech. Her research is in the area of adolescent development.

Robert W. Bell is a professor in the Department of Psychology, Texas Tech University. He received his doctorate in psychology from Purdue University in 1959. He has taught and conducted research at Allegheny College, Northern Illinois University, and, since 1973, Texas Tech University. His research has ranged from ultrasonic communication in small mammals to adolescent and adult vulnerability to alcoholism.

Joy G. Dryfoos is an independent researcher, writer, and lecturer, as well as Adjunct Professor, School of Public Health, Columbia University, New York, NY.

William Gardner is Associate Professor of Psychiatry, University of Pittsburgh School of Medicine, Pittsburgh, PA.

Charles E. Irwin, Jr., is Professor of Pediatrics and Director, Division of Adolescent Medicine, School of Medicine, University of California, San Francisco.

Lola L. Lopes is Pomerantz Professor of Business Administration and Professor of Psychology, Department of Management and Organizations, University of Iowa, Iowa City, IA.

Stephen Lyng is a faculty member in the Department of Sociology and Anthropology, Virginia Commonwealth University, Richmond, VA.

Susan G. Millstein recently spent two years as the Associate Director for the Carnegie Council on Adolescent Development. She currently is with the Department of Pediatrics, School of Medicine, University of California, San Francisco.

Brian L. Wilcox is the Director, Office of Public Interest Legislation, American Psychological Association, Washington, DC.

Margo Wilson and *Martin Daly* are faculty in the Department of Psychology, McMaster University, Hamilton, Ontario. Their chapter was completed while they were Fellows of the Center for Advanced Study in the Behavioral Sciences.

Authors of the final chapter are all members of the Institute for Multidisciplinary Research on Adolescent and Adult Risk-Taking Behavior at Texas Tech University, Lubbock, Texas. Faculty in the Department of Human Development and Family Studies are *Edward R. Anderson, Nancy J. Bell, Judith L. Fischer, Joyce Munsch,* and *Gwendolyn T. Sorell. Charles W. Peek* is a faculty member in the Department of Sociology.